FIFTY MAJOR POLITICAL THINKERS

Fifty Major Political Thinkers introduces the lives and ideas of some of the most influential figures in Western political thought, from Ancient Greece to the present day. The entries provide a fascinating and readable introduction to the major figures and schools of thought that have shaped contemporary politics. They include:

- Aristotle
- Simone de Beauvoir
- Jean-François Lyotard
- Mohandas Gandhi
- Jürgen Habermas
- Machiavelli
- Karl Marx
- Tom Paine
- Jean-Jacques Rousseau
- Alexis de Tocqueville

Fully cross-referenced and including a glossary of theoretical terms, this wide-ranging and accessible book is essential reading for anyone with an interest in the evolution and history of contemporary political thought.

Ian Adams is Honorary Fellow at the University of Durham.

R.W. Dyson is a Lecturer in Politics and Director of the Centre for the History of Political Thought at the University of Durham.

ROUTLEDGE KEY GUIDES

Routledge Key Guides are accessible, informative and lucid handbooks, which define and discuss the central concepts, thinkers and debates in a broad range of academic disciplines. All are written by noted experts in their respective subjects. Clear, concise exposition of complex and stimulating issues and ideas make *Routledge Key Guides* the ultimate reference resources for students, teachers, researchers and the interested lay person.

Ancient History: Key Themes and Approaches
Neville Morley

Key Writers on Art: From Antiquity to the Nineteenth Century
Edited by Chris Murray

Key Writers on Art: The Twentieth Century
Edited by Chris Murray

Business: The Key Concepts
Mark Vernon

Cinema Studies: The Key Concepts (Second edition)
Susan Hayward

Communication, Cultural and Media Studies: The Key Concepts (Third edition)
John Hartley

Cultural Theory: The Key Concepts
Edited by Andrew Edgar and Peter Sedgwick

Cultural Theory: The Key Thinkers
Andrew Edgar and Peter Sedgwick

Key Concepts in Eastern Philosophy
Oliver Leaman

Eastern Philosophy: Key Readings
Oliver Leaman

Gurdjieff: The Key Concepts
Sophia Wellbeloved

International Relations: The Key Concepts
Martin Griffiths and Terry O'Callaghan

Key Concepts in Language and Linguistics
R.L. Trask

Key Concepts in the Philosophy of Education
John Gingell and Christopher Winch

Popular Music: The Key Concepts
Roy Shuker

Post-Colonial Studies: The Key Concepts
Bill Ashcroft, Gareth Griffiths and Helen Tiffin

Social and Cultural Anthropology: The Key Concepts
Nigel Rapport and Joanna Overing

Sport and Physical Education: The Key Concepts
Timothy Chandler, Mike Cronin and Wray Vamplew

Sport Psychology: The Key Concepts
Ellis Cashmore

Television Studies: The Key Concepts
Neil Casey, Bernadette Casey, Justin Lewis, Ben Calvert and Liam French

Fifty Key Figures in Twentieth-Century British Politics
Keith Laybourn

Fifty Contemporary Choreographers
Edited by Martha Bremser

Fifty Key Classical Authors
Alison Sharrock and Rhiannon Ash

Fifty Eastern Thinkers
Diané Collinson, Kathryn Plant and Robert Wilkinson

Fifty Major Economists
Steven Pressman

Fifty Major Thinkers on Education
Joy Palmer

Fifty Modern Thinkers on Education
Joy Palmer

Fifty Key Thinkers on the Environment
Edited by Joy Palmer with Peter Blaze Corcoran and David A. Cooper

Fifty Contemporary Filmmakers
Edited by Yvonne Tasker

Fifty Key Thinkers on History
Marnie Hughes-Warrington

Fifty Key Thinkers in International Relations
Martin Griffiths

Fifty Key Jewish Thinkers
Dan Cohn-Sherbok

Fifty Key Figures in Management
Morgen Witzel

Fifty Major Philosophers
Diané Collinson

Fifty Major Political Thinkers
Ian Adams and R.W. Dyson

Fifty Key Contemporary Thinkers
John Lechte

FIFTY MAJOR POLITICAL THINKERS

Ian Adams and R.W. Dyson

LONDON AND NEW YORK

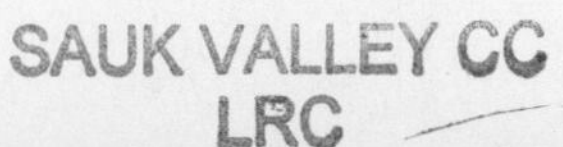

First published 2003
by Routledge
11 New Fetter Lane, London EC4P 4EE

Simultaneously published in the USA and Canada
by Routledge
29 West 35th Street, New York, NY 10001

Routledge is an imprint of the Taylor & Francis Group

Reprinted 2004

Typeset in Bembo by Taylor & Francis Books Ltd
Printed and bound in Great Britain by MPG Books Ltd, Bodmin

British Library Cataloguing in Publication Data
A catalogue record for this book is available from the British Library

Library of Congress Cataloging-in-Publication Data
Adams, Ian, 1943-
Fifty major political thinkers / Ian Adams and R. W. Dyson.
p. cm. – (Routledge key guides)
Includes bibliographical references and index.
1. Political science. 2. Political scientists. I. Dyson, R. W. II. Title. III. Series.

JA66.A314 2003
320′.092′2–dc21 2002045462

ISBN 0–415–22810–7 (hbk)
ISBN 0–415–22811–5 (pbk)

LIST OF CONTENTS

Alphabetical list of contents viii
Preface x

Plato (427–347 BCE) 3

Aristotle (384–322 BCE) 11

St Augustine of Hippo (354–430) 19

John of Salisbury (1120–80) 25

St Thomas Aquinas (1225–74) 28

Marsilius of Padua (*c.*1275–*c.*1343) 35

Nicolò Machiavelli (1469–1527) 38

Sir Thomas More (1478–1535) 47

Thomas Hobbes (1588–1679) 50

James Harrington (1611–77) 57

John Locke (1632–1704) 61

Montesquieu (1689–1755) 68

David Hume (1711–76) 73

Jean-Jacques Rousseau (1712–78) 78

Immanuel Kant (1724–1804) 85

Edmund Burke (1729–97) 88

Tom Paine (1737–1809) 92

Johann Gottfried Herder (1744–1803) 95

Mary Wollstonecraft (1759–97) 99

William Godwin (1756–1836) 101

G.W.F. Hegel (1770–1831) 104

Jeremy Bentham (1748–1832) 112

Charles Fourier (1772–1837) and Utopian Socialism 117

Karl Marx (1818–83) 121

Alexis de Tocqueville (1805–59) 130

John Stuart Mill (1806–73) 134

Herbert Spencer (1820–1903) 139

T.H. Green (1836–82) 142

Friedrich Nietzsche (1844–1900) 146

Prince Peter Kropotkin (1842–1921) and Anarchism 151

Georges Sorel (1847–1922) 155

Eduard Bernstein (1850–1932) 159

Max Weber (1864–1920) 164

Vladimir Ilich Lenin (1870–1924) 171

Benito Mussolini (1883–1945) and Fascism 175

Marcus Garvey (1887–1940) and Black Emancipation 181

Hannah Arendt (1906–75) 188

Sir Isaiah Berlin (1909–97) 190

Friedrich von Hayek (1899–1992) 193

Mohandas Gandhi (1869–1948) 196

Sir Karl Popper (1902–94) 199

Michael Oakeshott (1901–90) 203

Simone de Beauvoir (1908–86) and Second Wave Feminism 206

Herbert Marcuse (1898–1979) and the Frankfurt School 211

Michel Foucault (1926–84) 216

John Rawls (1921–2002) 220

Arne Naess (1912–) and Ecologism 224

Robert Nozick (1938–2002) 227

Jürgen Habermas (1929–) 230

Jean-François Lyotard (1924–98) 236

Glossary 241
Index 252

ALPHABETICAL LIST OF CONTENTS

St Thomas Aquinas (1225–74) 28
Hannah Arendt (1906–75) 188
Aristotle (384–322 BCE) 11
St Augustine of Hippo (354–430) 19
Simone de Beauvoir (1908–86) and Second Wave Feminism 206
Jeremy Bentham (1748–1832) 112
Sir Isaiah Berlin (1909–97) 190
Eduard Bernstein (1850–1932) 159
Edmund Burke (1729–97) 88
Michel Foucault (1926–84) 216
Charles Fourier (1772–1837) and Utopian Socialism 117
Mohandas Gandhi (1869–1948) 196
Marcus Garvey (1887–1940) and Black Emancipation 181
William Godwin (1756–1836) 101
T.H. Green (1836–82) 142
Jürgen Habermas (1929–) 230
James Harrington (1611–77) 57
Friedrich von Hayek (1899–1992) 193
G.W.F. Hegel (1770–1831) 104
Johann Gottfried Herder (1744–1803) 95
Thomas Hobbes (1588–1679) 50
David Hume (1711–76) 73
John of Salisbury (1120–80) 25
Immanuel Kant (1724–1804) 85
Prince Peter Kropotkin (1842–1921) and Anarchism 151
Vladimir Ilich Lenin (1870–1924) 171
John Locke (1632–1704) 61
Jean-François Lyotard (1924–98) 236
Nicolò Machiavelli (1469–1527) 38
Herbert Marcuse (1898–1979) and the Frankfurt School 211

Marsilius of Padua (*c.*1275–*c.*1343) 35
Karl Marx (1818–83) 121
John Stuart Mill (1806–73) 134
Montesquieu (1689–1755) 68
Sir Thomas More (1478–1535) 47
Benito Mussolini (1883–1945) and Fascism 175
Arne Naess (1912–) and Ecologism 224
Friedrich Nietzsche (1844–1900) 146
Robert Nozick (1938–2002) 227
Michael Oakeshott (1901–90) 203
Tom Paine (1737–1809) 92
Plato (427–347 BCE) 3
Sir Karl Popper (1902–94) 199
John Rawls (1921–2002) 220
Jean-Jacques Rousseau (1712–78) 78
Georges Sorel (1847–1922) 155
Herbert Spencer (1820–1903) 139
Alexis de Tocqueville (1805–59) 130
Max Weber (1864–1920) 164
Mary Wollstonecraft (1759–97) 99

PREFACE

The nature of political activity and how it may best be conducted is one of the perennial questions of human existence. In the West alone these matters have been the subject of philosophical discussion for more than 2,000 years, and the discussion is one to which many more than fifty thinkers have contributed. In choosing our fifty we have confined ourselves to Western political thought (with the exception of Mohandas Gandhi, whose ideas were influenced by the West). We have little expertise outside this field, and, besides, non-Western traditions are represented in other volumes in this series. Nor have we been concerned with theoretical debates concerning the 'scientific' study of politics. Even so, the business of choosing the best or most appropriate fifty was a difficult one.

Any shortlist of 'greats' compiled from such a wide and varied field will contain entries of three kinds. First, there will be those names it would be impossible to exclude: in this case Plato, Aristotle, Hobbes, Locke and so on. This part of the list almost compiles itself. Then there will be a penumbra of cases that, though discussable, would probably be included by most knowledgeable people. Finally, there will be a class of substantially controversial entries, where the choice really is a matter of editorial discretion. Anyone who undertakes to draw up such a list will therefore face some difficult decisions, and it is inevitable that the final selection will not be agreeable to everyone. Selection is particularly difficult when we come to the era after the French Revolution: the age of mass politics in which so many movements of political significance have emerged. The *Routledge Dictionary of Twentieth-Century Political Thinkers* (1998) has 178 entries and does not claim to be exhaustive. It is unavoidable that a volume purporting to deal with *major* political theorists will be 'thin' at its modern end, quite simply because, with some few distinguished exceptions, it is not possible to predict which very recent theorists will come to be regarded as 'major' by posterity.

A thinker may be 'major' on a number of grounds: power of reasoning, originality, extent of influence and so on. Choices are inevitably based on a balance of these things. However, for more recent centuries we have introduced a further criterion: that of representativeness. In the politics of the last two centuries there have been many movements which embody important political ideas. Sometimes such movements produce several thinkers of similar stature; or perhaps they produce no great thinker at all, yet the movement itself is important. Hence the decision was made to include some thinkers who are more representative than outstanding. This decision applies to movements such as anarchism, feminism, ecologism, black emancipation and – most controversially, perhaps – fascism.

Using these various criteria, we have tried to do justice to both the variety and the depth of Western political thought, and to encourage readers to explore beyond the fifty thinkers whom, for good or ill, we have chosen.

FIFTY MAJOR POLITICAL THINKERS

PLATO (427–347 BCE)

The philosophy of Plato has the curious property of being delivered almost entirely through the mouth of someone else. Nearly all his surviving works are 'dialogues': transcripts of real or imaginary conversations between groups of acquaintances, in which the chief protagonist is his teacher Socrates. In the dialogues, Socrates is the exponent of the doctrines that Plato wishes to recommend. In principle, it is possible to isolate Socrates' actual opinions from those attributed to him by Plato, but the distinction is problematical, and we shall not try to deal with it. Of Socrates himself we know only what can be gleaned from Plato's dialogues, from the writings of Xenophon, and from the fact that he is sent up in Aristophanes' comedy *Clouds*. A stonemason by trade, he preferred to spend his time discussing philosophy with friends. He wrote nothing. His 'dialectical' method consists in the clarification of concepts by a process of question and answer called *elenchos*. He sees himself not as teaching anything new, but as encouraging people to understand what they know already. He is also a self-proclaimed 'gadfly' whose mission is to pester people into realising that what they think they know is not really knowledge at all.

Plato was Socrates' friend and disciple from *c.*409 until Socrates' death. Plato is the author of three large-scale political works: the *Republic*, the *Politicus* or *Statesman* and the *Laws*. A number of his other dialogues – especially the *Crito* – contain or imply important political doctrines, but it is in the *Republic* that his political philosophy receives its most influential exposition. It is with the *Republic* that we shall be mainly concerned.

Plato's early adulthood coincided with the period of political dislocation following the defeat of Athens in the Peloponnesian War of 431–404 BCE. An immediate consequence of defeat was the overthrow of the democratic constitution of Pericles and the establishment of a ruling council of thirty oligarchs. Plato had high hopes that this oligarchy might preside over a successful post-war reconstruction, but such optimism soon foundered. Especially in the behaviour of Plato's uncle Critias, its most prominent member, the oligarchy was distinguished by an extreme disregard for ordinary standards of morality. Critias was by all accounts a brutal and cynical politician. The 'Thirty Tyrants' adopted methods of government so savage that they alienated many of those wealthy Athenians who had initially regarded their rule with favour. In 403 BCE, a counter-revolution under the leadership of Thrasybulus swept it away and reinstated the democratic constitution. It was under this new regime that Socrates perished, condemned on the curious and probably specious charge of 'not recognising the gods which the city recognises ... introducing new gods [and] corrupting young men' (Diogenes Laertius 2:40). It is likely that he was a political casualty. Although not personally associated with the excesses of the Thirty, he was known to be an associate of the hated Critias. The oligarch Charmides was also a member of his circle, and he was a close friend of Alcibiades, a man of pronounced anti-democratic tendencies. The orator Aeschines, speaking in 345 BCE, tells us that Socrates was condemned because of his association with Critias.

Socrates' condemnation was a defining moment in Plato's career. The celebration of his revered teacher's life became his mission. In 399 BCE, Plato left Athens and remained in voluntary exile until 386 BCE. It is not difficult to imagine his feelings. He had seen the oligarchy of the Thirty, which he had hoped might 'lead men out of a bad way of life into a good one', turn into a sanguinary fiasco. He had seen his friend and teacher condemned under the ensuing democracy. The conclusion formed in his mind that all existing states are bad. While still young, he came to believe that

> mankind's troubles will never cease until either true and genuine philosophers achieve political power or, by some dispensation of providence, rulers of states become genuine philosophers.
>
> (*Seventh Letter*)

Plato is much inclined to associate the political ills of his youth with the group of teachers and orators active in fifth-century Athens known as the Sophists. It is no accident that the literary device by which the *Republic* is got properly under way is a challenge to Socrates by the 'radical' Sophist Thrasymachus. Notionally, the dialogue is an enquiry into the nature of *dikaiosyne*: justice. After a few pages of amiable conversation, the floor is seized by Thrasymachus. He has been listening with irritation to the polite attempts of the protagonists to discover what justice is. Plato wants us to think him boorish and discourteous. Thrasymachus offers his own definition: 'Justice is nothing else than the interest of the stronger.' This dictum is clearly intended to exemplify the political amoralism that Plato associates with the younger generation of Sophists (of whom Callicles, in the dialogue called *Gorgias*, is another example). In the long discussion that occupies the rest of Book I, Thrasymachus is made to shift his ground several times. What he has in mind, it turns out, is not quite that justice is the interest of the stronger, but that it is in the interest of the stronger for *others* to be just and he himself unjust. His position can be reduced to the following four assertions:

1 The good life consists in disregarding all limit or restriction and enjoying a life of boundless gratification. People are happy to the extent that they do not have to consider anyone else's interests but their own. The same general sentiment is expressed by Callicles in the *Gorgias*.
2 'Justice' means 'compliance with the law'. It therefore involves accepting the limits or controls prescribed for one by a superior.
3 Laws are rules made by the strong and imposed by them on the weak. They are the devices by which the strong control the weak to their own advantage – or at any rate to what they believe is their own advantage.
4 The interest of the ruler is therefore best served when his subjects are just – that is, when they comply with his laws – and he himself is able to be 'unjust' in the sense of not limited by any will opposed to his own. In this sense, Thrasymachus thinks, injustice is better and stronger than justice.

Unsurprisingly, Thrasymachus is a frank admirer of tyranny. The good ruler will be the ruler who takes advantage of his subjects as fully and successfully as possible. Subjects, by contrast, will be people who live stultified and frustrated lives. This is precisely the kind of attitude to which Plato attributes the capricious and violent style of politics that he had experienced as a young man, and the whole of the rest of the *Republic* is an attempt, using Socrates as a mouthpiece, to rebut it.

Thrasymachus believes that injustice is preferable to justice because justice involves the acceptance of restrictions. The just man is a kind of amiable fool. The naturally superior man knows that the good life is a matter of disregarding all limits. But, Socrates points out, to characterise the good life in this way is obviously a mistake. If we aim at a life in which all limits are ignored, we shall simply not be able to get what we want. A musician who tunes his instrument has to tighten the strings to a suitable degree: neither more nor less. A physician who treats a patient has to give just the right amount of treatment: neither more nor less. Paradoxically, even robbers have to observe a kind of 'justice'. They have to act within the rules that govern the division of labour within the gang. If they do not, the gang will not be able to achieve the purposes for which it came together in the first place. The successful conduct of any human activity depends upon observing the limits that constitute the possibility of that activity. If remaining within limits is what we mean by justice, then, it seems that justice is not, after all, a conventional device invented by the strong to control the weak. 'Justice' is natural in the sense of being indispensable to any kind of coherent action, and injustice is not so much wrong as self-defeating. To the extent that human life is a purposive activity, justice is essential to its successful conduct.

Justice to the individual human being – to the individual soul, as Socrates expresses it – is therefore what sharpness is to a knife or keenness is to the eye. It is the 'virtue' that enables the soul to perform its function properly. Just as you can prune a vine after a fashion with a chisel or a blunt knife, so you can live, after a fashion, with an unjust soul; but it will not be the best kind of life. Clearly, then, it is important for us to understand what the justice of the individual soul actually is, or where in the soul it lies. In order to do this, Socrates says, we should first identify justice in the *polis* or state. By considering justice on a large scale, we shall be better able to understand it on the small or individual scale.

What, then, constitutes the justice of the state? Socrates answers this question not by analysing the constitution of any existing state, but by describing the development of an imaginary or 'ideal' state, which he calls Kallipolis ('Beautiful City'). Such a state would originate in the fact that human beings need to co-operate in order to meet their material needs. But the meeting of basic needs will inevitably produce more sophisticated needs, and so more complex structures will have to be devised to supply them. At the end-point of its evolution, Socrates suggests, the state will contain three occupational groups, between whom the state's 'virtues' will be distributed. These groups are called Guardians, Auxiliaries and Producers. The Guardians will embody the state's wisdom; the Auxiliaries or military class will embody its courage; the Producers will embody temperance or self-restraint, in that they will recognise that it is necessary for them to submit to the rule of the Guardians. Justice, Socrates argues, will not be a separate virtue in addition to courage, wisdom and self-restraint. It will be the relationship that holds when the Auxiliaries and Producers remain within the limits prescribed for them by the Guardians. Justice, in other words, will obtain when the Guardians, Auxiliaries and Producers function together in such a way as to secure the good of the whole community. Justice is a matter of everyone doing the job for which they are best suited and not interfering with anyone else.

Extrapolating from this, we can now say something about justice in the individual soul. The soul, Socrates suggests, has three parts or functions: reason, appetite and spirit or emotion. He does not explain why he believes there to be three and only three parts, but this does not affect his argument. What is important to the argument is that we accept that the soul does have parts, corresponding at least roughly to the parts of the state. Clearly, neither appetite nor spirit can function properly without the guidance of reason. A life of undirected appetite or of random and uncontrolled emotion would be a futile and frustrating one. By analogy with the state, then, Justice is present in the soul when appetite and spirit are guided by reason in such a way as to secure the good of the whole. The successful conduct of life – successful, that is, in terms of achieving the happiness that all individuals desire – depends upon our having a properly ordered soul; or, as one might nowadays express it, a well-integrated personality.

Is a version of justice that so emphasises the securing of individual happiness much of an improvement on the Sophist doctrine that self-gratification is really everybody's goal? This objection is developed in the *Republic* by the brothers Glaucon and Adeimantus. The arguments that occur to them are the obvious ones. Why should I not use my reason simply to direct my appetites and emotions so as to get what I want at someone else's expense? Why should I not pretend to be just when it suits me, and grab as much for myself as I can when I can do it without detection? If I could become invisible at will, would there still be any point in being just? Stated generally, Socrates' response to such questions is that people with properly integrated personalities – those whose wants and impulses are proportionate and not irrational and excessive – would *ipso facto* not *want* to grab as much as they could for themselves. The just man would be a happy, contented, well-adjusted individual whose desires would not outstrip his needs. He would have no reason for not spontaneously recognising the moral claims of others and willing their happiness and good as well as his own. Justice understood as a quality of soul certainly secures the interests of the just person, but it is other-regarding also.

In practice, however, we come across few individuals who are just in this sense. This is so, Socrates thinks, because most people lack *knowledge*. They do not *know* the nature of such things as justice, right, goodness and so forth. They therefore cannot conduct their lives according to fixed or stable principles of reason. Experience suggests that most people live in the kind of world described by the Sophists Protagoras and Gorgias: a world in which there is no certain knowledge, but only opinion or belief. Such a world is unstable because opinions or beliefs can so easily be changed. Especially, they can be changed by the influence of demagogues, of persuasive orators. This, Socrates suggests, is a particular danger in democracies, because the conditions of life that democracies furnish tend to produce weak-willed and indecisive people. The only truly just men, Socrates thinks, are those who have knowledge rather than opinion: those who are *philosophoi*, 'wisdom lovers', as distinct from 'lovers of sights and sounds'. Ideally, therefore, it is philosophers who should have responsibility for governing the state.

What, though, is knowledge as distinct from opinion? The Sophists were epistemological sceptics; they had denied the possibility of any such thing as knowledge. As far as they are concerned, we live in a world in which certainty is impossible because no single opinion can be shown to be truer than its contradictory. Socrates agrees that the world of ordinary sense experience is full of uncertainty, but he believes that the right kind of education – a philosophical education – can lead the mind away from the concrete world of appearance into a 'real' world of 'forms' or 'ideas'. This 'theory of forms', as it is called, is a strange and problematical doctrine that is never fully expounded in any of Plato's dialogues, but to which he often refers. (It should be remembered that we are here having to state it very simply.) Every just act, every beautiful object is, he thinks, just and beautiful because, and only because, it 'participates' in a pure idea of justice and beauty: an idea capable of being apprehended by the trained mind only. These ideas, as Socrates depicts them, are capable of enlightening the mind as to the true nature of the things of which they are the ideas. The ambiguity exhibited by so many things in the 'world of sight' is due to the fact that they are only imperfect copies of the ideas in which they participate. Most people only experience the copies, and do not realise that they are copies. Such people suppose mere appearance to be reality. But the philosopher, by definition, is one who has grasped the ideas themselves, and whose activity is therefore now informed by true knowledge rather than unstable opinion. He is like a prisoner who has escaped into the sun from a cave in which his fellow men are bound in darkness. He has gone beyond the veil of shadowy belief and understood the true nature of things. For this reason, he is uniquely able to rule others.

For Socrates, then, the best state would be an aristocracy presided over by those who have transcended the world of appearance which most of us occupy and who therefore do what is good because they *know* what is good. They will not legislate; they will govern at their own personal discretion. Despite the Sophists' typical assumption, they will not exploit their subjects to secure their own interests. Quite apart from the fact that they are enlightened beings whose acts are informed by knowledge, the educational and social system of the ideal city will require them to live in such a way as to abolish from their minds any thought of private gain or glory. They will have no families and no property. They will seek only the common good, and they will act in such a way as to secure a life of virtue and happiness for all, according to the abilities and station of each.

In recent times, commentators have tended to deplore Plato's mistrust of democracy. Such critics deprecate his lack of belief in the capacity of ordinary human beings to organise their lives without paternalistic supervision. They complain that the regime over which Plato's philosopher-rulers preside is a totalitarian one: that they are despots who, on the strength of the knowledge that they claim, control every aspect of their subjects' lives, by methods just as disreputable as those for which Plato is so ready to reproach the Sophists. The kind of knowledge that Plato values is not used to make people free, but only to create the kind of unfreedom that he regards as benign.

This kind of criticism hardly deserves to be taken seriously. For one thing, it is pointless to censure Plato for not having had the kind of values and opinions that modern liberals applaud. For another, such criticism does not pay heed to what Plato's intentions really are. On the one hand, it is certainly his view that only a few people will have the talent to become rulers, and that the ignorant should follow the leadership of the wise. It is also true that, as far as Plato is concerned, the Guardians will, where necessary, use myth, persuasion and deception as devices for governing the commonwealth. They will lie when they have to; they will secretly fix the ballots that allot mating partners in order to bring about the best combinations; they will perpetuate the 'noble lie' that the gods have made men of gold, silver and bronze and that each should know his place. But, on the other hand, Plato is quite clearly sincere in his belief that these things will be done not for the sake of the rulers themselves, but in order to achieve a collective and long-term good. The Guardians will do such things because they have to shape into a semblance of virtue those who are not equipped with the resources to be virtuous spontaneously. They themselves, however, will be men of supreme goodness of intention. They will live lives of austerity and disinterest; they will deploy all their considerable resources of intellect for the well-being of the community over which they preside; they will strive to see to it that those subject to them live happy and complete lives within the limits of what is possible for them.

In his later political thought, as represented in the *Politicus* and *Laws*, Plato somewhat revised his faith in the sovereign rule of the wise, although he never wholly relinquished it. This later development is usually thought to be related to two things. First, misgivings about his epistemological doctrines may have led Plato to question what he had once taken to be the straightforward link between abstract knowledge and political practice. It is clear that, with the passage of time, he began to have second thoughts about his 'theory of forms'. His revaluation of it is exemplified in the late dialogue called *Parmenides*. This is a remarkable essay in self-criticism, in which Plato anticipates a number of objections later voiced by **Aristotle** in his *Metaphysics*. Second, and possibly more important, in 367 BCE Plato became the political adviser of Dionysius II, the young tyrant of Syracuse. Here, he thought, might be an opportunity to mould a real-life version of the philosophically enlightened statesman. The experiment proved a dismal failure. Plato found himself involved in a series of political imbroglios that left his faith in the idea of a philosopher-ruler much deflated. In the *Politicus* he is still committed in principle to the notion of an ideal statesman, but his theme now is that such a statesman is unlikely to be found and that, in his absence, the second-best form of government will be that of conscientious rulers whose actions are circumscribed by law. Such rulers do not have knowledge strictly so-called. They do not themselves understand the art or science of politics. But wise laws can at least give them true opinion, and the rule of true opinion is better than arbitrariness and favouritism. It is, however, not entirely clear where such wise laws are to come from. Plato's last dialogue, the *Laws*, probably completed shortly before his death, represents the apotheosis of law in his political thought. The ideal state described in it – called 'Magnesia' – is governed in minute detail by laws devised and administered by a 'Nocturnal Council'. The members of this Council are recognisably like the Guardians of the *Republic*, but it is no longer supposed that their wisdom will enable them to rule the state by personal discretion alone. Plato's final position is that the best attainable kind of state is one governed by laws embodying, albeit imperfectly, a kind of collective and accumulated wisdom. Under such an arrangement, civic virtue is the will to obey laws that regulate every detail of life, even down to the most trivial.

Further reading

Primary sources

Republic, ed. F.M. Cornford (Oxford: Oxford University Press, 1941).

Statesman, ed. J.B. Skemp (New York: Liberal Arts Press, 1957).
Laws, ed. T.J. Saunders (Harmondsworth: Penguin, 1970).

Secondary sources

Annas, J.: *An Introduction to Plato's Republic* (Oxford: Clarendon Press, 1981).
Coleman, J.: *A History of Political Thought*, vol. 1 (Oxford: Blackwell, 2000).
Cross, R.C. and Woozley, A.D.: *Plato's Republic: A Philosophical Commentary* (London: Macmillan, 1964).
Klosko, G.: *The Development of Plato's Political Theory* (London and New York: Methuen, 1986).
Sayers, S.: *Plato's Republic: An Introduction* (Edinburgh: Edinburgh University Press, 1999).

ARISTOTLE (384–322 BCE)

Aristotle was born at Stagira, a Greek colony of Thrace. He became a member of Plato's Academy in 367 BCE. It is said that he expected to be made head of the Academy when **Plato** died. Disappointed in this expectation, he left Athens. After three rather mysterious but decisively formative years spent in the court of Hermias at Assos, in 343 BCE he accepted a post at the court of Philip of Macedon, as tutor to the future Alexander the Great. He returned to Athens in 335 BCE and opened his own school, the Lyceum. His connection with Alexander made him unpopular with Athenian patriots after Alexander's death in 323 BCE, and he again left the city. He died at Chalcis in Euboea. Of his numerous philosophical, logical and scientific works, the ones directly of interest to us are the *Nicomachean Ethics* and *Politics*. Like nearly all his extant works, these were posthumously assembled from literary remains by his family and students (the Nicomachus of the *Nicomachean Ethics* was Aristotle's son). This fact has given rise to serious textual complications.

The naturalness, and therefore the rightness, of political life is a constant theme of Aristotle's political and ethical writing. 'Man is *by nature* a political animal. Whoever is outside the state is either greater than human or less than human' (*Politics* 1:2). The state – the *polis* – is, he thinks, the only setting within which human beings can live the sort of lives appropriate to their kind. Aristotle's *Politics* is devoted to a technical analysis of the ways in which states can be organised. The ethical presuppositions that inform this analysis are mostly found in the *Nicomachean Ethics*.

Aristotle's general view of the world is of the kind known as *teleological*. Everything in the universe has a *telos* – an 'end' or 'purpose'

– peculiar to itself. By this, Aristotle does not mean that everything has a 'purpose' in the way that it is the purpose of a knife to cut or a pen to write. Things which are not artefacts, which have not been made to do something, have *teloi* in the sense of having a state of full or final development towards which it is their nature to unfold. The *telos* of an acorn is to become an oak tree. The process whereby it does so is its *ergon*, its work or task. The natural capacity it has for engaging in and completing this process is its *dynamis*. Finally, what we mean when we call a thing 'good' is that it has achieved its *telos* successfully. A good pen is a pen that writes well, a good oak tree is a fully grown specimen, and so on.

What is the *telos*, and hence the good, of man? It is, Aristotle says, the achievement of a state of *eudaimonia*. The customary translation of *eudaimonia* is 'happiness', but 'happiness' means less than Aristotle does by *eudaimonia*. For Aristotle, the word denotes a lifelong state of active ethical well-being considered as the goal of human activity. How do we know that 'happiness' is man's 'end' in this sense? We know it because we know both that we desire happiness and that we do not desire it for the sake of anything else. If someone asks why we want money or power, we might say that we want them because they will make us happy. But if anyone asks why we want to be happy, we do not reply in terms of some objective lying beyond happiness. Happiness is the 'end' in the uncomplicated sense of there being no further desideratum to which it is a means. Moreover, happiness is only properly such when it is continued or continuous throughout life. Happiness cannot be something evanescent or trivial. We cannot really say that a man's life has been 'happy' until it is over, since only then can it be reviewed in its entirety.

By what means, then, are we to accomplish this end, and hence this good? It is, Aristotle thinks, only by identifying some mode of activity in which no other creature is equipped to engage that we can identify a *telos* peculiar to human beings. We need, therefore, to find a capacity, a *dynamis*, that we and only we have. This *dynamis* cannot consist merely in the processes of living, for plants are alive; nor can it consist in being alive and sentient, for then we should have no *telos* separate from that of the beasts. It must, Aristotle concludes, have to do with *reason*, the capacity, which no other creature has, to engage in connected and purposive thought. And it must lie in the use rather than the possession of reason: musicians are not musicians because they own, but because they play, their instruments. Again, it cannot lie in the *mere* use of reason: someone is a good harpist not because they play the harp, but because they play it well. We shall not, therefore, call someone a good man unless he uses his reason well: unless he uses it 'according to virtue'. The 'point' of human life is to achieve 'happiness' through rational activity according to virtue. This is the 'end' prescribed for us by our nature.

Aristotle uses the word 'virtue' to mean two different but related things. He speaks of moral virtues, which are virtues in the usual sense, and *dianoetic* or intellectual virtues, of which two are of interest to us: *sophia* and *phronesis*. Difficulties inherent in the texts as they have been transmitted to us sometimes make Aristotle's meaning less than obvious, but he seems to think that happiness is associated in different ways, or at different levels, with the deployment of both types of virtue. On the one hand, happiness in the fullest sense lies in the contemplation of abstract ideas and their logical relations. Such activity requires the deployment of the intellectual virtue called *sophia*: 'theoretical' or 'demonstrative' wisdom. Demonstrative reasoning has no practical outcome. It is the activity of philosophical thought pure and simple, divested of any connection with the material world. To practise such reasoning is to enjoy happiness of the most sublime kind, removed from all change and uncertainty. The philosopher, in so far as he is a philosopher, is without want and without pain, rapt as the gods are in the calm and desireless contemplation of the eternal and changeless. 'The human activity that most resembles the activity of the gods will most of all have the character of happiness' (*Nicomachean Ethics* 10:8). On the other hand, the happiness of philosophical contemplation, precisely because it is so sublime, cannot be the normal condition of anyone's life. No one can live permanently in a state of abstraction to the exclusion of everyday activity. Are we, then, to say that so exclusive a form of happiness is the only sort of happiness? Clearly not, since we want to discover a happiness capable of being achieved by mankind in general and throughout life as a whole. We need to look for a kind of happiness that is, so to speak, more mundane or everyday.

It is here that the moral virtues come in. Happiness for most of us, most of the time, is to be found not in abstract reasoning, but in the practice of good or honourable behaviour in everyday life. This statement is not inconsistent with the view that the philosophical life is the most sublime of all.

> But in a secondary degree, life according to the other kind of virtue [moral virtue] is happy; for activity according to this is suitable to our human condition.
>
> (*Nicomachean Ethics* 10:8)

'Secondary' or everyday happiness, then, consists in the practice of the moral virtues, the moral virtues being such things as courage, temperance, generosity and justice. But in what specific kinds of action does the practice of these virtues consist? It is in this connection that Aristotle proposes his doctrine of the mean. Morally virtuous activity, he says, is

> a habit of choice lying in a mean, relative to ourselves, determined according to a rational principle in the way that a man of practical wisdom would determine it . . . between two vices, the one of excess and the other of defect.
>
> (*Nicomachean Ethics* 2:6)

The principle is clear enough. Courageous behaviour lies somewhere between the foolish courting of danger and the timorous shirking of it. The man of temperance neither suppresses his natural appetites altogether, nor does he wallow in them swinishly: he enjoys what is enjoyable in the right measure and at the right time. An important part of the definition is the phrase 'relative to ourselves': that is, 'relative to the kind of person we are and the position in which we find ourselves'. The practice of moral virtue is a matter of doing what is suitable to person, time and place while avoiding extremes. One cannot prescribe hard and fast rules in advance. The specific and appropriate manifestations of courage, temperance and so on will be different at different times and in different circumstances, and will be subject to the judgement of the agent. Sometimes, indeed, it will be appropriate to be intensely pleased or intensely angry. What the doctrine of the mean prescribes is not the avoidance of intense feeling or strenuous action, but the avoidance of responses that are excessive in the sense of unsuitable to the occasion.

The practice of moral virtue brings into play an intellectual virtue different from the *sophia* that we deploy when philosophising. In order to find the mean, one needs to be 'a man of practical wisdom', a *phronimos*. *Phronesis*, 'practical reasoning' or 'prudence', is the type of thinking that we engage in when we debate with ourselves what to do in any given situation. The aim of *phronesis* as distinct from *sophia* is not abstract and universal knowledge, but action of a practically or morally beneficial kind. *Phronesis* does not identify moral goals as such. These are given by our disposition to seek the mean, and this disposition is formed not by reason or deliberation, but by habit. But *phronesis* specifies for us what our conduct should be in given circumstances if we are to achieve our moral goals. 'Virtue makes us aim at the right mark, and practical wisdom makes us take the right means' (*Nicomachean Ethics* 6:13).

Our 'end', then, is *eudaimonia*, 'happiness'. We accomplish it by living well throughout life as a whole, and living well is a matter of rational activity well performed. Supreme happiness is found in abstract contemplation by means of the intellectual virtue of *sophia*, undistracted by mundane concerns; but this is hardly an attainable goal for life considered at large. For ordinary purposes, happiness lies in the consistent practice of moral virtue, calling upon the intellectual virtue of *phronesis* to guide us in our specific acts. This teleological analysis is, we recall, an analysis in terms of nature. The end that man has is the end appropriate to his nature. We recall also that 'man is by nature a political animal'. What, then, is the connection between our natural end as moral creatures and our natural existence as political ones? Just as Plato does in his discussion of the beginnings of political association, Aristotle makes the point that, as a preliminary to any kind of moral activity at all, we need material conditions of life that depend upon a division of labour. It is a fact of nature that no individual can supply himself with all the necessaries of life. Thus all forms of human association are natural in so far as they meet a particular level of material need: the household is natural; so is the village; so is the *polis*. But it is the *polis* that is the most completely sufficient, and therefore the most completely natural, community. Unlike less developed forms of association, the *polis* enables all our needs to be met in their entirety. Aristotle has in mind here not only economic needs, but also the full range of moral needs that we have as rational creatures. 'The state comes into existence so that men may live; it remains in being so that they may live well' (*Politics* 1:2). The following points will amplify this maxim.

First: the *polis* provides the economic prerequisites of morality. Economic and moral needs are intertwined. Neither the supremely happy life of contemplation nor the balanced, rational and moral life of the kind that Aristotle identifies with 'ordinary' happiness can be lived in conditions of want. Too plentiful a supply of external goods is bad for us: it encourages laziness and arrogance. We should engage in economic activity only to the extent necessary to meet our needs. Economic activity for profit alone is unnatural; as is usury, the use of money to create merely paper values. But a sufficient level of material prosperity is necessary if we are to live well. We cannot engage in pursuits suitable to rational creatures if we are distracted by care or if we lack health and leisure. We cannot be generous unless we have the means with which to be generous, or just unless we have the means to pay our debts. The processes of production and distribution that the *polis* makes possible therefore have moral as well as economic dimensions.

Second: the *polis* provides the educational conditions upon which the cultivation and realisation of moral virtue depend. For Aristotle, education in moral as distinct from intellectual virtue is a matter of acquiring habituated modes of behaviour through training and repetition. It is by *doing* virtuous acts that we learn to be virtuous, just as it is by practising music that we become accomplished musicians. It is therefore an important function of legislation to make men good by requiring or encouraging them to form good habits. Aristotle believes that law can in this way make men good, as distinct from merely inducing conformity. This, at least partly, is why he says that 'Man, when perfected, is the best of all creatures, but when isolated from law and justice he is the worst of all' (*Politics* 1:2). Also, it is by associating with others like ourselves and participating in a common life that we develop *phronesis*, that we become accomplished in the practice of deliberating and acting correctly. The life of the *polis* – life as part of a social community governed by law – provides the conditions of our moral education and practice.

Third: the *polis* provides the social preconditions of our ethical good. This is because it is not in our nature to be solitary, nor is it in our nature to find satisfaction or happiness solely in ourselves and our own interests. We take pleasure in and achieve fulfilment through interaction with other human beings. In its everyday, attainable sense, happiness will be incomplete unless it is involved to some extent with the happiness of others. Aristotle does not mean that human beings are natural altruists who put the good of others before their own; nor does he think that our interest in the welfare of others can or should be limitless. What he means is that the good of others can make an important contribution to our own good. We derive pleasure and satisfaction from the concern that we feel for our friends and from the shared activities that friendship makes possible. Friendship takes a number of different forms, not all of them disinterested, but the love of friends for their own sake is one of the highest pleasures that life affords. On the other hand, if we take no interest in the welfare and happiness of others, we cut ourselves off from relationships of shared concern and trust that are necessary to the fulfilment of our natural capacities as social beings. Also, since the moral virtues are pre-eminently social virtues, it is clear that moral virtue cannot be practised alone: one cannot be generous or just without other people to be generous or just to.

The *polis* as Aristotle depicts it, therefore, is a natural community in that it meets all the needs, both moral and material, attaching to the natures of those who occupy it. Severed from the *polis*, human beings lose their identity, just as a hand does if severed from the body. We are defined by the organic relations existing between us and the whole of which we are parts. By the same token, because the *polis* is an all-sufficient community in this sense, it must be true that the study of politics is the master science by which all other studies bearing on human happiness are defined. Political science is the study of the common good: 'its end must be the good for man' (*Nicomachean Ethics* 1:2).

This idea of politics as a systematic and practical investigation accounts for Aristotle's interest in the comparison and classification of constitutions. Aristotle defines a constitution as 'the organisation of a *polis* with respect to its offices generally, but especially with respect to that office which is sovereign over all matters' (*Politics* 3:6). He does not wish to argue, as Plato does, for one ideal constitution from which every other is necessarily a decline. He knows that, in practice, states have devised many ways of organising themselves and that we have to deal with what exists rather than with what ought to exist. He knows that even the worst arrangements can be improved, and that what is best for one *polis* may not suit another. All these conclusions are largely the result of a determinedly comparative approach. Aristotle is said to have written (or supervised the writing of) treatises on 158 Greek city-states, although only one of them, on *The Constitution of Athens*, is extant.

The most general conclusion to which his comparisons lead him is that constitutional types are classifiable into three broad categories: rule by one, by few and by many. Aristotle deals in detail with these three types and their possible permutations. He is largely concerned with technical questions of stability and change. With considerable impartiality, he recommends ways in which even bad or dysfunctional constitutions can be made more stable. The stability of a constitution is, he thinks, secured by balancing elements of 'fewness' and 'manyness' in such a way as to ensure that as few people as possible are excluded or alienated. In general, the more moderate and broadly based a constitution is, the more stable it will be. By the same token, 'pure' forms of constitution have instability built into them because they will always contain disaffected groups. Oligarchies will antagonise the poor, who are numerous; democracies will antagonise the rich, who are few but influential. Thus, oligarchies can protect themselves by admitting as many people as possible to some share of political power; democracies can make themselves more stable by pursuing moderation with regard to the redistribution of wealth and by placating the wealthy with dignified and expensive offices. The most stable constitution will be one in which political power rests with a large middle class: that is, one that is a government of neither the wealthy few nor the propertyless many, but somewhere between the two. The members of the middle class are not wealthy enough to be resented, but they are sufficiently well off not to want to dispossess the rich. This is the political expression of Aristotle's doctrine of the mean.

But, as we might expect, given the close connection that he draws between politics and ethics, Aristotle's interest in constitutions is not purely analytic and taxonomic. He is concerned with constitutions not simply as organisational, but as moral phenomena. To that extent, the designation 'political scientist', with its implication of value-freedom, does not belong to him. The *moral quality* of a constitution, considered as something apart from stability and longevity, is, he thinks, not a matter of structure but of what one might call intentionality. It is a matter of the *good* at which the ruler or ruling group aims. Aristocracy and monarchy are good constitutions, oligarchy and tyranny are bad or degenerate ones; yet aristocracy and oligarchy both involve rule by the few. Outwardly, in terms of the visible distribution of power, they look the same. But aristocracy is rule by the best men for the good of all, whereas oligarchy is rule by the wealthy for their own good. Similarly, monarchy and tyranny are both rule by one, but a monarch rules for the good of all and a tyrant for his own good. What Aristotle calls 'polity' is rule by the many for the common good; its bad counterpart, democracy, is, in effect, mob rule: rule by the many for the good of the many. Good constitutions answer to the true nature of a constitution by securing the good of all their members; bad or degenerate constitutions fail to do so because they secure the good of a part or group only.

Notwithstanding Aristotle's 'scientific' interest in political forms and dynamics, then, he thinks that politics is ultimately worthwhile as a mode of human experience only in so far as political arrangements secure not a narrow or sectional good, but the interests of those whose arrangements they are. Genuine monarchies and aristocracies are rare. It may happen that individuals appear on the scene who are so superior by nature that it is obviously right to hand over responsibility for government to them, but such individuals are, in the nature of the case, seldom found. Thus, although he is prepared to regard any constitutional form as good if it aims at the good of all the citizens, Aristotle considers that, on the whole, the best achieveable kinds of political association will be those that involve as many people – or, at any rate, as many free, non-foreign males – as possible in the processes of government. Similarly, the best kind of *polis* will be large enough to be self-sufficient, but small enough for everyone to be able to participate in its life. Where the citizens are united under a good constitution, governed by just and impartial laws, and all play a part in bringing about the good of the whole community, the virtue of the good man and the virtue of the good citizen will be the same. The moral purpose of the commonwealth will be realised most fully.

Between them, Plato and Aristotle furnish what subsequent political philosophy was to regard as 'the' classical doctrine of the state. Virtually all subsequent Western political theory has owed something, acknowledged or unacknowledged, to their efforts. Their broad conclusion, that the state exists by nature to enhance the lives of its members, was, if not the sole, at least the dominant, theory of political association down to the establishment, in the fifth century, of a new and Christianised version of politics. This in itself is a measure of their achievement.

Further reading

Primary sources

Nicomachean Ethics, ed. W.D. Ross (Oxford: Oxford University Press, 1980).
Politics, ed. C. Lord (Chicago, IL, and London: University of Chicago Press, 1984).

Secondary sources

Coleman, J.: *A History of Political Thought*, vol.1 (Oxford: Blackwell, 2000).
Davis, M.: *The Politics of Philosophy* (Lanham, MD: Rowman & Littlefield, 1996).
Hardie, W.F.R.: *Aristotle's Ethical Theory* (Oxford: Oxford University Press, 1968).
Kraut, R.: *Aristotle* (Oxford: Oxford University Press, 1995).
Mulgan, R.G.: *Aristotle's Political Theory* (Oxford: Clarendon Press, 1977).

ST AUGUSTINE OF HIPPO (354–430)

Augustine was born at Thagaste (modern Suk Ahras, in Algeria). His mother was a Christian, but he did not respond well to her efforts to educate him in the faith. As a young man he admired Cicero and Plotinus, and flirted with Manichaeism and Scepticism. His mature intellectual position may be described as Christian Neoplatonism. Having in 384 accepted a position at Milan as a teacher of rhetoric, he came under the influence of prominent Christians in that city. After a long mental struggle, recounted in detail in his *Confessions*, he was baptised by St Ambrose on Holy Saturday, 387. He was ordained priest in 391, and in 396 became Bishop of Hippo (the modern Algerian town of Annaba), where he remained until his death. Augustine's literary output was immense, but he is not a political 'theorist' in the ordinary sense. The political doctrines with which he is associated emerged largely as by-products of the controversies in which he engaged as a Christian bishop and intellectual. The belief that his huge work called *The City of God* is the repository of a completed political philosophy, though common, is false. His political thought needs to be assembled from a range of literature – letters, sermons, scriptural commentaries, polemical works, doctrinal treatises – produced during a span of more than thirty years. A brief summary of it inevitably makes Augustine look more systematic than he is.

To the extent that summary is possible, it must begin with Augustine's doctrines of original sin, grace and predestination. Adam and Eve were created with free will. In eating the forbidden fruit they sinned precisely because they *chose* to disobey God's command. In doing so, they disrupted the natural order of justice: they placed love of self before love of God. They were punished by expulsion from Eden and by the penalties of death and pain. But their sin has had grave consequences for all their offspring also. Each subsequent member of the human race is a vessel made from the same lump of clay, and the impurities introduced into that lump are in us too. Each of us is born guilty of the original sin. Moreover, we have inherited from our first parents a defective will. We are born incapable of acting in any way that is not actuated by avarice, pride and self-love. All that is left of our free will is the freedom to choose which of the many available sins actually to commit. Considered simply as such, we come into this world deserving only damnation. Augustine does not try to deal with the obvious difficulties that this account of the human condition involves. His warrant for it is Holy Scripture, or at any rate his interpretation of Holy Scripture, and the testimony of scripture is, he thinks, beyond question.

Because God is omniscient, He knew from all eternity that Adam would sin, and in His mercy He resolved to rescue a few, but only a few, members of the human race from the wreck. He does this by bestowing upon them the grace that enables them truly to place love of God before love of self, and so to act from motives other than greed, pride and lust. This grace cannot be earned or deserved. It is a free gift of God, bestowed upon the predestined few by His own unmotived choice. These predestined ones, the Elect, are members of the *civitas Dei*, the City of God. The rest of mankind are members of the Earthly City, the *civitas terrena*. They are the unchosen, the reprobate, doomed to damnation without hope of reprieve. We do not know why God has predestined some and not others, or some rather than all, or a few rather than many, but we are not entitled to question His judgement. The fact that God damns the majority of mankind shows His justice; the fact that he saves a few shows His mercy.

Augustine's medieval admirers tended to regard the City of God as a metaphor for the institutional Church, and the Earthly City as symbolising the power of kings and emperors. It is important to understand that this is not what Augustine means. The City of God is not in a particular place or time. It consists partly of the Elect who are alive on earth, but it consists also of the souls of the Elect who have died and gone to heaven, and of those angels who remained loyal to God after Satan's rebellion. It is the *communio sanctorum*, the whole community of those who love God. Similarly, the Earthly City is the community of those united by 'love of self extending even to contempt of God' (*De civitate Dei* 14:28). It includes those of the reprobate who are currently alive, the souls of the reprobate who have died and now suffer in hell, and the demons or fallen angels.

Everyone is a member of one or other of the Cities, depending on how God has predestined them. On earth, however, the two cities are for the time being mingled together. Their members share the same resources and undergo the same tribulations. No one can tell by any outward sign who belongs to which, and all earthly communities, including the Church, contain members of both. The two cities will remain thus mingled until the Final Judgment, when Christ will separate the saved from the damned and each contingent will receive 'the end to which there is no end' (*De civitate Dei* 18:54).

What, then, of politics? **Plato** and **Aristotle** had held that political life is natural to man. They considered the life of the *polis*, the city-state, to be peculiarly appropriate to human nature as rational, deliberative and co-operative. But Augustine departs from this principle fundamentally. When God created man, He gave him dominion over the beasts, but not over others of his own kind. Human beings were intended to live together in harmony and equality under a natural law having a single precept: do not do to others what you would not want to have done to you. But the entry of sin into the world corrupted human nature in such a way as to make spontaneous social co-operation impossible. The avarice and self-love that distinguish the behaviour of fallen man manifest themselves above all in what Augustine calls *libido dominandi*: the desire to rule and control. It is this human drive that has brought the state into existence. The state is the institutionalisation of the human lust for dominion.

But the state has positive functions also. If it were not for its controlling and limiting influence, men would destroy one another in their struggle to master each other and control the earth's resources. To the extent that it prevents this by holding human destructiveness in check, the state is a remedy for the material consequences of sin as well as being one of those consequences. Inevitably, it will achieve its purposes largely by terror and pain. Human power, to Augustine's mind, is embodied in the hangman and the torturer. Also, its legal and judicial mechanisms are all too fallible. Often the innocent are condemned and the guilty go free. But here again the state has a divinely intended purpose. The harshness and injustice associated with it serve to punish the wicked for their sins and test and refine the righteous on their earthly pilgrimage. As is His wont, God uses evil to bring forth good.

For Augustine, then, the state is to be understood under three aspects. It is a result of sin, a means of limiting the material damage done by sin, and a disciplinary order. Augustine's opinion of political activity as such is not high. At *De civitate Dei* 4:4 he relates with approval the anecdote (derived from Cicero) of the pirate arrested and brought before Alexander the Great. 'How dare you infest the sea?' the emperor demands. 'I do exactly the same as you,' retorts the pirate, 'but I have only one ship, and you have a navy.' In his lengthy critique of Cicero at *De civitate Dei* 2:21 and 19:21, Augustine argues that no earthly state can embody *vera iustitia*, true justice. Justice, according to the classical definition, consists in rendering to each their due. But the population of all earthly states, even those that are notionally Christian, will contain a majority of individuals who belong to the Earthly City and who therefore withhold from the true God the worship that is His due. Clearly, then, no such state can be just collectively, even if some of its individual members are just. The state is not a moral community. It has no bearing on our inner lives. The earthly justice which it can enforce is only a pale copy of *vera iustitia*. Earthly justice consists in suppressing strife and enforcing conformity to an external order so that the saved and the damned can live some kind of common life. True justice, by contrast, is a condition from which strife is entirely absent. It is the condition under which those live who are united in fellowship by the love of God. But true justice will only prevail at the end of history, when the City of God, finally divested of all impure associations, enters into its inheritance of bliss.

Not even Christian states, then, can embody *vera iustitia*. None-theless, they can achieve a better semblance of justice than non-Christian states can, for two reasons. First, Christian rulers can and should live in such a way as to set a good example to their subjects. Second, Christian rulers should be ready to place their power at the Church's disposal, to defend it against its enemies and further its work. It is important to be clear, however, that Augustine does not say or imply that rulers as such are formally subordinate to the Church or subject to its command. His point is simply that all men, no matter who they are, should serve God in whatever capacity they happen to find themselves. Christian princes should take the opportunities that their office affords to assist the Church's work: as should Christian shoemakers, carpenters or soldiers. By the eleventh century, this kind of reasoning had burgeoned into the claim that the Church, or the pope, can command and depose emperors. Augustine himself certainly has nothing like this in mind.

Augustine's understanding of the duties of Christian princes, particularly in regard to religious persecution, evolved largely during the controversy with the schismatic Donatist church in North Africa in which he was involved from *c.*391 to 417. Originally, he thought that religious differences should be dealt with only by reason and argument. After *c.*400, he became increasingly convinced that the Church is justified in calling upon the secular authorities to enact and enforce laws against heretics and schismatics: partly, indeed, to protect it against acts of violence directed against Catholics and their property, but also to maintain the unity and doctrinal integrity of the Church. His emphasis on this latter aspect becomes increasingly prominent after 406. In this year, he first says outright that he would support a policy of coercion

> even if I were opposing men who were only involved in the darkness of error and who had not dared to assault anyone with insane violence.
>
> (*Epistulae* 89:2)

His fullest justifications of religious persecution occur in long letters written in 408 and 417. He does not, of course, believe that genuine changes of heart can be effected by coercion, but he did come to think – on the basis, as he tells us, of his own experience and that of colleagues – that stern measures and the fear of them can induce those subject to them to re-examine their beliefs for themselves. In this secondary sense, persecution can bring benefit to those who undergo it. Those brought forcibly into contact with teachers of the truth may thereby come to see the truth; coercion by the Catholic Church may counteract the fear of coercion by one's fellow heretics; coercion can break the bonds of habit and lethargy. Characteristically, Augustine holds that coercion of those outside the Church is, when carried out with the correct intentionality, an act of love. No love can be greater than Christ's; yet when he wished to summon St Paul into His service, He first struck him blind. In Christ's parable of the Great Supper, when the servants are sent out to hunt for guests, their master's instruction to them is significant: 'Go out into the highways and hedges and compel them to come in.'

Augustine does not, strictly speaking, offer a theory of political obligation. On the whole, the question is not an issue for him. He believes that most people's relationship with the state is explicable simply in terms of prudence or self-interest. Most citizens obey the state not from any sense of duty, but either out of fear of what would happen to them otherwise, or in order to secure the rewards – riches, office, glory – that come to those who serve their country well. In their case, matters of obligation do not really arise. Christians, on the other hand, must recognise a genuine obligation to obey the state and uphold the institutions of society, but this obligation is not distinctively political. It is our duty to submit to government not because government as such has any moral claim on us, but because it is God's will that we should submit. The state is the outcome of sin, but its existence and operation are in accordance with God's plan for the world. He uses even flawed institutions to bring forth at least a tolerable degree of peace and order. The Christian recognises this, and acts accordingly. No earthly ruler has any cause to complain about the standards of citizenship enjoined by the Christian faith.

Augustine recognises the traditional distinction between political and despotic rule, but he accords no particular significance to it in terms of its bearing on our duty as subjects. No matter how wicked or oppressive our ruler, rebellion or active resistance cannot be justified. If he requires of us something that positively contravenes the will of God, our proper course is passive resistance. We should politely decline to comply and willingly suffer the consequences; Augustine never suggests more than this. He is clear that all political power – even the power of wicked emperors like Nero – comes from God.

Subjects cannot remove what they have not conferred. Augustine is also clear that bad rulers are our just punishment. If the emperor harms us or persecutes us, he does not cease to be our rightful ruler. If he commands us to worship false gods, we must decline to obey not because we do not acknowledge his authority, but because we are all, including the emperor, bound to acknowledge an authority higher than his. Christians' political behaviour in both giving and withholding obedience is governed by no principle other than their allegiance to God. Obedience and refusal both arise out of an obligation that is not political, but religious.

Further reading

Primary sources

The City of God Against the Pagans, ed. R.W. Dyson (Cambridge: Cambridge University Press, 1998).

Political Writings, ed. E.M. Atkins and R.J. Dodaro (Cambridge: Cambridge University Press, 2001).

Secondary sources

Brown, P.: *Augustine of Hippo: A Biography* (London: Faber & Faber, 1967).

Deane, H.A.: *The Social and Political Ideas of St Augustine of Hippo* (New York: Columbia University Press, 1963).

Dyson, R.W.: *The Pilgrim City* (Woodbridge: Boydell Press, 2001).

Markus, R.A.: *Saeculum: History and Society in the Theology of St Augustine* (Cambridge: Cambridge University Press, 1970).

JOHN OF SALISBURY (1120–80)

John of Salisbury, also called John Little, was born in Salisbury, England, and educated largely in France. After ordination to the priesthood he joined the household of Theobald, Archbishop of Canterbury, in a secretarial capacity. His duties brought him into contact with senior figures in the ecclesiastical and secular life of England and continental Europe, including Pope Eugenius III (1145–53) and Nicholas Breakspear, who in 1154 became Pope Hadrian IV. John was a lifelong friend of Thomas Becket and supported him against Henry II after Becket became Archbishop of Canterbury in 1162. In consequence, John spent the years between 1163 and 1170 in exile, either in France or at the papal court. He continued to promote Becket's cause from abroad until the latter's assassination in 1170, whereupon he returned to England. In 1176, by which time his health seems to have been failing, he was consecrated Bishop of Chartres, where he remained until his death.

John's political principles are most fully stated in his *Policraticus*, a rambling treatise of some 250,000 words which he finished in about 1159 and dedicated to Becket. Much of it is devoted to a discussion of the follies and weaknesses of courtiers. From our point of view, its interest lies chiefly in the picture that it presents of the Church as sovereign over all aspects of life, temporal and spiritual, public and private. As is characteristic of twelfth-century political thought, his argument is not about 'Church and state' considered as discrete entities, but about how, within the same community or corporation, two functioning parts are related: *regnum* and *sacerdotium*, the temporal power of kings and the spiritual power of priests.

It is with a view to elucidating this relationship that John develops his 'organic analogy'. He conceives the political community as a kind of macrocosm – a large-scale counterpart – of the human body.

> [T]he place of the head in the body of the commonwealth is filled by the prince ... The place of the heart is filled by the Senate ... The duties of eyes, ears and tongue are claimed by the judges and governors of provinces. Officials and soldiers correspond to the hands ... The husbandmen correspond to the feet, which always cleave to the soil.
>
> (*Policraticus* 5:2)

The imagery is self-consciously classical, but it is, of course, biblical as well. As St Paul tells us, we are all one body, with Christ as the head. This is a language with which John's contemporary audience would have been entirely familiar.

If the prince is its head, the soul of the body politic is the Church. The soul gives life, unity and purpose to the whole, and the prince must acknowledge himself subject to the Church just as, in the human body, the head is subject to the soul. By this, John does not mean merely that the prince must submit to the Church in spiritual or religious respects. In his secular office also he is bound to respond to the Church's supervision and direction, translating the law of God into the law of the civil community. John wishes to argue, indeed, that the prince's power is actually conferred on him or delegated to him by the Church. More strictly, it is bestowed on him by God acting through the agency of the Church. In developing this argument, he draws upon the symbolism of medieval coronation ritual. The prince receives

> the sword of blood [his temporal power] from the hand of the Church, although she has no sword of blood at all; or, rather, she has this sword, but she uses it by the hand of the prince, upon whom she confers the power of bodily coercion, retaining to herself authority over spiritual things in the person of the pontiffs.
>
> (*Policraticus* 4:3)

One implication of this argument is clear: what the Church confers, the Church can also remove.

What, though, of the time-honoured Roman law doctrine that the prince is *legibus solutus*, 'not bound by the law'? There is, John concedes, an obvious sense in which the prince is not bound by the law: in the sense, that is, that no one is in a position to enforce it against him. But the good prince subjects himself to the law voluntarily, and by serving it seeks the common good that it is the purpose of law to secure. He functions as a 'head' should, and directs the whole body to its corporate advantage. The tyrant, by contrast, disregards the law and seeks his own private good at the expense of his subjects. If the prince is or becomes a tyrant, the Church may discipline him or depose him. The Church can dispense his subjects from their oath of fealty to him, preach a crusade against him, or even sanction his assassination by his subjects. John is prepared to say explicitly that those who usurp or misuse the 'sword of blood' may rightly and justly be slain: 'the priests of God regard the slaying of tyrants as a godly deed' (*Policraticus* 8:20). It should be noted, however, that John sanctions tyrannicide only in extreme circumstances. For the most part, it is better to suffer and pray for deliverance; experience shows that tyrants usually come to bad ends anyway.

In comparative terms, John is not a political philosopher of the first rank. Strictly speaking, he is not a political 'philosopher' at all. The *Policraticus* is more a compendium of classical and biblical anecdotes and quotations than a developed argument. John's humanist learning is impressive, and the *Policraticus* was valued in the later Middle Ages as a storehouse of such learning, but his relationship with the literary past is largely second-hand and not, indeed, entirely honest. One of his ostensible sources, a treatise attributed to Plutarch called *Institutio Traiani* ('The Instruction of Trajan'), is almost certainly an invention of his own, devised to lend the authority of antiquity to his thesis. The *Policraticus* does, however, represent the earliest medieval attempt to state, in a way that is recognisably theoretical rather than merely controversial or assertoric, the political claims that the Church had been formulating since the fifth century. It is this fact that gives the work its status as a 'landmark' in the history of political thought.

Further reading

Primary source

Policraticus, ed. C.J. Nederman (Cambridge: Cambridge University Press, 1990).

Secondary sources

Leibeschütz, H.: *Medieval Humanism in the Life and Writings of John of Salisbury* (Nendeln: Kraus, 1968).
Webb, C.C.J.: *John of Salisbury* (London: Methuen, 1932).
Wilks, M. (ed.): *The World of John of Salisbury* (Oxford: Blackwell, 1984).

ST THOMAS AQUINAS (1225–74)

St Thomas was born in the castle of Roccasecca near Aquino in Italy, into a wealthy and aristocratic family. He was educated at the Benedictine Abbey of Monte Cassino, where his uncle was abbot. In 1245, despite family opposition, he joined the Dominican order and went to the University of Paris to study under the German theologian Albertus Magnus. He took his master's degree in 1256 and spent the next eighteen years teaching and studying at Paris, Naples, Orvieto, Viterbo and Rome. His *Summa contra gentiles* – a manual for missionaries to Muslims and Jews – was completed in 1264. He began the enormous *Summa theologiae* in 1266 and worked on it until his health failed in 1273. He died on his way to the second Council of Lyons. Most of his political doctrines emerge incidentally, during the theological and moral discussions of the *Summa theologiae*. His only exclusively political work is a longish fragment called *De regimine principum*: part of a much larger work which he abandoned in about 1267 and which was subsequently completed by his pupil Tolommeo of Lucca.

The most obvious feature of St Thomas's philosophy is the extent to which it is influenced by the ideas and thought-patterns of **Aristotle**. Largely thanks to the triumph of Neoplatonism as mediated through the writings of **Augustine**, Aristotle's ethical and political writings were effectively unknown in the West from late antiquity to the end of the eleventh century. The study of these writings had for many years been the province of Arab commentators, most notably Averroes (1126–98). That they again came to be studied in the West is due to a handful of translators and exegetes, mostly working at the University of Paris; it was there, under the tutelage of Albertus Magnus, that St Thomas was introduced to them. Not surprisingly, the Church regarded this 'recovery' of Aristotle with disfavour. Apart from his own paganism, the fact that Aristotle had been so much studied by Arab scholars was enough to infect him with the taint of Islam. Matters came to a head in 1277, with the formal condemnation of a long list of Aristotelian doctrines by Bishop Tempier of Paris. Despite – perhaps because of – the climate of opposition to Aristotelianism that prevailed throughout his professional career, St Thomas was convinced from the beginning that Aristotle's teachings could be reconciled with the Christian faith. Aristotle – 'the Philosopher' – had carried intellectual investigation as far as it can go without the advantage of divine revelation. When his conclusions are divested of error and supplemented by revealed truth, the resulting synthesis of reason and revelation will yield an intellectually complete system. So St Thomas believed. To produce such a synthesis through the kind of minute philosophical analysis exemplified in the *Summa theologiae* became his life's work.

As we might expect, then, his political thought departs fundamentally from the Platonist and Augustinian orientation of earlier generations. Augustine, with his eyes fastened on the world to come – the transcendent other-world of the Christian Neoplatonist – had found the present world sin-laden and disordered, and its politics merely harsh and coercive. To Augustine, the individual is aligned either with earth or with heaven. To be the ally of one is to be estranged from the other. St Thomas, by contrast, finds nothing to quarrel with in the rational, humane and ordered world depicted by Aristotle. He sees no irreconcilable tension between the acquisition of present goods on earth and the achievement of eternal ones in heaven, provided only that the former are directed towards the latter and the latter are not neglected in favour of the former. To be sure, man has a true and final end – eternal beatitude with God in heaven – of which Aristotle knew nothing; but earthly happiness also is possible and desirable. Life on earth is not the welter of misery that St Augustine depicted, and the achievement of temporal well-being is an end that, though limited and secondary, is valid and worthwhile.

The achievement of such well-being requires government, but this is not 'Augustinian' government, ordained to suppress human destructiveness by force and fear. It is a benign administration suited to the kind of sociable and co-operating creature that man is. Nobody is able to provide themselves with all the necessaries of life: we need to co-operate in order to secure the benefits of a division of labour. There may be more than one way to achieve our ends, and we need to be guided wisely towards them just as a ship needs to be steered into harbour. These are facts that have nothing to do with sin. They are simply facts of human nature. They are the facts that make it necessary for a human community to be knit together in a common purpose by wise leadership directed to the common good.

In *De regimine principum*, St Thomas holds that the kind of leadership our condition requires is best provided by a king. Kingship, because it is government by one, is the most natural kind of government. Its archetype is God's government of the universe, and we see it mirrored everywhere in nature. It is the most efficient kind of government because a king's power is undivided and his freedom of action unlimited. The discussion of governmental forms in *De regimine principum* is incomplete. In the *Summa theologiae*, St Thomas again recommends kingship, but this time a kingship tempered or limited by elements of democracy and oligarchy. This, of course, is an Aristotelian prescription, borrowed from Aristotle's account of mixed government in the *Politics*. St Thomas follows Aristotle in supposing that this kind of government will derive stability from the fact that it will please all sections of the community.

But the king must understand that his function is not merely to rule externals. In the final analysis his task is to create conditions of life conducive to the virtue and salvation of his subjects. Whatever he does should have material well-being only as an intermediate goal. His true reward is not any material gain, nor is it the passing glory that comes from human renown. It is the eternal blessedness of heaven. This kind of thing is, of course, a stock in trade of ecclesiastical writers. It is a curious fact, however, that St Thomas does not develop an explicit theory of 'Church and state'; or, at any rate, he is somewhat vague and non-committal in what he has to say. He states in a general way that the Supreme Pontiff – the pope – is Christ's earthly representative, that the king should submit to the spiritual guidance of the priesthood, that in certain unspecified cases the king is subject to the temporal authority of the Church, and that spiritual and temporal power coincide in the Supreme Pontiff. But he does not draw out the detailed implications of these statements, for reasons about which we can only speculate – possibly because he was not personally involved in any political controversy.

Because, for St Thomas, politics is a benign and positive activity and civic happiness a worthwhile end, he takes a view of tyranny different from the 'traditional' Augustinian one. His thought on the subject is not wholly divested of Augustinian elements, but he tends not to regard tyranny as a divinely intended punishment, nor does he hold that the right to disobey a tyrant extends only to those commands that manifestly flout God's will. Kings exist to do more than merely suppress wickedness and test faith: they exist to secure a common good or a public interest. If, therefore, instead of this, the king devotes himself to his own private good – if he becomes a tyrant in the sense specified in Book III of Aristotle's *Politics* – he has betrayed the purpose for which God has appointed him, and his people have no obligation to obey. What action St Thomas thinks them entitled to take is not entirely clear, at least partly because he himself does not think the question amenable to a clear-cut answer. Some commentators have thought him inconsistent or pusillanimous on this issue. In his relatively youthful *Scripta super libros sententiarum*, speaking with apparent approval of the assassination of Julius Caesar, he seems to subscribe to a version of tyrannicide, at least when the tyranny is extreme and no other course of action is available. In *De regimine principum*, he takes the view that action may be taken against tyrants, but only by those who are in some sense authorised to do so: either because they have a formal 'kingmaking' role, or because they are carrying out the will of an oppressed community. Tyrants may not be overthrown merely on the private judgement of someone who happens not to like the king. Again, in *De regimine principum* and the *Summa theologiae*, St Thomas holds that tyranny of a relatively mild kind should be tolerated and that action should be taken only where the harm and scandal involved is not greater than the advantages that doing so may be expected to secure. We may read these statements in conjunction with what he says elsewhere about war and violence: that wars waged to repel aggression or escape oppression, and reasonable force used in self-defence and without malice, are morally justified, but one must always be careful not to do more damage than one averts. His position is not really inconsistent; nor, strictly, does he fudge the issue. His remarks, taken together, add up to a position of cautious conservatism, which recognises that extreme measures may be justified but should be avoided if at all possible.

The best-known part of St Thomas' political writings is the section of the *Summa theologiae* in which he develops his fourfold typology of law as eternal law, natural law, human law and divine law. He conceives law as being a rational pattern somewhat after the fashion of Plato's 'forms' or 'ideas'. Any relationship between a superior and an inferior involves, as it were, a picture in the mind of the superior of what the inferior should do or be, just as, before he actually makes anything, the craftsman has in his mind an idea of what his product will be like. In the case of a relationship between ruler and subjects, the idea that the ruler has in his mind of what his subjects should do is what we call law. It is the 'rule and measure' that, when formulated and promulgated, governs their acts; when the subjects act as they should, they 'participate' in the law in the way that a table 'participates' in the idea of a table which the carpenter has in his mind. Because God is the supreme governor of everything, the pattern of the government of the universe that exists in His mind is 'law' in the most general and comprehensive sense: it is the 'law' that makes the universe orderly and predictable rather than chaotic and irrational. This rational pattern is what St Thomas calls the 'eternal law', and to it everything in the created universe is subject.

Inasmuch as humankind is part of the order of the universe, it follows that there must be a portion of the eternal law that relates to human conduct specifically. This is the *lex naturalis*, the 'law of nature' or 'natural law'. The idea is a very ancient one, but St Thomas expounds it in unprecedented philosophical detail. There is a broad sense in which all animals have a 'natural' law: the sense, that is, in which all sentient creatures have an instinctive urge to protect and reproduce themselves. But the natural law to which humans are subject is not a mere instinct to survive and breed. It is prescriptive also: it tells us what to do. It tells us to do good and avoid evil; it tells us to live at peace with our neighbours. It is 'natural' to us in the sense that we are by nature creatures to whom its prescriptions are rationally obvious. We do not have to learn about them or have them legislated for us: to all human beings, pagans included, they simply 'stand to reason'.

But why, in that case, is it also necessary to have 'human' or 'positive law'? The reason is that the provisions of the law of nature, though clear to us, are too general to furnish us with sufficiently specific guidance. We know that we ought to do good and avoid evil, but we do not know what actually is good or evil in specific circumstances; nor do we know what to do with people who do evil: what punishments should there be and who should incur them? Human laws are particular rules deduced by practical reasoning from the general principles of the natural law. They are derived from it in much the same way as, in scientific or speculative reasoning, we arrive at particular conclusions by deduction from first principles. All human law, properly so-called, takes its character as law from the fact that it is derived from the natural law. Human laws can be changed or dispensed from in order to suit changing times or exceptional circumstances, but the general principles of natural law cannot be changed and must always be honoured. By the same token, 'laws' that are not derived from the natural law – laws that are unjust in the sense that they oppress those subject to them or fail to secure their good – are not really laws at all, and so we are not bound to obey them. They have, St Thomas says, more the character of force than of law. And so a similar condition here arises to the one that we noted in connection with tyranny. We should obey even unjust or tyrannical laws if the consequences of disobedience would be worse than any good that disobedience might secure. But we are not *obliged* to obey, simply because the 'laws' in question are not really laws, and so cannot oblige. (The point is more obvious in Latin than in English, inasmuch as *lex*, 'law', is related etymologically to *ligare*, 'to bind'.)

The fourth and final kind of law is 'divine law'. The divine law differs from human law in that it is not derived by a process of rational inference from the more general principles of nature, and not all of its precepts 'stand to reason'. It is part of the eternal law, but it is the law of revelation, made accessible to us through the teaching of scripture and the Church. Why do rational creatures need a revealed law over and above the natural and human laws? The answer to this is that human law is concerned only with the external aspects of conduct. Eternal salvation, on the other hand, requires that we be inwardly virtuous as well as outwardly obedient. The divine law regulates our inner lives; it regulates those aspects of conduct that no one can see; it punishes us in so far as we are sinners rather than merely criminal; it guides us in those duties which are religious rather than civic.

Broadly speaking, then, St Thomas's theory of law is of the kind called 'intellectualist' rather than 'voluntarist'. He thinks that law derives the morally important aspects of its character not from the will or command of a legislator, but from the rational content that it embodies; legislative pronouncements that depart from, or fail to institutionalise, the natural law simply do not have the character of law. Promulgation and command are important parts of what make law a reality, and there is a formal or technical sense in which even bad laws are laws; but no one who commands or promulgates something that is against nature makes law in the proper sense. Ultimately, the value and validity of law depends upon its conformity to eternal and invariable moral principles.

The fact that he was for so long the semi-official philosopher of the Roman Catholic Church has tended to insulate St Thomas from criticism. It is fair to say that he has been somewhat overrated as a philosopher. His literary style is difficult. He is apt to set off in pursuit of elaborate and distracting side issues. His arguments tend to be clouded by needlessly subtle and sometimes trivial distinctions: this is a criticism that has perhaps been levelled too much against scholasticism in general, but it is not wholly undeserved. He is committed in advance to a closed system of religious and moral beliefs, and his 'philosophical' arguments are devised with a view to supporting and confirming those beliefs. Having said this, we can hardly fail to admire his persistence and diligence and the ambitious scale of his philosophical thinking. Specifically in regard to political theory, we may make three remarks. First, St Thomas was responsible, almost if not quite single-handedly, for reintroducing the political and ethical thought of Aristotle into the educational curriculum of the Latin West. This, in itself, is a fact of considerable significance. Second, and as a direct consequence of the rehabilitation of Aristotle, he was responsible for a large-scale re-evaluation of political activity and participation as worthwhile activities apart from any connection with the Church. We may say that, in this respect, he helped to make 'modern' normative political theory possible. Third, although he himself abstains from any extended treatment of 'Church and state', he made available the intellectual equipment with which his immediate successors were to begin to unravel the long-established interweaving of secular and spiritual themes in European political writing. These facts establish him in a place of the first importance in the history of political thought.

Further reading

Primary source

St Thomas Aquinas: Political Writings, ed. R.W. Dyson (Cambridge: Cambridge University Press, 2002).

Secondary sources

Coleman, J.: *A History of Political Thought*, vol. 2 (Oxford: Blackwell, 2000).

Finnis, J.: *Aquinas: Moral, Political and Legal Theory* (Oxford: Oxford University Press, 1998).

McInerny, R.: *Ethica Thomistica: The Moral Philosophy of Thomas Aquinas* (Washington, D.C.: Catholic University of America, 1982).

O'Connor, D.J.: *Aquinas and Natural Law* (London: Macmillan, 1967).

Weisheipl, J.: *Friar Thomas d'Aquino: His Life, Thought and Works* (Oxford: Blackwell, 1974).

MARSILIUS OF PADUA (*c.*1275–*c.*1343)

Marsilius of Padua – Marsiglio dei Mainardini – was born shortly after the death of St Thomas **Aquinas**, in Padua, Italy. He studied medicine at the Universities of Padua and Paris, and became Rector of the University of Paris in 1312 or 1313. His major political work, a long and complex treatise called *Defensor pacis*, was finished in 1324 and dedicated to the German king Ludwig of Bavaria. He subsequently wrote two shorter works, *De translatione imperii* (*c.*1326) and *Defensor minor* (*c.*1340), the latter being, as one might expect, a condensed version of *Defensor pacis*. *Defensor pacis* was at first published anonymously, but in 1326, in circumstances that are not clear, the identity of its author became known and Marsilius thought it prudent to leave Paris. He and a colleague, John of Jandun, took refuge in the court of Ludwig of Bavaria, who had been in conflict with Pope John XXII since the disputed imperial election of 1314. Marsilius seems to have accompanied Ludwig on his Italian expedition of 1328. *Defensor pacis* was formally condemned by John XXII in the Bull *Licet iuxta* in 1327.

Marsilius, like St Thomas, is steeped in **Aristotle**; but while St Thomas has relatively little to say on the subject of 'Church and state', Marsilius uses Aristotelian modes of thought to strike at the root of the medieval Church's claim to fullness of power in temporal matters. The Church's interference in such matters is, he says, one of the most notorious causes of civil strife, and his purpose is to offer a remedy for such strife. *Defensor pacis* is the antithesis of the arguments put forward by **John of Salisbury** in the *Policraticus*. On the analogy of body and soul, John of Salisbury had argued that the government of a kingdom ought to be entirely subject to ecclesiastical supervision and that the prince should be subject, if necessary, even to deposition at the Church's behest. Marsilius, by contrast, wishes not merely to reduce the Church's role or curb its pretensions, but to exclude the Church entirely from all part in the conduct of temporal affairs.

A kingdom or state is, Marsilius argues, a sufficient or 'perfect' community. By this, he means exactly what Aristotle means when he describes the *polis* in similar terms: a community within which human beings can live to the full the kind of life appropriate to their kind. If such a life is to be achieved and enjoyed in peace, the various occupations in which men engage must be harmonised with one another for the common good. Following Aristotle, Marsilius mentions six such occupations: farmers, artisans, merchants, soldiers, priests and magistrates. Social harmony is achieved when the magistrates govern the other groups for the good of all according to law. Although he has a preference for elective kingship, it does not much matter to Marsilius whether government is in the hands of one, few or many, provided that the object sought by government is the common good rather than a sectional or individual good. In this, again, he follows Aristotle's analysis of constitutional forms. We note that, as with St Thomas, this new Aristotelian political thought is entirely divested of 'Augustinianism': there is no suggestion that human association and its ends are in themselves base or sin-laden. Granted that they are not our final ends, the ends at which organised human life aims are nonetheless worthwhile.

Marsilius thinks that government should be government according to law. The rule of law is the best safeguard against the perversion of government by individual or partial interests: another Aristotelian motif. Unlike St Thomas, Marsilius is a legal positivist. Whereas St Thomas is an 'intellectualist', holding that the authority of law comes from the rationality of its content, and ultimately from its association with divine reason, Marsilius is a 'voluntarist' who defines law simply as the will or command of a human legislator, a *legislator humanus*, reinforced by the threat of coercive sanctions. A not-unintended effect of this definition is to exclude the possibility of a law being declared invalid by the Church because of some alleged defect of moral content. Law, Marsilius thinks, should emanate from the *universitas civium*, the 'universality of the citizens': that is, from the people, or at least from the 'weightier part' of the people (what he means by 'weightier part' is not entirely clear). There are several reasons for this. If law is made by one or a few, it can more easily become subservient to particular interests. People are more ready to obey laws if they feel they have made those laws themselves. The purpose of law is to secure the common good, and the people themselves are the best judge of what is in the common good. Finally, if the law is to be enforced successfully against transgressors, the co-operation of the whole community is required for this to be done effectively. Also, and for similar reasons, Marsilius favours a republican form of government. Princes or magistrates – the *pars principans*, the 'ruling part' – should be elected by the people over whom they are to exercise authority. In making these recommendations, Marsilius has the model of the Italian civic republics in mind, although he seems to intend his political prescriptions to have universal application.

If a state is a sufficient community governed by law, it follows that none of its citizens can claim exemption from the law. Priests are no longer a people set apart, as the medieval Church had insisted for so long. The priesthood is just another occupational group within the community. Its members, *qua* citizens, have no more claim to be exempt from the civil law because they are priests than builders do because they are builders. By the same token, there is no reason why ecclesiastical property should be exempt from taxation merely because it is the property of the Church rather than of any other association within the state. For Marsilius, because individual members of the clergy are just as much citizens as anyone else, their traditional claim to be beyond the reach of secular jurisdiction carries no weight. This is not to deny that the clergy are ministers of the divine law. Moreover, Marsilius does not dispute that the divine law is law in the proper sense. It is the command of a Legislator, Almighty God, and it is reinforced by the threat of coercion in the form of eternal damnation. But the good to which the divine law is directed is not of this world, nor will the sanctions by which it is reinforced apply in this world. The role of the clergy is to prepare us, by instruction and admonition, for the life that is to come after this one. The affairs of this world are entirely in the hands of the secular authorities; the affairs that are in the hands of the ecclesiastical authorities are not of this world. The ecclesiastical authorities therefore have no right to interfere in temporal matters, and no right to coerce any member of the community. Like physicians, they may teach and advise, but they may not compel. Heretics, simply in so far as they are heretics, may not be coerced at all; in so far as their heresy involves criminal behaviour, they should be coerced by the secular power only.

Marsilius is not content merely to exclude the clergy from temporal affairs. He wishes to challenge the whole way in which the Church is governed. Just as sovereignty in the political community should lie with the universality of the citizens, the *universitas civium*, so should the Church be governed by the *universitas fidelium*, the 'universality of the faithful'. The hierarchical organisation of the Church is a matter of convenience only. It has no supernatural origin. Apart from a certain pre-eminence in dignity, the pope is in a position of equality with other bishops. Final authority in matters of doctrine and scriptural interpretation should be vested not in the pope, but in a General Council, which should include secular as well as ecclesiastical delegates. The Council should be elected by the citizens of the various sovereign states, and its decisions should be enforced, in so far as enforcement is necessary, by the secular governments of those states. The pope should be chosen by the people as represented in the Council, and the Council should have the right to depose him.

Marsilius wrote at a time when the Church was demoralised by the migration of the papal curia to Avignon, and when the emergence of nation-states in Europe was in any case eroding the traditional supranational claims of the papacy. He is an early precursor of the 'conciliar movement' associated with Jean Gerson (1363–1429), Nicholas of Cusa (1401–64) and Aeneas Sylvius (1405–64): this movement sought, albeit without ultimate success, to replace the authority of the pope with that of a representative Church council. Without too much simplification, we can say that *Defensor pacis* began to sound the death-knell of the 'high' medieval ideal of papal monarchy and to prepare the way for the increasing secularisation of political thought during the fifteenth and sixteenth centuries.

Further reading

Primary sources

Defensor pacis, ed. A. Gewirth (New York: Columbia University Press, 1980).
Defensor minor and De translatione imperii, ed. C.J. Nederman (Cambridge: Cambridge University Press, 1993).

Secondary sources

Black, A.: *Political Thought in Europe, 1250–1450* (Cambridge: Cambridge University Press, 1992).
Coleman, J.: *A History of Political Thought* (Oxford: Blackwell, 2000).
Gewirth, A.: *Marsilius of Padua and Medieval Political Philosophy* (New York: Columbia University Press, 1951).

NICOLÒ MACHIAVELLI (1469–1527)

Nicolò Machiavelli was born in Florence, Italy, into an ancient but impoverished family. He entered the service of the republic of Florence in 1494 and was employed on diplomatic missions to France, the Holy See and Germany. When the republic fell in 1512, he was briefly imprisoned and tortured. He retired into private life and devoted himself to political analysis, military theory and the study of history, producing *The Prince* in about 1513, *The Discourses* in about 1516 and *The Art of War* in about 1520. Part of his purpose in writing *The Prince* was to ingratiate himself with Lorenzo de' Medici, to whom it is dedicated; but it was not until 1525 that he was recalled to government service. With the overthrow of the Medici in 1527, Machiavelli was again excluded from office. In the last years of his life he completed a *History of Florence*, a commentary on the historical records of Florence, offering a remarkably sophisticated account of causal relationships rather than mere chronology.

Machiavelli is not interested in the religious and ecclesiastical issues so characteristic of medieval political thought. He is on the whole hostile to Christianity, believing that a people genuinely committed to the Christian virtues of meekness and submission would not thrive in the cut-throat world of politics. He is a republican and a patriot interested in the establishment and maintenance of a strong state in the face of foreign aggression and domestic upheaval. This interest expresses itself in two main ways. In *The Prince*, Machiavelli's concern is with how one man can maintain his sway over subjects; in *The Discourses*, he addresses the question of how a republic can be made to endure and prosper by channelling the fundamentally selfish vigour of its citizens in publicly beneficial ways. Machiavelli's method is historical and comparative, relying especially upon illustrations furnished by classical antiquity. His purpose is to show how events are conditioned by the circumstances in which they occurred, to identify their causes, and to lay bare the general principles underlying human relationships and behaviour. His underlying hope seems to be that a strong prince will one day unify Italy and that a republican form of government will thereafter emerge.

Throughout his writings, Machiavelli subscribes to a consistent theory of human nature. An important aspect of this theory is the assumption that human nature is changeless. It is this that enables us to make generalisations about politics. Although their behaviour is always in some respects modified by their conditions of life, human beings exhibit the same essential characteristics, and these characteristics are not of the kind traditionally admired. Machiavelli says in *The Prince*,

> One can make this generalisation about men: that they are ungrateful, fickle, liars and deceivers; they shun danger and are greedy for profit; while you treat them well they are yours . . . but when you are in danger they turn against you.
>
> (*The Prince* ch.17)

In *The Discourses* (3:4) he remarks that

> all men are bad, and ready to display their vicious nature whenever they find occasion for it. If their evil disposition remains concealed for a time, this must be attributed to some unknown reason, and we must assume that it has lacked occasion to show itself; but time, which has been said to be the father of all truth, does not fail to bring it to light.

The root of man's 'evil disposition', Machiavelli believes, is inveterate selfishness. This selfishness manifests itself primarily in the desire for self-preservation and security; then, when security has been achieved, it becomes a single-minded devotion to personal power and the glory inseparable from it. Also, power means freedom: this is one of the main reasons why people value it. Even those who do not wish to rule others at least wish to have enough power to prevent themselves from falling too completely under the control of others. The world is divided into those who dominate and those who strive not to be dominated.

It is because this desire for power plays so prominent a part in human behaviour, Machiavelli believes, that political life has always been characterised by strife. Politics is not, and cannot be, about the kind of co-operation and organic interdependence that **Plato** and **Aristotle** assumed to be possible. People are able to co-operate, but they do so only in so far and for as long as co-operation serves their turn. The traditional suggestion that the point of politics is to achieve a harmonious common good is humbug. Politics necessarily involves struggle. In a monarchy, Machiavelli suggests, the struggle is that of one man to dominate all others. It is true that the prince's private gratification can also be a public good. The decisive qualities of the ruthless Italian prince Cesare Borgia are just what is needed to unite Italy. But the prince's primary purpose is his own secure tenure and free enjoyment of power. The struggle can be seen most clearly in the case of the prince who has just seized power, and whose position is therefore not buttressed by custom, apathy or the people's veneration for his family. The 'new' prince has to maintain and consolidate his position by his own adroitness alone. Ostensibly, *The Prince* is a treatise on how he may do so.

Machiavelli suggests that the prince must rely chiefly on the judicious use of force and deceit. Because we must assume that man is the slave of his own selfish passions, it is pointless and unsafe to suppose that subjects may be ruled by obtaining their rational consent or setting them a good moral example. Wherever there is a choice, men will respond to the dictates of passion rather than to the requirements of moral reason. It is therefore by manipulating the passions of others that they can be made to do what one wants them to do. There is, in politics, no such thing as an effective appeal to reason. Machiavelli suggests that there are four passions that govern human behaviour: love, hatred, fear and contempt. Love and hatred are mutually exclusive: clearly it is not possible simultaneously to love and hate someone. By the same token, it is not possible to both fear and despise someone: fear and contempt are also incompatibles. However, love and fear are compatible; so are hatred and contempt, hatred and fear, and love and contempt. The passions that the prince will most obviously seek to inspire are the compatibles of love and fear. If people hate and despise their ruler, they cannot be controlled and they will, indeed, be anxious to act against him. Love and fear are therefore to be induced, and contempt and hatred avoided. The worst thing that can happen to a ruler in seeking to maintain his power, Machiavelli suggests, is that he be despised. Thus, though love and fear are best, hatred and fear are to be preferred to love and contempt. Any combination with fear will be good because it will mean that subjects can be controlled through their fear. Any combination with contempt, however, even if that combination is love, is to be avoided because it will rob the ruler of his power to coerce: fear and contempt are incompatibles. It is not essential to be loved, but it is essential to be feared – and it is even more essential not to be despised.

What this means, in plain terms, is that the foundation of the prince's power is force and his willingness to use it ruthlessly. This accounts for Machiavelli's assertion that the only arts that the prince need acquire are the military arts. Many of Machiavelli's Renaissance contemporaries, and many of his forebears in the history of political thought, had taken it as a truism that the prince should be a cultivated and humane man: a patron of the arts, godly, wise, learned and so forth. To Machiavelli, though, the proper study of the prince is the art of war. This is because, for Machiavelli, politics itself is only a kind of muted or ritualised warfare. His takes it for granted that, in quality if not in scale, the relations between a ruler and his subjects are the same as those between sovereign states. It is as if subjects are perpetually at war with their ruler, just as states are always potentially or actually at war with one another. The prince's correct general policy, therefore, is to ensure that there is no one who has sufficient power to challenge him, because, if such persons exist, he must assume that lust for power will induce them to challenge him indeed. Moreover, war between states, Machiavelli thinks, can never be avoided, only postponed; the prince who does not realise this is heading for disaster. If there are neighbouring powers capable of challenging the power of the prince, war is inevitable, because neither side can rest secure until the threat from the other is removed. So it is always best to attack if one has the advantage or to destroy the other's advantage by diplomacy if not. War should never be postponed to one's own detriment. Above all, if the prince is forced to injure others, he should do it in such a way as to deprive them of power permanently or destroy them altogether. If he does not do this, desire for revenge will augment their natural ambition and they will leave no stone unturned in their efforts to undermine him.

Machiavelli's view of morality and politics is, then, very different from the traditional insistence that the good ruler is necessarily also a good man: that he will exhibit moral virtue in his own life and conduct; that he will set a good example to his subjects; that he will seek to secure the common good rather than his own good merely; that he will submit to the guidance of the Church. To the Machiavelli of *The Prince*, politics is simply about getting and keeping power. He attaches to the word 'virtue' a quasi-technical meaning. Virtue, to Machiavelli – it is the custom in discussing his view to retain the Italian spelling, *virtù* – is not moral virtue; rather, it is a particular kind of skill or aptitude, combined, of course, with the will to use it.

We can amplify this idea by examining the relationship, which Machiavelli sketches in *The Prince*, between *virtù* and *fortuna*. There is, he remarks, a considerable extent to which we are all in the hands of the fickle goddess Fortuna, and experience teaches us that there is no necessary connection between the traditional moral virtues and the incidence of good and ill fortune. An honest and skilful merchant may have all his ships sunk in a storm, and his honesty will not help him. A diligent and godfearing farmer may still have all his crops destroyed in a storm. Life does not run in comfortable grooves; unpredictable and unexpected things happen; we inhabit a morally incoherent world in which there is no necessary relation between what one deserves and what one gets. And nowhere is this unpredictability and moral incoherence more evident than in the political forum. Those who occupy the shifting and unstable world of politics are pre-eminently in the hands of fortune. For them, there is certainly no connection between desert and reward. They do not know from one day to the next what will happen, how loyalties will change, how the balance of force will alter, and so on.

In contrast to the unstable and contingent world of practical affairs, however, stands the fact that, on the whole, human beings have rigid and inflexible temperaments. A man's character and disposition, Machiavelli observes, and therefore his mode of procedure, are normally fairly fixed and constant. Indeed, what might be termed a traditional moral education calls upon one to cultivate such a fixed and constant disposition (one is not brought up, after all, to be virtuous only sometimes or when it serves one's purposes). But what is the good of having an inflexible mode of procedure in a world where the necessities under which fortune places one are subject to such variation? Always to act in the same way regardless of the circumstances in which you find yourself is, Machiavelli insists, a recipe for disaster. This is particularly true, of course, if you are a prince – especially a new prince – trying to survive in the volatile and merciless world of politics.

In a nutshell, then, we can say that, for Machiavelli, *virtù* is that quality or prowess which enables an individual to encounter the blows of fortune and overcome them by whatever means are necessary. Fortune, he tells us, uttering in the process a celebrated piece of political incorrectness, is like a wilful and headstrong woman. A man should cope with her, just as he would with any wilful and headstrong woman, by beating her into submission. In his encounters with fortune, it will not do for the prince to be bound by a rigid moral temperament. He must be adaptable. He must be ready and able to use both the lion and the fox in him: he must be able to be both man and beast. When mercy is appropriate, let him be merciful; but when it is appropriate for him to be merciless, savage and terrifying, let him be these things too. Let him be honest and truthful where necessary; but let him lie and break faith if he must. The prince must do whatever circumstances require, and if those circumstances require him to disregard traditional moral values and Christian ways of behaving, then so be it. It is self-defeating to behave in ways that will increase one's chances of losing power or to omit to behave in ways that will increase one's chances of keeping it.

Many of Machiavelli's contemporaries held, and many of his subsequent critics have held, that he is a teacher of evil. By the early seventeenth century, Machiavelli's name had become a synonym for tyranny and perfidy. But it is easy enough to see that Machiavelli does not counsel wickedness and that his prince is not a wicked man. Machiavelli is quite ready to concede that, from the point of view of ordinary morality, necessity requires political actors to do deplorable things. This may be regrettable, but the fact remains that the prince who cannot alter his mode of procedure to suit changing circumstances will not be a prince for long. This is a fact of life and there is no point, Machiavelli thinks, in wringing one's hands about it. Most people cannot deviate from what their character or education predispose them to; or perhaps, having prospered by walking in one path, they cannot persuade themselves to adopt another. If one could change one's mode of procedure and character to suit the varying conditions of one's life, one's fortune would never change. The successful prince, Machiavelli thinks, is a man who can do precisely this. The ability by which he counteracts the effects of fortune is the ability to be infinitely flexible, to bend with the breeze. Everything he does is done because circumstances require it; he does nothing merely because his character or moral principle dictate it. We might, therefore, most easily describe the prince as amoral. He is neither good nor bad, neither wicked nor the reverse. He has *no* moral character in the traditional sense of the term. He does not have a fixed disposition or habit of mind to act in a certain way. Unlike most men, who do have such fixed dispositions, he is able to be either completely virtuous or utterly vicious, and he knows how to be both. The traditional moral virtues are simply no part of his character. They are not absolutes to which he adheres through thick and thin. They are simply modes of action, which he can pick up and discard at will.

Machiavelli's assumptions about human nature and behaviour lead him to conclude that, though power is most easily studied in the case of the new prince, a republic is a healthier and more successful form of government than a monarchy. This is the theme of *The Discourses*: a quite different work from *The Prince*, but resting on the same presuppositions. In a monarchy, one man has supreme power. One man is in a position to stifle – and, if he is to survive, must stifle – the manly impulses of all those subject to him. In a republic, every individual is a prince: every individual is able to develop and deploy his own *virtù* in defence of his security, freedom and property, thereby producing a kind of collective or public *virtù* that conduces to the welfare and safety of all. In a monarchy, Machiavelli says, only one man is free; in a republic, all are free. This collective *virtù* does not arise out of friendship or altruism. Men co-operate because they know that collective wisdom and effort is, on the whole, better than that of any individual. Each man co-operates with others so far as is necessary to secure his own good, while at the same time competing with others for the things that men value – glory, honour, riches. A republic furnishes everyone with both the benefits of co-operation and the opportunity to develop *virtù* by striving with others to assert himself in an open forum. Republics will be more stable than monarchies, more able to defend themselves and more successful at extending their territories by war, not because they somehow submerge or counteract human self-assertiveness, but because they give it freer range and so produce sturdy, indomitable, self-reliant individuals.

Human nature being what it is, the problem confronting a republic is that of ensuring that it does not become a tyranny; or, at any rate, of delaying the process of deterioration for as long as possible. Republics can only be stable if they enable men to compete with one another creatively without allowing anyone to acquire so much power that he can simply dominate everyone else. There is bound to be conflict between the aristocracy or commercial elites and the mass of the people. The former will wish to dominate the latter; the latter will wish to remain free. Such conflict is inevitable and energising. The struggle between the plebeians and the Senate in the Roman republic is the example to which Machiavelli looks. Opposing interests produce the force by which good laws are generated, provided such conflict is kept in bounds by properly designed political institutions. Machiavelli realises that actual governmental forms will vary according to the circumstances of the people in question, but the best form of state, he thinks, will be a republic with a mixed constitution rather like that favoured by Aristotle. Where the people have a meaningful share in government, all are able to feel secure in their honour, property and person. The laws must be clear and made known: the citizens must know with a high degree of certainty what they can and cannot do with impunity. General economic prosperity should be encouraged, but excessive individual wealth and luxury prevented by the laws. Due recognition must be given to the merits of citizens, and advancement in the service of the state should be open to those who seek honour and glory. There should be a state religion for the inculcation and maintenance of civic virtue. This religion should not, however, be Christianity, which encourages weakness and submission. There should be a citizen army, both to defend the republic and to extend its possessions by wars of aggression. The army should serve an educational as well as a military purpose: it should instil in citizens a respect for authority, patriotism and martial virtues. It will also provide a means for individual ambition to find its natural and healthy expression. Life in a republic should not be too comfortable. Social cohesion and vigour are most readily secured in conditions of hardship and crisis. Such conditions bring out the best in a people and encourage them to work together. Ease and security are inconsistent with public *virtù* not because they make people selfish, but because they turn their natural selfishness inwards and make it destructive.

In short, Machiavelli regards political activity as being the activity of individuals with power of various kinds and degrees who are trying to keep what they have and acquire more. *The Prince* and *The Discourses* are not radically different; nor are they contradictory. Both share a view of human nature as individualistic, competitive and, where necessary, ruthless and unscrupulous. *The Prince* is an essay on how the prince is to control the forces of human nature to his own advantage; *The Discourses* is a treatise on how these forces can be harnessed in such a way as to secure unity and public safety. But the forces involved in each case are the same. It is often said that Machiavelli is the first political theorist to give serious attention to the idea of *raison d'état*. This may be so, but it is not the whole story. Machiavelli admires the combination of practical qualities that he calls *virtù*, even where no particular *raison d'état* is at stake. He does so because, at heart, he is fascinated not so much by outcomes as by the phenomenon of power itself. One cannot help forming the impression that, for Machiavelli, the ends to which power is applied are of secondary importance. He admires Cesare Borgia – an individual who, by all ordinary standards, is a cruel and vicious tyrant – for his effectiveness, not his moral character. Unlike the great majority of his forebears and contemporaries, Machiavelli really does believe that politics is a morally neutral art. The fact that he, more than anyone, established this as a respectable view of how political events and relationships are to be analysed is what gives his career its significance in the history of political thought.

Further reading

Primary sources

The Discourses, ed. L.J. Walker and B. Crick (Harmondsworth: Penguin, 1970).
The Prince, ed. Q. Skinner and R. Price (Cambridge: Cambridge University Press, 1988).

Secondary sources

Pocock, J.G.A.: *The Machiavellian Moment* (Princeton, NJ: Princeton University Press, 1975).
Skinner, Q.R.D.: *The Foundations of Modern Political Thought*, vol. 1: *The Renaissance* (Cambridge: Cambridge University Press, 1978).
— *Machiavelli* (Oxford: Oxford University Press, 1981).
Viroli, M.: *Machiavelli* (Oxford: Oxford University Press, 1998).

SIR THOMAS MORE (1478–1535)

Thomas More was born in London in 1478, the son of a successful lawyer. He spent part of his upbringing in the household of John Morton, Archbishop of Canterbury and Lord Chancellor. More also seems to have spent some years living among Carthusian monks and the religious life always held strong attractions for him. He was widely educated and trained as a lawyer. As well as practising law, he became a Member of Parliament in 1504, and attracted the attention of the king. He became an official and diplomat in the court of Henry VIII, and after a number of royal appointments became Lord Chancellor of England, the head of the legal system, in 1529 (he was the first layman to hold the post). In addition to his public life, More was a considerable classical scholar, a leading figure in the Northern Renaissance and a close friend of Erasmus.

More was a man of considerable charm and wit, and this is reflected in his most famous work, *Utopia*, written in Latin and published in 1516. However, More was also a deeply religious man and the advent of the Reformation in the years immediately following this publication brought out another side of his personality: he persecuted heretics with the greatest vigour. His *Utopia* was later repudiated and he refused to have it translated into English (apart from anything else, the society it portrays is a model of religious toleration). More's religious convictions eventually brought him into conflict with the king, with him refusing to accept the king's position as supreme head of the Church. He did not seek martyrdom and defended himself by every legal means. In the end, however, he would not submit and was beheaded for treason in 1535. The Roman Catholic Church beatified him in 1886, canonised him in 1935 and subsequently declared him the patron saint of politicians.

More's contribution to political theory lies entirely with his short book, *Concerning the Best State of a Commonwealth and the New Island of Utopia*, better known simply as *Utopia*. Despite its brevity, it is a very complex and enigmatic work, reflecting the personality of its author. What precisely his intentions were is still the subject of considerable scholarly debate. The ambiguities of *Utopia* begin with the title. It is a play on two Greek words *u-topia*, meaning 'no place', and *eu-topia*, meaning 'happy place'. The ambivalence continues in the name of the central character, Raphael Hythloday, with Raphael meaning 'messenger of God' and Hythloday meaning 'talker of nonsense'. Yet the two characters to whom he tells his story are More himself and a friend who did exist, and on an occasion (a diplomatic mission to the Low Countries) that really happened. These and many other puzzles, jokes and ironies make the book ambiguous as to how seriously it should all be taken and just what the author is trying to do.

After the main characters have been introduced, there is a discussion of the pros and cons of entering public life, and of some of the social problems officials of Henry VIII might face, especially poverty, vagrancy and crime. The account of Utopia that follows could be viewed as an answer to these ills, but this is far from clear.

The central character of the book is a returning traveller who tells of his visit to a wondrous land – a perfectly plausible story in that age of discovery. He tells of an island-society called Utopia, founded around the middle of the third century BCE by King Utopus. It is not a state, but rather a federation of fifty-four largely independent, though remarkably uniform, city-states. Representatives meet once a year to discuss common problems, but there is no island-wide executive. In each city the people, or at least households, choose officials who organise work and form an assembly of around 200, which in turn selects higher officials to form a senate of around twenty. A prince is elected for life (dependent on good behaviour), having been chosen by the whole body of officials from popular nominations.

Utopia is a prosperous island, although no one has any personal wealth. Precious metals and stones are treated with ostentatious contempt, yet everyone is provided for: food, shelter and other needs are fully met from communal sources, there is communal eating and all must work. There are no hereditary social classes in Utopia, which is a highly egalitarian and meritocratic society. But there is a class of scholars from which all officials and priests are chosen. Children of scholarly promise are picked out at an early age, although many of the population cultivate scholarly pursuits in their spare time. The scholars are exempt from manual work, but everyone else must work for up to six hours per day, alternating between agriculture and some town-based craft.

At the same time, Utopia is a highly authoritarian society and there is tight social discipline. The permission of elders or officials is necessary for practically everything out of the normal routine. Law is strict, although executions are rare. More serious crimes result in slavery, and slaves supplement the work of the rest.

The Utopians are remarkably tolerant when it comes to moral and religious beliefs, there being a variety of forms of worship. Yet there is a broad consensus about the existence of an all-creating deity, and a list of moral principles to which virtually all subscribe. The Utopians seem to readily take to Christianity because it is close to their own moral ideas. The implication here, deriving from **Aquinas**, is that religion and morality are essentially rational, needing revelation to reach completion. The Utopians, being a highly rational people, have worked these things out for themselves, as had the Ancient Greeks.

With their rational and sensible approach to every question, the Utopians have created a world of perfect harmony and happiness. But yet it cannot be More's personal vision of a perfect society, if only because it is not a Christian society. This returns us to the question of why it is written.

Utopia is very much a work of Renaissance Humanism. It manifests a higher opinion of what human beings can achieve by their reason than prevailed in most of the Middle Ages. Utopians are remarkably like the Ancient Greeks as Humanists saw them. The work expresses More's deep admiration for Greek thought and literature, especially **Plato**'s *Republic*, which was a major inspiration. The community of goods and the communal life relate directly to Plato's Guardians, only here they are extended to everyone. And instead of the rather bleak intellectualism of the Platonic Guardians, we have a thirst for, and veneration of, scholarship. Utopia is a Renaissance Humanist's paradise.

In terms of religion and ideas the book is as tolerant and eclectic as was the Renaissance. It is very much a Renaissance Humanist exercise in moral philosophy, discussing issues in a light and literary yet serious way. How far it relates, or was meant to relate, to the actual conduct of affairs is difficult to gauge. It is a commentary on the ills of contemporary society, which are discussed with considerable passion. Yet the book is also partly a satire. It is clearly not More's ideal society, though it is certainly ideal in some respects, reflecting what might be possible if only humans were rational. As such it is a vehicle for More's views on a great range of topics, from church music to the conduct of war.

There are many elements mixed together. But whatever More's aims may have been, utopian literature has since been used for all these purposes and more. While More's *Utopia* is not the first picture of an ideal society (examples can be found particularly in the literature of the classical world) he did coin the word 'utopia' and began a self-conscious tradition of utopian writing that continues to this day. In keeping with More's own character, it is a complicated and ambiguous tradition. The nature and purpose of utopian literature is an open and contested question that continues to be debated by scholars.

Further reading

Primary source

Utopia (Cambridge: Cambridge University Press, 1989).

Secondary sources

Cousins, A.D. and Grace, D. (eds): *More's Utopia and the Utopian Inheritance* (Lanham, MD: University Press of America, 1995).
Hexter, J.H.: *More's Utopia: The Biography of an Idea* (Harper, 1965).
Kenny, A.J.P.: *Thomas More* (Oxford: Oxford University Press, 1983).
Logan, G.M.: *The Meaning of More's Utopia* (Princeton, NJ: Princeton University Press, 1983).
Olin, J.C. (ed.): *Interpreting Thomas More's Utopia* (New York: Fordham University Press, 1989).
Surtz, E.: *The Praise of Wisdom* (Chicago, IL: Chicago University Press, 1957).

THOMAS HOBBES (1588–1679)

Thomas Hobbes was born at Westport near Malmesbury in Wiltshire, England. A wealthy uncle paid for his education and sent him to Magdalen Hall, Oxford. Hobbes lived at a time of immense intellectual excitement, and the universities of his day were far from being at the cutting edge of intellectual advance. The Oxford curriculum still consisted largely of scholastic logic and metaphysics, which he regarded as sterile pedantry and for which he had nothing good to say. On taking his degree in 1608, he became tutor to William Cavendish, eldest son of the Earl of Devonshire. His lifelong connection with the Cavendish family brought him into contact with the leading intellectuals of the day, notably Sir Francis Bacon, by whom he was greatly influenced. It also gave him the leisure and means to devote himself to study. He was something of a late developer. John Aubrey tells us in his *Brief Life* of Hobbes that

> He was forty years old before he looked on Geometry, which happened accidentally. Being in a gentleman's library, Euclid's *Elements* lay open ... He read the Proposition. *By G—*, says he (he would now and then swear an emphatical oath by way of emphasis), *this is impossible!* So he reads the demonstration of it, which referred him back to such a Proposition; which proposition he read. That referred him to another, which he also read ... This made him in love with Geometry.
>
> (Aubrey, *Brief Lives*, p.309)

Henceforth geometrical or demonstrative reasoning – reasoning that leads by clear logical steps to indubitable conclusions – was to be one of the mainstays of his philosophical method. Its influence is already clear in a little work produced in about 1630 called *A Short Tract on First Principles*. Much later he would call Geometry 'the only science which it hath pleased God hitherto to bestow on mankind' (*Leviathan* 1:4).

In 1634 he set off on a tour of Europe with the young Earl of Devonshire (the son of his original pupil). At Paris, he met Marin Mersenne, who was the centre of a scientific circle including Descartes and Gassendi; at Florence he met Galileo. Returning to England, he wrote a work called *The Elements of Law Natural and Politic*. This was not published as a whole until 1889, but in 1650 its first thirteen chapters appeared under the title *Human Nature*, and the remainder as a separate work called *De Corpore Politico*. In November 1640, with the Civil War imminent, Hobbes returned to France and resumed his former friendships. Mersenne invited him to contribute to a collection of responses to Descartes's projected *Meditationes de prima philosophia*. Hobbes's contributions, with Descartes's replies, appeared as the third set of *Obiectiones* when the treatise was published in 1641. Further correspondence followed on the *Dioptrique*, which had appeared along with the *Discours de la methode* in 1637.

By this time, Hobbes had devised the plan of his own *magnum opus*. It was to be a work in three parts, dealing respectively with matter or body, with human nature, and with society. His original intention was to deal with these subjects in order, but because England was then on the brink of civil war and, as he judged, in urgent need of political counsel, he decided to deal with the third part first, and published *De cive* in Paris in 1642. (*De corpore* came out in 1655 and *De homine* in 1658.) In 1651, stability having been restored by the Commonwealth, he returned to England, where he remained for the rest of his life. In that year he published an English translation of *De cive* called *Philosophical Rudiments Concerning Government and Society*, and his acknowledged masterpiece, *Leviathan*. He remained active to the end of his life, producing several more works of interest – in particular a history of the Civil War called *Behemoth* and a treatise called *The Questions Concerning Liberty, Necessity and Chance*. A revised edition of *Leviathan* in Latin came out in 1668.

Hobbes's political theory, then, is that of someone who experienced both the English Civil War and the scientific revolution of the seventeenth century. This fact is important to our understanding of it. He formulated his political ideas several times, but it is in *Leviathan* that they find their most complete and influential statement. His approach to politics is self-consciously scientific. His technique of enquiry is derived partly from the 'resolutive-compositive' method associated with Galileo and Bacon, and partly from the deductive reasoning that had so impressed him in Euclid. If we are to arrive at a sound understanding of politics, we must first analyse or 'resolve' social wholes into their smallest component parts: namely, individual human beings. Then, having studied the properties and behaviour of those parts in isolation, we can deduce from them, as it were from first principles, rational conclusions about social and political organisation. In this way, Hobbes thinks, politics can be put on as sure a footing as any other science, and we can arrive at an account of politics that will furnish us with indubitable means of securing stability and peace.

What are we to make of the individual human being, of the 'natural' human being, unmodified by manners and civilisation? Hobbes had become convinced as early as 1630 – largely thanks to Bacon's influence – that the whole of the natural order can be explained in terms of 'body' without invoking such things as mind or spirit. The task of science, he argues in *De corpore*, is to examine and describe the effects of various types of corporeal motion; this, he thinks, is as true of physiology and psychology as it is of physics. His materialism – which earned him the condemnation of his contemporaries for 'atheism' – is central to his account of human behaviour. The body of each human being is, he thinks, only a complex mechanism, somewhat like a clock. He develops this imagery at length in *De corpore*. The heart is a spring; the nerves are wires; the joints are the wheels that give motion to the whole. Its behaviour is a series of responses to the stimuli received through the senses from the outside world. Some stimuli are pleasurable because they enhance our 'vital motion'. These we call good. Our feeling towards them is one of desire, and we endeavour to maximise and prolong them. Our condition when we are in a state where pleasure predominates is called 'felicity'. Other stimuli, which impede our vital motions, are painful. These we call evil; our feeling towards them is one of aversion, and we endeavour to avoid them. 'Good' and 'evil' have no other meaning than 'pleasurable' and 'painful': they are the names we give to what we desire and shun respectively. (Hobbes is, generally, a nominalist in his view of language: 'Words are but wise men's counters, they do but reckon with them, but they are the money of fools' (*Leviathan* 1:4).) 'Reason' is the calculative faculty by which we are enabled most effectively to achieve felicity and avoid the reverse. What we fear and seek to avoid more than anything else is death, death being precisely the event that makes the further continuance of felicity impossible. It is a truth of experience that individuals invariably act in such a way as to maintain themselves in being for as long as they can and by all possible means. In the light of this observation, we are, Hobbes thinks, to attribute to each man a 'right of nature' – an inherent right – 'to use his own power, as he will himself, for the preservation of his own nature' (*Leviathan* 1:14). To infer a 'right' – an entitlement to act – from what purports to be a factual generalisation about how people actually do act may seem a questionable logical procedure; but Hobbes is prevented by his materialist psychology from giving any other account of what it is to have a right, and he wishes to operate with the idea of right because it is, he thinks, by giving up our 'right of nature' that we create society and government.

Hobbes's materialist and hedonist psychology is worked out with remarkable thoroughness and consistency (although it raises questions about determinism and free will that he never satisfactorily answers). It is associated in his mind with, although it does not strictly imply, a destructive egoism. This feature of his thought is essential to his understanding of the nature and purposes of government. Given that each individual is no more than a self-contained mechanism operated by the attracting and repelling forces of pleasure and pain, no one has any reason to will anything but the greatest possible pleasure for themselves and the least possible pain. Hobbes does not believe that we are incapable of such things as benevolence. We can, after all, take pleasure in another's pleasure. But he thinks that other-directed passions tend to be overridden by immediate and self-centred ones, particularly in circumstances where there is danger, or where there is a shortage of those things that people want and need. If people lived in a world in which there were no government – in what Hobbes calls 'a State of Nature' – the result would be chaos, or at least it would be if the resources in the state of nature were scarce (which is what Hobbes assumes). People unrestrained by government would constantly come into conflict with one another in their efforts to maximise their own pleasure and avoid pain and death. Because they would constantly live in fear of losing what they have, no one would be free from the incessant urge to place themselves beyond the control of others and to achieve control over others. Everyone is naturally in the grip of 'a perpetual and restless desire of power after power, that ceaseth only in death' (*Leviathan* 1:11). In the absence of government, no one would be required to recognise any restraint or any obligation to anyone else, and so each would regard his natural right 'to use his own power, as he will himself, for the preservation of his own nature' as extending to everything whatsoever. The right of nature would, in effect, be a right to everything. 'And therefore if any two men desire the same thing, which nevertheless they cannot both enjoy, they become enemies' and 'endeavour to destroy or subdue one another' (*Leviathan* 1:13).

The state of nature, therefore, would be a condition of incessant conflict: 'a war ... of every man against every man' (*Leviathan* 1:13). Even in the absence of actual conflict, there would be the ever present fear of it, because no one would trust anyone else not to attack them. No one is so much stronger than everyone else as to be immune from threat. What some lack in physical strength they make up for in guile, and the weak can in any case band together to overcome the strong. In the state of nature there is no safety for anyone. Unlike some of the other political theorists who adopted it, Hobbes does not seriously suppose that the state of nature was ever a historical reality. But we can, he thinks, imagine only too clearly what life would be like if all restraint on us were absent. Even in civilised society, he remarks, no one trusts anyone else: when we go out, we lock our doors and carry arms; we hide our belongings away in chests; even where we have law to protect us, we take it for granted that anyone could be a thief.

If human beings really were ungoverned, then, their condition would be one of fear and wretchedness. Life would, in Hobbes's most quoted phrase, be 'solitary, poor, nasty, brutish and short' (*Leviathan* 1:13). But this fact in itself is enough to ensure that people in the state of nature would be led by their powerful instinct of self-preservation to seek the quickest and most effective way out of it. Each individual would understand that the only way of evading the perils of the state of nature would be to act according to certain rational maxims that Hobbes calls 'laws of nature', a law of nature being defined as

> a precept, or general rule, found out by reason, by which a person is forbidden to do that which is destructive of his life, or takes away the means of preserving the same; and to omit that by which he thinks it may be best preserved.
>
> (*Leviathan* 1:14)

He would understand (1) that it is rationally necessary to seek peace; (2) that the way to secure peace is to enter into an agreement with others not to harm one another; and (3) that having entered into such an agreement, it would be irrational, in the sense of self-defeating, to break it for as long as the others kept it. By this chain of reasoning, society would be created. It would be created by an agreement – a 'compact', as Hobbes calls it – made by individuals, no one of whom has any interest in anyone else's good *per se*, but each of whom realises that his own good can be secured only by agreeing not to harm others in return for their agreement not to harm him.

But '[t]he force of words [is] too weak to hold men to the performance of their covenants' (*Leviathan* 1:14). A *mere* compact, a compact not enforceable against anyone, would be of no value because no one of the parties to it could ever be sure that the others would not break it. 'Covenants without the sword are but words, and of no strength to secure a man at all' (*Leviathan* 2:17). The parties will need to insure themselves against this possibility by including in the compact an agreement to appoint a sovereign power to defend them collectively and punish those who violate its terms. The compact into which Hobbes imagines men entering therefore takes the following form:

> I authorise and give up my right of governing myself to this man, or to this assembly of men, on this condition, that thou give up thy right to him, and authorise all his actions in like manner.

This, he goes on,

> is the generation of that great Leviathan, or rather (to speak more reverently) of that Mortal God, to which we owe, under the immortal God, our peace and defence.
>
> (*Leviathan* 2:17)

Primarily by making and enforcing law, the sovereign power thus created will establish and maintain the kind of public order and security that it is not possible to enjoy in the state of nature. It will not (contrary to the impression that Hobbes sometimes gives) achieve its ends by coercion alone. It will also inculcate a moral sense into the citizens through education. In Book II of *Leviathan*, called 'Of the Commonwealth', Hobbes describes the various possible constitutional forms. In principle, sovereign power could be vested in any kind of government; but it would, he thinks, be best exercised by a monarch; and by this Hobbes means an absolute monarch. Monarchical power is efficient and enduring because undivided. Human nature being what it is, where power is shared, all who have a share in it will want a larger share than they have and will promptly fall into trying to wrest power from their colleagues, and so the very security and permanence that sovereign power is supposed to achieve will be lost.

The sovereign is created by, but is not a party to, the compact. He therefore cannot be got rid of because he is in breach of the compact. If he could be, his power would not, after all, be sovereign. His power is, however, conditional in a sense. It is conditional upon his continued willingness and effectiveness in relation to the defence and protection of his subjects. For as long as this condition is met, no one has any right of disobedience or resistance; but the subject's 'right of nature' to defend himself reasserts itself if the sovereign threatens his life or fails to protect it. No one can be expected to relinquish this natural right entirely. It was, after all, precisely in order to protect their lives that men submitted to government in the first place. The subject who finds his life threatened by the sovereign is therefore entitled – even if he is a criminal under sentence of death – to escape or resist if he can. Similarly, subjects are no longer obliged to obey a ruler who is defeated by an invading enemy. In such a case the sovereign would not longer be sovereign, and his subjects would be perfectly entitled to transfer their allegiance to the conqueror: that is, to someone who is better able to protect them than the defeated former sovereign.

The sovereign will be prevented from becoming a tyrant by the fact that, like everyone else, he naturally wishes to preserve a state of affairs favourable to himself. He will therefore allow his subjects as great a degree of freedom as is compatible with protecting them against internal threat and external disorder. Similarly, he will see to it that material goods and other benefits are distributed in such a way as to create the least possible discontent. Everything in the commonwealth must be organised so as to damp down the possibilities of conflict that are always latent in human transactions. It is particularly important, Hobbes thinks, that there be one state religion and that the head of state is also the head of the Church. Any other arrangement – and he is, of course, speaking in the light of his experience of civil war in England – will lead to faction and strife. Religious belief in the strict sense is a private matter, but the public aspects of religion must be completely subordinate to public authority. Where the Bible is ambiguous, the interpretation of the sovereign is to be final; the sovereign is to decide which books of scripture are canonical; he is to decide how religious observance is to be conducted; he is to decide how the Church is to be organised. The Roman Catholic Church – to which Hobbes turns his attention in Part IV of *Leviathan*, significantly called 'Of the Kingdom of Darkness' – is inimical to the autonomy of the commonwealth precisely because it requires of its votaries a loyalty that goes beyond their loyalty to the state.

Hobbes is in the curious position of having developed a theory of absolute government based on the reasoned consent of those subject to it and aimed at their common good. The clarity, force and pungency of his writing and the incisiveness of his arguments have impressed students of politics for more than three centuries. Reduced to its essentials, his doctrine is extremely simple. Taking the worst view of human behaviour, men can only live together in large numbers and for any length of time if they are subject to a government strong enough to control their destructive tendencies. Salvation lies in the fact that we are rational enough to know this. Attempts at refutation and reply – some of them impressive, some unimpressive, some laughable – began almost as soon as *Leviathan* was published; but it seems in the highest degree unlikely that anything will dislodge it from its place in the canon. Hobbes remains one of the most impressive and influential of English political theorists. He is also, though he several times twits himself on his own timidity, a writer of considerable intellectual courage, who expressed unpopular views at a time when it was dangerous – mortally dangerous, indeed – to do so. Virtually all subsequent attempts to treat politics and political behaviour philosophically have in some sense had to take Hobbes into account.

Further reading

Primary sources

De cive, ed. H. Warrender (Oxford: Clarendon Press, 1983).
Leviathan, ed. R. Tuck (Cambridge: Cambridge University Press, 1991).

Secondary sources

Aubrey, J.: *Brief Lives*, ed. O.L. Dick (Harmondsworth: Penguin, 1982).
Hampsher-Monk, I.: *A History of Modern Political Thought* (Oxford: Blackwell, 1992).
Raphael, D.D.: *Hobbes* (London: Allen & Unwin, 1977).
Skinner, Q.: *Visions of Politics*, vol. 3: *Hobbes and Civil Science* (Cambridge: Cambridge University Press, 2002).
Warrender, H.: *The Political Philosophy of Hobbes* (Oxford: Oxford University Press, 1957).
Watkins, J.W.N.: *Hobbes's System of Ideas* (London: Hutchinson, 1973).

JAMES HARRINGTON (1611–77)

James Harrington was born in Lincolnshire, England. He inherited a large fortune from his father while still a young man. After studying at

Oxford, he made the customary Grand Tour of Europe. He was much impressed by the Republic of Venice and returned home in 1635 a convinced republican, though he remained a loyal supporter and friend of Charles I. After the king's execution, Harrington's financial independence enabled him to devote himself to his major work, *The Commonwealth of Oceana*, published in 1656. After the Restoration, Harrington was suspected of plotting to reinstate the Commonwealth. Arrested in 1661 and imprisoned for a time in the Tower, he suffered a breakdown in health from which he never fully recovered, although the rumour that he died insane is probably without foundation.

Harrington shows little respect for the political thinkers of his day. He esteems **Hobbes** as a philosopher, but dislikes his politics. His political models are **Plato**'s *Laws*, **Aristotle**'s *Politics*, Polybius's *Histories* and the writings of **Machiavelli**, whom he especially admires. *Oceana* is a description of the government of a purportedly imaginary commonwealth, but the events, places and people depicted are only lightly disguised: 'Emporium' is London, 'Hiera' is Westminster, 'Leviathan' is Hobbes, 'Panurgus' is Henry VII, 'Parthenia' is Elizabeth I, 'Olpheus Megaletor' is Cromwell, and so on.

An important and original principle of Harrington's political thought is the causal link that it posits between economic distribution and political power. The form and operation of government inevitably depends, he thinks, on the distribution of property, especially of land. When the control of land rests with a monarch who lets it to numerous tenants in exchange for military service, the result is absolute monarchy. When the land is in the hands of a relatively small number of nobles who maintain large bodies of retainers, the result is a mixed or feudal monarchy. Feudal lords are able to limit the power of the monarchy, but are prevented by their own mutual quarrels from overthrowing it altogether. When the great feudal estates are broken up and the nobles are no longer able to support their retainers, the result is a commonwealth or republic. In short, government follows property: one form of government turns into another in response to changes in land distribution. Not surprisingly, therefore, Harrington's account of English history is primarily economic. The old feudal order had depended upon the division of property and power between kings and nobility. This division was unbalanced by the Wars of the Roses and the economic changes effected by the Tudors. Henry VII redistributed the great feudal estates among a relatively large number of proprietors. Henry VIII, in dissolving the monasteries, redistributed the property of the largest landowner of all – namely, the Church. The result was the creation of an increasingly numerous class of yeomen from whom, as they became collectively aware of their own power, the demand for political rights was bound to come. Hence the Civil War, the conflict that arose as political realities adjusted themselves to economic realities.

Given, Harrington continues, that recent English history has witnessed a redistribution of property in favour of the people, it follows that the form of government now appropriate – indeed, inevitable – in that country is a republican one. Harrington's project is to devise for 'Oceana' a constitution that will create what he calls an 'equal' commonwealth: namely, a balanced and stable commonwealth within which there are no serious conflicts between self-interest and public interest, so that it is in no one's interest to subvert it. Such a commonwealth must, he thinks, rest upon the impartial rule of law rather than upon the inconstant and partial will of men. Its most fundamental basis will be an agrarian law that will protect popular ownership of land against the natural tendency of property to accumulate in the hands of the few. This agrarian law would, as far as possible, restrict land ownership to holdings having an annual value of not more than £2,000. Harrington's idea of popular ownership is, however, rather different from what we should nowadays call popular. He thinks that as few as 5,000 landed proprietors would be enough to make the commonwealth stable.

The government should, Harrington thinks, embody three features that will secure responsiveness to the popular will. First, there is to be rotation in office, to ensure that the members of the community all have a chance to play their part in government. Magistrates are to be elected for short terms only, usually not exceeding one year, and they should not be eligible for immediate re-election. Second, elections should be conducted by secret ballot, so that neither fear nor favour can play a part in the result. Third, there is to be a bicameral legislature. The deliberative or policy-forming function is to be performed by a Senate consisting of a few persons of wisdom and experience. The acceptance or rejection of the Senate's legislative proposals is to rest with a larger body called the 'Prerogative Tribe', which is, however, to have no deliberative authority of its own. Both parts of the legislature are to be elected by the citizens through an elaborate system of indirect election involving ascending tiers of government – parishes, hundreds and 'tribes' – and property qualifications.

Harrington restricts citizenship to persons of independent means. Wage-earners or servants – people whose livelihood depends on someone other than themselves – cannot, he thinks, have a disinterested political will. The citizens or freemen are divided into those under thirty, who are the active military class, and the elders – the 'orb' of the commonwealth – who form the military reserve and are the main repository of political wisdom. Citizens with incomes of £100 a year or more are to serve in the cavalry when required; those with incomes of less than £100 a year will be infantrymen. No one is exempt from military service, and there is to be conscription if necessary. Suitable arrangements are to be made for the care of the old and infirm.

Education is to be an important feature of the commonwealth. Schools should be provided at public expense, and attendance is to be compulsory between the ages of nine and fifteen. Harrington understands that the viability of a government depends largely on the belief and understanding of those subject to it. Education is therefore to include weekly classes for the purpose of explaining the constitution and maintaining political awareness. Harrington also gives much thought to how the religious life of the commonwealth is to be organised. There is to be a non-compulsory state religion, overseen by a council of religion elected by the Senate. Each congregation is to be free to choose its own minister. When a vacancy arises, two representatives of the parish are to request one of the two universities to appoint a minister, who will hold his office on probation for one year. The parishioners will then vote on whether his appointment is to be confirmed, such confirmation depending on a majority of two-thirds. The clergy will not be allowed any occupation apart from their parochial duties, but in order to ensure that there will be no shortage of candidates for the ministry, no benefice is to be worth less than £100 a year. There is to be freedom of worship for everyone except Jews and Catholics, and no religious coercion of any sort. When disputes over religious matters arise, they are to be referred to the divines of the two universities, who will settle them by debate and discussion.

Much of what he says is derived, as he happily admits, from 'ancient prudence', but Harrington has considerable ability as a political theorist. As a designer of constitutions, he was admired in eighteenth-century America. It has been suggested that he influenced the drafting of the constitutions of Carolina and Pennsylvania. Marxist historians have found support in his writings for the theory that the English Civil War was a bourgeois revolution caused by the so-called 'rise of the gentry'. Many of the devices that he recommended have become established as standard features of liberal government: a written constitution; the election and rotation of magistrates, with short terms of office; guarantees of religious freedom; popular education at the public expense. Harrington is often congratulated on his objective treatment of political problems. He himself conceived political theory to be a science comparable to the anatomical work of William Harvey. The degree of rational detachment that he achieves is all the more remarkable in view of the political turmoil by which his lifetime was distinguished.

Further reading

Primary source

The Political Works of James Harrington, ed. J.G.A. Pocock (Cambridge: Cambridge University Press, 1977).

Secondary sources

Blitzer, C.: *An Immortal Commonwealth: The Political Thought of James Harrington* (New Haven, CT: Yale University Press, 1960).

Macpherson, C.B.: *The Political Theory of Possessive Individualism* (Oxford: Oxford University Press, 1962).

Raab, F.: *The English Face of Machiavelli* (London: Routledge & Kegan Paul, 1964).

Tawney, R.H.: *Harrington's Interpretation of His Age* (Oxford: Oxford University Press, 1942).

JOHN LOCKE (1632–1704)

John Locke was born into a Puritan family in Somerset, England. His father was a country lawyer who raised a troop of horse and fought on the parliamentary side in the Civil War. Locke went up to Christ Church, Oxford, in 1652. Like **Hobbes** before him, Locke found the old-fashioned Scholastic curriculum uncongenial, though his association with Christ Church was to last, with interruptions, for more than thirty years. He became a senior student – that is, a Fellow – in 1659. His earliest political work, *Essays on the Law of Nature*, was written (in two Latin versions) in 1660, though not edited until the 1950s. He considered, but rejected, the idea of taking orders, and in 1666 was given a dispensation by the college to enable him to hold his studentship without doing so. He began to be interested in medicine in the 1660s and in 1675 took the degree of Bachelor of Medicine, although he never practised medicine as a profession. He was acquainted with many members of the newly formed Royal Society, and was himself elected Fellow in 1668. In 1667 he became medical adviser and general factotum of Anthony Ashley Cooper, created first Earl of Shaftesbury in 1672. When Shaftesbury was appointed Lord Chancellor in 1672, Locke became his secretary. His association with the exclusionist politics of Shaftesbury and his circle meant that when James II succeeded to the throne in 1685, Locke thought it wise to exile himself to Holland. While there – often in real danger of arrest by agents of the British government – he worked on his *Essay Concerning Human Understanding*. In 1689, a year after the accession of William of Orange, Locke returned to England and published the *Essay*. In the same year he published his *Two Treatises of Government* and his first *Letter Concerning Toleration*. His *Thoughts on Education* came out in 1693 and *On the Reasonableness of Christianity* in 1695.

Although Locke's reputation as a philosopher rests almost entirely on the epistemological doctrines expressed in *An Essay Concerning Human Understanding*, he made a great and lasting contribution to political thought. This contribution consists mainly in his *Two Treatises of Government*, especially in the *Second Treatise*. It was for many years assumed that the treatises were written as *ex post facto* justifications of the Glorious Revolution of 1688. Thanks largely to the researches of Professor Peter Laslett, it is now accepted that the *Two Treatises* were composed some ten years before they were published. In all probability Locke withheld them from publication for reasons of prudence. They would have been treasonable beyond doubt had they been published at the time when they were written.

The *First Treatise* is a response to the version of the divine right of kings theory developed by the Royalist author Sir Robert Filmer in his book *Patriarcha* (published in 1680, though probably written in about 1630). Locke's purpose is to rebut Filmer's claim that royal power is patriarchal in nature, and therefore neither conferred nor revocable by the people over whom it is exercised. Filmer had contended, by appeal to the Old Testament, that Adam and his heirs were divinely appointed as rulers of the world and that all subsequent kings somehow derive their authority from this fact. Locke dismantles this argument with ease. In its place he advances the principle that no one is intended by God to be the natural ruler of anyone else. (We may remark in passing that Filmer has more ability as a political thinker than Locke credits him with. It is a little unfortunate that, largely thanks to Locke's smiting of him in the *First Treatise*, Filmer has been consigned so effectively to the ranks of the unregarded.)

It is usual to regard the *First Treatise* as being mainly of antiquarian interest. It is in the *Second Treatise* that Locke presents his own ideas. The proper title of the treatise is 'An Essay Concerning the True

Original, Extent and End of Civil Government'. It takes its departure from the point that it was the purpose of the *First Treatise* to establish: no one is by nature or by the divine will subject to anyone else. All men are born equal; each individual is, as it were, the sovereign ruler of his own person. In curious but intentional language Locke speaks of each man having a 'property' in his own person. From this it follows that no one can become subject to anyone else, or to any law, save by his own consent.

> The liberty of man in society is to be under no other legislative power but that established by consent in the commonwealth, nor under the dominion of any will, or restraint of any law, but what the legislative shall enact, according to the trust put in it.
>
> (*Second Treatise* ch.4)

How, then, are we to account for the existence, or at any rate the legitimacy, of present-day governments?

Like Hobbes, Locke makes use of the idea of a state of nature as an explanatory conceit upon which to build his political theory. As with Hobbes, and despite some ambiguity of language, the argument is not really a historical one. It is an attempt to infer the proper structure of government – and above all to develop a theory of political obligation – from a consideration of what rational people would invent if they were living without a government and wanted to devise one. We are to imagine an original condition, social but non-political, in which human beings are subject only to the law of nature. This is a law, given by God and discernible by human reason, that 'teaches all mankind ... that being all equal and independent, no one ought to harm another in his life, liberty or possessions' (*Second Treatise* ch.2). (The fact that the law of nature seems to be the kind of 'innate idea' that Locke is elsewhere so unequivocal in denying has been noted as a serious difficulty, but it is a difficulty to which he offers no solution.) We are then to consider why and how individuals would move from this condition of virtually complete freedom into political society, and what the moral and practical consequences of their doing so would be.

Locke holds that the law of nature confers upon mankind natural rights of life, liberty and property; but it is the natural right to property that interests him most, and to it he devotes most attention. God gave the earth and its fruits to men as a common possession. Labour is the origin and justification of, and confers value on, private property.

Private property (by which Locke means landed property) arises when individuals 'mix their labour' with what God has provided (ch.5). In a certain sense they add what they mix their labour with to the original property that they have in their own persons. Their property becomes part of themselves. This process of expropriation is legitimate under the law of nature provided that no one violates anyone else's right: provided, that is, that no one takes more than he needs and so allows resources to spoil which might have been enjoyed by someone else. The right to acquire private property is therefore not unrestricted. No one may take more than he can use, and enough and as good must be left over for others. This proviso fixes a natural limit to property acquisition; it suggests moreover, given that each man's needs and capacity for consumption are roughly the same, that the amount of property that anyone may claim as his own is governed in principle by a standard of approximate equality. But this equality was long ago overridden in practice by the invention of money as a means of exchange. Money allows any given individual to own and profit from more land than he could himself consume the produce of, and for the livelihood of some to depend not directly on the fruits of the earth, but upon cash payments made in exchange for their labour. Again, this arrangement does not violate the law of nature provided that those who sell their labour do so under contracts into which they have entered freely. Given that the amount of land available for enclosure is not infinite, it is inevitable that some such conventional system of exchange will arise.

Theoretically, all these economic processes could take place spontaneously, without the intervention or regulation of government. Locke does not take Hobbes's pessimistic view of how ungoverned human beings would behave in relation to each other. Unlike Hobbes, he does not depict the state of nature as an intolerable condition in which the amenities of civilisation are impossible. It is not a 'state of war' from which fear would drive men to escape even at the cost of submitting to absolute government. The drawbacks of Locke's state of nature would be no worse than 'inconveniences'. It is inevitable that disputes would arise, especially with the growth of inequalities of property distribution, and in the state of nature there would be no settled and reliable way of resolving such disputes. Men who were, in effect, judges in their own cause would be unduly vigilant of their rights, and would tend to punish with excessive severity those who infringed them. Conscious of these inconveniences, individuals would agree to unite into a community for the purpose of defending one another's rights. There would, in short, be a 'social contract'. Clearly, such a contract would require the consent of each of the parties to it. The community, once established, would then set about creating for itself legislative and other institutions, although Locke thinks that majority consent would be enough to do this. Such institutions would need to be supported by means of taxation, but taxation would be strictly subject to the agreement of property owners, given in person or by means of a representative assembly. This requirement arises from the fact that, since the point of setting up government in the first place was to protect property and other rights, government may not remove or redistribute property without the consent of those whose property it is. It seems, then (although Locke's description is not entirely clear), that the 'social contract' would have three stages: the establishment of a community by the contracting parties, the setting up of governmental institutions, and the authorisation of taxation.

The executive institutions of government would be subject to the rule of law. This, as one might expect of an opponent of divine-right claims, is an important point for Locke. The business of government must be conducted according to fixed and known legal and procedural standards and not by means of fiat or prerogative. Locke does allow a certain degree of prerogative power, but such power is to be exercised only in exceptional circumstances and only for a manifest public good. Absolute rulers, he thinks – he does not mention Hobbes, but the allusion is clearly to him – would be in a state of nature relative to their subjects. Also, Locke thinks it desirable for the various functions of government to be in different hands, and he insists that the executive must be subordinate to the legislature. He does not, however, discuss the 'separation of powers' in detail, nor does he apply the principle consistently. To regard him, as some commentators have, as an early exponent of the doctrine is something of an exaggeration.

Locke's insistence on consent as the basis of political obligation encounters a rather obvious objection. The keystone of his argument, we recall, is that because no one is naturally subject to government, the legitimacy of government depends upon the individual's voluntary submission to it. At what point and by what means, though, does this voluntary submission actually take place? How and when is consent given? This is a difficulty that all versions of the consent theory of authority encounter sooner or later. The fact that there is no plausible sense in which most people can be said to have given active or deliberate consent to be governed is on the face of it a serious obstacle to the kind of argument that Locke wishes to develop. He solves it by recourse to the dubious, if common, expedient of 'tacit' – silent – consent. Actual or explicit consent, he considers, is not necessary.

Anyone who enjoys or uses property under the protection of a government or makes free use of the facilities and protection that the government provides, even if this means 'barely travelling freely on the highway', is deemed to be consenting to its authority not actively, indeed, but tacitly. In short, we give our consent merely by remaining where we are. The weakness of this version of consent was to be pointed out by David **Hume**.

Locke's political theory is, above all, a theory of resistance. Ultimately, it is a theory of revolution, published, after all, to defend or in some sense celebrate the removal of James II from the throne of England. Men establish government to defend their natural rights and uphold the natural law with a degree of reliability and impartiality impossible in the state of nature; but government does not supersede the natural law and may not infringe or ignore the rights that the natural law confers. Government has the nature of a trust. We entrust the defence of our rights to it, but we do not relinquish those rights to it. A government that violates natural rights is therefore in breach of its trust, and its subjects are entitled to defend their rights and liberties by resisting it: with violence if necessary. In a sufficiently gross case of breach, the people actually have a right of revolution: that is, a right to take back the authority originally conferred on the government. Revolution, Locke thinks, is a kind of appeal to heaven for judgment by the people who consider themselves oppressed by tyrannical government. If the revolution is successful – if the divine judgment is given in favour of the people – sovereignty reverts back to the community constituted by the original agreement that took men out of the state of nature, and the process of creating political institutions can begin again.

> In these and like cases where the government is dissolved, the people are at liberty to provide for themselves by erecting a new legislative, differing from the other by the change of persons or form or both, as they shall find it most for their safety and good.
>
> (*Second Treatise* ch.19)

If a people can simply remove authority from governments if it sees fit, is not this a recipe for anarchy? Locke has two responses to this objection. First, it is not his suggestion that governments are to be overthrown for every trifling offence that they may give to subjects' sensibilities. Tyrants will not be resisted unless large numbers of people are damaged by their exactions. Second, there is in any case a sense in which a tyrannical government overthrows itself, by failing to perform the only functions that justified its existence in the first place.

> [W]henever the legislators endeavour to take away or destroy the property of the people, or to reduce them to slavery under arbitrary power, they put themselves into a state of war with the people, who are thereupon absolved from any further obedience, and are left to the common refuge, which God hath provided for all men against force and violence: resistance.
>
> (*Second Treatise* ch.19)

Locke is interested also in the question of religious toleration; a question that was, of course, topical throughout his lifetime. He produced an *Essay on Toleration* as early as 1667, and later published three *Letters Concerning Toleration* (1689, 1690, 1692; a fourth letter was published after his death). His defence of religious freedom has three aspects. First, persecution and religious intolerance are at odds with the spirit of the Gospel. Second, the duty of government is to preserve a public and external order only. The business of the law, he says, is not to regulate people's opinions, but to provide for the safety and security of the commonwealth. Religious observance and belief are private matters: the practice of religion affects no one but the individual whose practice it is. Magistrates therefore have no right to require anyone to act against conscience in any matter of religion. Third, religious faith is in any case a matter of belief, and belief is not an act of will. Since, therefore, magistrates can only coerce the will, it is irrational and futile to try to enforce religious belief. It may be thought that this last argument rather misses the point, inasmuch as what magistrates try to enforce is not religious belief, but religious conformity; but Locke's arguments considered generally are familiar liberal ones, reminiscent in a number of ways of those of J.S. **Mill**. As *The Reasonableness of Christianity* shows, Locke does not understand Christianity to be an edifice of elaborate and subtle doctrine. The minimum requirements of the Christian faith are not much more than belief in God and in Jesus as the Son of God. He therefore does not find it difficult to ignore the theological niceties that separate the various kinds of dissenters from one another and from the Anglican establishment. Toleration should not, he thinks, be extended to Roman Catholics and atheists: not because of any religious consideration, but because the former owe allegiance to a foreign power and the latter, because they do not believe in a God who is the ground of moral obligation, cannot be relied upon to honour obligations.

Locke – jointly, perhaps, with Hobbes – is the most influential of all English political theorists. His political writing, like all political writing, is a response to the issues and events of a specific time and place, and reflects a particular perception of those issues and events. He is an opponent of the specific ideological claims of the Stuart kings. Arguably, the apparently universal principles and values for which he argues are really no more than the interests of an emergent capitalist class. This is a view that was argued persuasively by C.B. Macpherson in his influential book called *The Political Theory of Possessive Individualism*. Nonetheless, Locke's thought has been promoted into timeless significance by the admiration of generations of liberals. The impact of his ideas on the American Constitution and upon the declarations of the French Revolutionaries is clear, and his theory of property continued to influence liberal political thinkers – Robert **Nozick** is an obvious example – into the twentieth century.

Further reading

Primary sources

A Letter Concerning Toleration, ed. R. Klibansky and J.W. Gough (Oxford: Clarendon Press, 1968).

Two Treatises of Government, ed. P. Laslett (Cambridge: Cambridge University Press, 1988).

Essays on the Law of Nature, ed. W.M. von Leyden (Oxford: Clarendon Press, 2002).

Secondary sources

Cranston, M.: *John Locke: a Biography* (London: Longman, 1957).

Dunn, J.: *The Political Thought of John Locke* (Cambridge: Cambridge University Press, 1969).

Gough, J.W.: *John Locke's Political Philosophy* (Oxford: Clarendon Press, 1973).

Hampsher-Monk, I.: *A History of Modern Political Thought* (Oxford: Blackwell, 1992).

Macpherson, C.B.: *The Political Theory of Possessive Individualism* (Oxford: Oxford University Press, 1962).

MONTESQUIEU (1689–1755)

Charles-Louis de Secondat, Baron de la Brède et de Montesquieu, was born at La Brède, France. He was educated at the Oratorian collège de

Juilly from 1700 to 1705 and thereafter at the University of Bordeaux, where he read law. In 1716 he inherited from his uncle the barony of Montesquieu and the office of Président à Mortier of the Parlement de Guyenne at Bordeaux. His literary reputation was established in 1721 with the publication of his *Lettres persanes* (*Persian Letters*), a satire on French life, customs and political institutions in the form of letters supposedly written by two bemused Persian travellers. In 1728 he was elected, though by no means unanimously, to the Académie française. He spent the years between 1728 and 1731 travelling in Europe. He lived for a short time in England, and his experience of English life and politics left a deep impression on his mind. In 1734 he published his *Considérations sur les causes de la grandeur et de la décadence des romains* (*The Causes of the Greatness and Decline of the Romans*). Part of the purpose of this work is to emphasise the extent to which Roman history was the product of the external circumstances that shaped the Romans' lives and actions. This emphasis on external circumstances foreshadows one of the important themes of the work for which Montesquieu is best remembered, *De l'esprit des lois* (*The Spirit of the Laws*, 1748).

Reading *De l'esprit des lois* is an arduous task. It is very long, and it exhibits a notorious lack of form and coherence. Its literary peculiarities are to some extent, though only to some extent, deliberate. Montesquieu wrote obscurely partly to shield the susceptibilities of plain folk from the possibly unsettling effects of his doctrines, partly to set his readers the challenge of unravelling his meanings for themselves, and partly to evade censorship (of which he seems to have been inordinately fearful: all three of his major works were at first published abroad and anonymously). Thanks to these peculiarities, *De l'esprit des lois* is not an easy work to summarise without distortion. This should be borne in mind throughout the following account.

The universe, Montesquieu observes, exhibits as part of its nature the kind of regularities that we call laws. Laws in this sense are 'necessary relationships deriving from the very nature of things'. Even God is bound by the 'laws' – the necessary conditions – that make creative activity possible. Those parts of the law of the universe that pertain to human behaviour are, predictably enough, called 'natural laws'. Natural laws relate to the achievement of such basic imperatives of human existence as protection and reproduction, but they are not mere instincts. They prescribe what we should do, and what they prescribe is discoverable by human reason. By nature, however, men are solitary and fearful, and their reason is developed only to a very rudimentary degree. It requires pressure or stimulus to activate and refine reason. Sociability develops as they begin to discover the pleasures and advantages of life with others of their own kind; but the development of sociability is immediately productive of strife, as men begin to exhibit their natural tendency to exploit one another. For Montesquieu, as for **Hobbes**, the primitive or ungoverned condition of mankind – the 'State of Nature' – would be a state of misery and terror. It is under the impulse of such terror that man's hitherto torpid reason teaches him that it is necessary to devise and enforce positive laws that will enable him to achieve peace and security. This, at the most basic level of explanation, is how government emerges. Montesquieu's argument is, it will be noticed, something of a blend of **Rousseau** and Hobbes, and his account of law owes something to St Thomas **Aquinas**.

Government as a general phenomenon, then, is created by common humanity and its needs, but the particular ways in which government manifests itself are diverse. This diversity arises from the fact that human needs, though universal, will be expressed and met in different ways by different peoples, according to their different circumstances. The form taken by government and law will depend on the 'general spirit of each nation', and this spirit will itself be determined by a number of variables: climate, soil, occupation, history, geographical location, religion and so forth. It is commonly said that Montesquieu's emphasis on the physical, environmental and cultural factors that give a society its character is the earliest attempt to write a sociology of politics. It may fairly be pointed out, however, that, in emphasising how different circumstances favour and produce different constitutional forms, Montesquieu is really only pursuing the kind of analysis pioneered by **Aristotle**. Montesquieu identifies three main types of government, although these types will be modified by environmental influences: despotisms, republics and monarchies. Each kind of government has what he calls a 'nature' and a 'principle'. Its 'nature' is defined by where sovereign power is located in it; its 'principle', in the absence of which it will not work successfully, is a suitable disposition or condition of mind – a 'modification of soul' – on the part of those subject to it. Despotism, again predictably enough, is in its 'nature' arbitrary and capricious government by one person. It is an unnatural form of government from which law is absent. It tends to be characteristic of large empires and hot climates. Its 'principle' is the fear or servility of those under it. Republican government is a blend of aristocracy and democracy, requiring of its citizens a strong sense of civic virtue or public spirit, which will motivate them to subordinate private interests to public or patriotic ones. Montesquieu admires republics, but he considers that the standards of selflessness and public service that they demand are often achieved at the cost of institutionalising a rigid morality that stultifies the individualism of their citizens. Life in a virtuous republic is, he says, rather like life in a monastery. Monarchy is government by one man tempered by the countervailing influence of 'intermediate powers' such as the parlements, chartered towns, nobility and clergy. It will depend, Montesquieu thinks, on a sense of honour, by which he seems chiefly to mean a strong sense of rank and distinction, and, in particular, a taste for military accomplishment. Again, the dependence of Montesquieu on Aristotle's description of constitutional forms and their variations is clear enough. Although he believes himself to be engaging in a value-free analysis of political forms, he cannot in practice separate his analyses from his own convictions about the contemporary political evils of France. A monarchy is what Montesquieu thinks France should be; a despotic regime is what he thinks it has become under the centralising tendencies of Richelieu and Louis XIV.

What form of constitution, then, is most compatible with liberty: that is, what constitutional arrangements will best enable individuals to live their lives without interference and enjoy their property in peace? The answer, Montesquieu thinks, is monarchy, and, in particular, monarchy of the kind observable in England. His famous discussion of the English constitution comes in Book XI of *De l'esprit des lois*. Old-fashioned feudal monarchies derived their stability from the uneasily balanced distribution of power between king, nobles and clergy. In contemporary England, this equipoise has come to express itself in a formal 'separation of powers'. Legislative, judicial and executive functions are in different hands, and the various mechanisms through which these functions are expressed operate as 'checks and balances' upon one another. Power cannot therefore achieve unwholesome concentrations, despotism cannot arise, and the liberty of all is guaranteed. Montesquieu also thinks that the English dedication to commerce is a civilising influence. Quite apart from the material benefits of prosperity, commerce broadens outlooks; it tends to overcome destructive religious and national differences; the desire to engage in peaceful trade cures human beings of their addiction to military exploits; it inculcates the virtues of thrift, diligence, moderation, prudence and order. Montesquieu believes that the political ills of France, where the executive, legislative and judicial powers are concentrated in the king's hands, are in principle capable of being cured by the importation of the main features of English government; though he understands, of course, that any imitation by one nation of the customs and practices of another would have to take full account of differences of history and culture.

It is not easy to give a brief evaluation of Montesquieu. *De l'esprit des lois* tends to be regarded as the classic work of French Enlightenment political thought, but there is nothing truly original in it; nor is his analysis of the English constitution a very accurate account of what the English constitution was like in the middle of the eighteenth century. He claims to have studied it first-hand, but most of what he says seems to depend on **Locke**, **Harrington** and Bolingbroke. Even the famous 'separation of powers' doctrine is really no more than a version of the 'mixed' constitution discussed by **Plato**, Aristotle and Polybius. Montesquieu's erudition is wide but not deep, his analyses are often prejudiced and subjective, and the writing and organisation of *De l'esprit des lois* is incoherent in ways that often suggest a failure of literary skill rather than intentional policy. Despite all negative comments, however, it is impossible not to admire the size and ambition of his undertakings. He was the first modern thinker to attempt an investigation of the effects of geography, environment and other externalities upon political institutions. His reputation also owes much to the esteem in which he was held by the draftsmen of the Constitution of the United States. His influence has been immense, and on the strength of it he holds a place of great importance in the history of political thought.

Further reading

Primary sources

The Political Theory of Montesquieu, ed. M. Richter (Cambridge: Cambridge University Press, 1977).

The Spirit of the Laws, ed. A.M. Cohler, B.C. Miller and H.S. Stone (Cambridge: Cambridge University Press, 1989).

Secondary sources

Durkheim, E.: *Montesquieu and Rousseau: Forerunners of Sociology*, ed. R. Mannheim (Ann Arbor, MI: University of Michigan Press, 1960).

Pangle, T.L.: *Montesquieu's Philosophy of Liberalism* (Chicago, IL: University of Chicago Press, 1973).

Shackleton, R.: *Montesquieu: A Critical Biography* (Oxford: Oxford University Press, 1961).

DAVID HUME (1711–76)

David Hume was born near Berwick into the minor landed gentry of Scotland. He was educated at the University of Edinburgh, where he read law, though his interest presently turned towards literature and philosophy. In early manhood he abandoned the Presbyterian beliefs of his family, and opposition from the Scottish religious establishment prevented him from securing the Chairs of Philosophy at Edinburgh in 1745 and Glasgow in 1752. His first and most important philosophical work, *A Treatise of Human Nature*, was written in France and published in 1739–40. To his great disappointment, the *Treatise* was not a success. He published a revised and more accessible version of its main doctrines in two works: *An Enquiry Concerning Human Understanding* (1748) and *An Enquiry Concerning the Principles of Morals* (1751). He was an elegant and versatile essayist, producing *Essays Moral and Political* in 1742 and *Political Discourses* in 1752. His *History of England* was published in eight volumes between 1754 and 1761, while he held the post of Keeper of the Advocates' Library at Edinburgh. He was an easy and cheerful man, who made friends easily and enjoyed their affection, though **Rousseau** treated him with characteristic ingratitude when they met. His *Dialogues Concerning Natural Religion* were published posthumously, in 1779.

The starting-point of Hume's political and moral thought is his conviction that human beings are primarily creatures not of reason, but of passion or feeling. Reason, he tells us in a much-quoted aphorism,

> is, and ought only to be, the slave of the passions, and can never pretend to any other office than to serve and obey them.
>
> (*Treatise of Human Nature* 2:3:3)

This is an odd way of putting it (if reason *is* the slave of the passions, there seems no point in adding that it *ought* to be so), but what Hume intends to do is challenge the supposition that our moral beliefs are grounded in, and demonstrable by, reason. This supposition appeals to those who, like **Locke**, wish to repudiate the idea that political authority must be accepted as a given and not subjected to the scrutiny of reason or required to conform to rational standards. But, Hume maintains, it rests on a misunderstanding of the causal relation between reason and feeling. Moral belief, he thinks, is a species of feeling. But we do not have the feelings that we do because we have reasoned in a certain way. On the contrary, we reason as we do because we have the particular kind of feelings that we have. Some people might prefer the destruction of the whole world to some trifling inconvenience to themselves; someone else might choose total ruin to spare another a trifling inconvenience. We might think such preferences odd, but they are not *irrational*: that is to say, no logical contradiction is involved in holding them. Moral convictions are positions chosen because one feels as one does, not logical conclusions that one has thought one's way to. In so far as government institutionalises moral beliefs, it is a creation not of reason directly, but of reason in so far as reason is the 'slave' of a certain kind of feeling.

What this implies for politics is that government and political obligation are to be understood as originating not in some such abstraction as a social contract or law of nature, but in the practical responses of human beings to felt needs and desires. Men are, Hume thinks, naturally sociable. They are drawn to live with others of their own kind. But their goodwill towards others – their 'benevolence' – is limited. It is limited in the sense that they think first of themselves and their own families and only then of other people. Given that this is so, and given also that the material resources of the world are scarce, it is inevitable that disputes will occur wherever human beings come together. It is in order to keep such disputes to a minimum that men have over the years generated what Hume calls 'rules of justice': rules intended to maintain the security of possessions and the honouring of contracts. We cannot point to a legislator who formulated these rules first, nor is there any need to try to do so. They have arisen more or less spontaneously in the course of human transactions. They are not 'natural laws' discovered by abstract reason; they are merely conventional, and have no intrinsic merit. They are the productions of practical reason responding to the sentiments to which the possibility of conflict gives rise. Because human beings are all more or less the same in how they feel and think, the rules of justice by which men live show a high degree of uniformity. They are logically prior to government. Government comes about because, human nature being what it is, we cannot live by the 'rules of justice' unless we have over us some agency with coercive power. The rules of justice need to be enforced because we are short sighted; we value short-term goals at the expense of our long-term interests. In our calmer moments, we realise that it is in our true interest to support an authority that can enforce the rules of justice effectively. It is this collective realisation on the part of passionate, short-sighted but ultimately rational human beings that accounts for the existence and authority of government.

When and in what precise circumstances did government originate? Hume does not understand why political authors have attached so much importance to this question. We cannot, he thinks, possibly know the answer to it, and no good purpose can be served by speculation. It is probably best to regard government as having evolved over time and become established by the authority of custom, but it is enough for us to know that we have it and that it answers successfully to its purpose. Like **Burke**, Hume recommends a policy of leaving well enough alone. If the existing regime does what we want of it, it is as well not to tamper with it. He believes that government conducted according to uniform and general laws will be the most satisfactory, because it is the form of government most likely to please everyone under it. Hume's own preference is for a form of mixed monarchical and republican government of (what he takes to be) the British variety, where the two kinds of power check and limit one another. But the form of government does not much matter, as long as it works and the people consider that their purposes are served by supporting it.

> I look upon all kinds of subdivision of power, from the monarchy of France to the freest democracy of the Swiss cantons, to be equally legal if established by custom and authority.
>
> (*New Letters*, p.81)

Hume is impatient of social-contract arguments. He offers a pertinent critique of them in his essay called 'Of the Original Contract' – an essay that every admirer of **Locke** ought to read. If all our obligations are held to rest on an original contract, what does the obligation to keep the original contract rest on? Since no one can identify the occasion when an original contract was actually concluded, why does it make more sense to appeal to consent than to tradition or custom as the source of obligation? Locke had appealed to 'tacit' consent. The mere fact that individuals do not leave the community in which they live is, he had argued, evidence that they are consenting to the arrangements by which it is governed. But this, says Hume, will not do. He invites us to consider the press-ganged seaman who wakes up and finds himself on a ship in the middle of the ocean. According to the social contractarians, all authority is constituted by, and only by, the individual's consent to it; but that consent, says Locke, does not have to be explicit. What, then, is the individual taken to sea against his will to do? He can either throw himself over the side, which is obviously not an eligible possibility, or he can remain where he is; in which case, according to the tacit consent argument, he is *ipso facto* accepting the captain's authority. This, says Hume, is exactly the predicament of the 'poor peasant or artisan' who hates the government under which he finds himself, but has no means of removing himself from its jurisdiction. Tacit consent is an argument that takes no account of the fact that there may be people living under a government whose only reason for doing so is that they cannot leave; this is hardly a sensible version of consent.

Hume also has a telling argument against the type of natural law doctrine that deduces its prescriptions from what purport to be facts about human nature or the nature of the world in general. This kind of derivation, Hume suggests, involves a straightforward fallacy.

> In every system of morality which I have hitherto met with, I have always remarked that the author proceeds for some time in the ordinary way of reasoning, and establishes the being of a God, or makes observations concerning human affairs; when of a sudden I am surprised to find that instead of the usual copulations of propositions 'is' and 'is not', I meet with no proposition that is not connected with an 'ought' or 'ought not'. This change is imperceptible; but is, however, of the last consequence. For as this 'ought' or 'ought not' expresses some new relation or affirmation, 'tis necessary that it should be observed and explained, and at the same time that a reason should be given, for what seems altogether inconceivable: how this new relation can be a deduction from others, which are entirely different from it.
>
> (*Treatise of Human Nature* 3:1:1)

Hume's point in this passage is that the sort of moral reasoning he is describing involves what we should now call a category-mistake. In this respect he is, of course, correct. From the fact that (say) all men naturally starve without food, it clearly does not *follow* that anyone has a 'natural right' to food. The consequences of Hume being correct are not, however, as radical as is sometimes supposed. The fallacy of deriving 'ought' from 'is', as it tends to be described nowadays, is a fallacy if and only if the derivation is a formal deduction. We can perfectly well formulate a list of 'natural rights' *in the light of* what we know about natural needs, but without purporting to make a deduction; there is nothing whatsoever fallacious about this. It is, indeed, difficult to see how we might formulate such a list other than in the light of what people actually need. To this extent, Hume's point is not as damaging to natural-law type arguments as has sometimes been thought; although it has, it must be admitted, prompted moral philosophers to think about exactly what kind of claim is being made when they talk about natural or human rights.

Hume may fairly be described as a proto-utilitarian. Jeremy **Bentham** was impressed by the *Treatise* and clearly influenced by Hume's ideas about what motivates us to act as we do, although it is unlikely that Hume would have approved of Bentham's narrow hedonism. Hume believes that we are to account for government, and evaluate it, not by trying to measure its conformity to some such abstract idea as consent, contract or natural law, but in terms of its historical, organic development, and by reference to the consequences that make it worth our while to accept and support it. Also, although he deliberately kept himself aloof from political parties – the common assertion that he was a Tory is erroneous – he is temperamentally a conservative in much the same mould as Burke, upon whom it is hard to believe that he did not have an influence.

Further reading

Primary sources

New Letters of David Hume, ed. R. Kilbansky and E.C. Mossner (Oxford: Clarendon Press, 1954).

Enquiries Concerning Human Understanding and Concerning the Principles of Morals, ed. E. Selby-Bigge (Oxford: Clarendon Press, 1975).

A Treatise of Human Nature, ed. L.A. Selby-Bigge (Oxford: Clarendon Press, 1978).

The History of England from the Invasion of Julius Caesar to the Revolution of 1688, ed. W.B. Todd (Indianapolis, IN: Liberty Classics, 1983–5).

Essays Moral, Political and Literary, ed. E. Miller (Indianapolis, IN: Liberty Classics, 1985).

Secondary sources

Forbes, D.: *Hume's Philosophical Politics* (Cambridge: Cambridge University Press, 1975).

Mackie, J.L.: *Hume's Moral Theory* (London: Routledge & Kegan Paul, 1980).

Miller, D.: *Philosophy and Ideology in Hume's Political Thought* (Oxford: Clarendon Press, 1981).

Whelan, F.G.: *Order and Artifice in Hume's Political Philosophy* (Princeton, NJ: Princeton University Press, 1985).

JEAN-JACQUES ROUSSEAU (1712–78)

Rousseau was born in Geneva in 1712, the son of a Calvinist watchmaker. It was his father who brought him up, his mother having died in childbirth. His father also gave Rousseau a great love of books, but otherwise he had little formal education. At the age of fifteen he ran away from home and began a life of solitary wandering. His was a difficult, hypersensitive personality, with a towering sense of his own genius. Although capable of intense friendship, his relationships never lasted.

After leaving Switzerland, Rousseau lived in Savoy and worked in Italy, before gravitating to Paris, at the time the leading intellectual centre in Europe. There he associated with the Enlightenment thinkers – the *philosophes* – and particularly Diderot. Rousseau contributed articles (mainly on musicology) to their great project, the *Encyclopedia*, but although he subscribed to some of their beliefs he was never a committed member of the group. He developed his own ideas that differed radically from their fashionable cult of reason and from establishment orthodoxy. Indeed, Rousseau's most striking characteristic is his originality. He changed the thinking of Europe, having an impact on political theory, education, literature, ethics, ideas about the self and its relationship to nature, and much else. These influences, together with his elevation of emotion and will above reason, make him the major precursor of the Romantic movement.

His early 'Discourses' offended the *philosophes*, while his two most famous works, *Emile* and *The Social Contract* (both 1762), outraged the authorities, particularly because of their religious content. They were burned by the public executioner in both Paris and Geneva, and Rousseau's arrest was ordered. He fled France and spent several years seeking refuge in various countries, but returned in 1767 under an assumed name. The authorities turned a blind eye so long as he did not publish. He spent his final years living in solitude on the estate of an admirer-patron near Paris. Here he studied botany and continued to write, mainly autobiographical works. The *Confessions* and *Reveries of a Solitary Walker* were both published after Rousseau's death in 1778.

In his first major published work, *A Discourse on the Arts and Sciences* (1750), Rousseau sketched a conception of history that would be central to all his later works, in which he endorsed neither traditional views nor the fashionable ideas of progress developed by Enlightenment thinkers. Instead he astounded everyone by claiming that what were thought to be advances in civilisation, far from representing the development of reason and human happiness, were in fact making human beings corrupt, dishonest and unhappy. Rousseau attacked and denigrated all that the *philosophes* held dear: reason, science, philosophy, progress and intellectual sophistication. He extolled the virtues of the common man, his loyalty and patriotism and sense of community, and admired dour, militaristic, anti-intellectual Sparta at the expense of intellectually glittering Athens. As against the orthodox doctrine of original sin, Rousseau insisted that human beings are essentially good, and that it is only society that corrupts them.

These themes were taken up again in his next significant work, *A Discourse on the Origin of Inequality* (1755). Here he makes use of a common device of Enlightenment thinkers, the state of nature, but portrays human beings not as essentially rational and social, but as free solitary individuals who engage with each other occasionally and who are capable of self-love and sympathy. Under pressure of population this idyllic natural freedom is destroyed, private property is introduced, and with it exploitation, inequality and all the ills of human society. Social inequality becomes the basic cause of injustice and moral corruption. The *Discourses* suggest that the prospects for humanity are unrelievedly bleak. Yet Rousseau nonetheless makes clear that he believes in the possibility of human perfectibility, of human improvement. This leaves him with the questions of whether, first of all, it is possible to live an individual human life that is not corrupted by society, and, second, whether it is possible to create a non-corrupt society.

Rousseau's answers to these questions constitute his mature social and political philosophy and are set out in the two books published in 1762. The first of these was *Emile*, in which Rousseau put forward his educational ideas and in so doing transformed the European understanding of childhood and how children should be treated and educated. It is a didactic novel, showing how an individual could be educated 'according to nature' away from the corrupting influences of society. However, there comes a point when Emile reaches manhood and his education is complete. It seems that then he will have to suppress his natural self in order to cope with corrupt society, leaving the reader wondering quite what the point of his elaborate education was.

The alternative possibility – of creating a society that is not corrupt – is explored in the second book of 1762, *The Social Contract*, which takes up more directly where *A Discourse on the Origin of Inequality* leaves off. Chapter 1 famously opens with the words 'Man is born free, and everywhere he is in chains.' This, of course, immediately follows from the picture of corruption, exploitation and domination coming with society and its inequalities, and imposed upon natural man. But behind the famous slogan there is also a deeper philosophical point that goes to the heart of Rousseau's understanding of human nature. He believed that what makes human beings genuinely human is not, as most previous philosophers had argued, our capacity for reason, but rather it is our capacity for moral choice. It follows from this that, unless human beings have the freedom to make such choices, they cannot live fully human lives; their humanity is being denied. In Rousseau's melodramatic phrase, they are slaves. This raises a dilemma. If human beings are by nature free, and are in fact free in the state of nature, then how can they be free in society, which involves unfreedom (whether as the domination and exploitation that tends to come with social life, or merely in the form of having to live according to laws imposed by others)? How is it possible for men to live in society, yet live full, free human lives? This is the problem that Rousseau sets out to solve in *The Social Contract*.

Rousseau is clear that it is not possible for men to return to the freedom of the state of nature, but it is possible, he insists, to exchange that freedom for the freedom of the citizen. This is done through an act of association that creates the social entity and in which all give up rights and become subjects while at the same time receiving rights as citizens and members of the sovereign. This is the 'social contract', although the manner in which the sovereign expresses itself through laws and government is left to a separate constitution-making process. So long as each person is both a subject and a participating citizen, there can be freedom.

Men can live in freedom if they live according to rules they have made themselves. This means that they must be citizens of a state where they make their own laws: a democracy. However, Rousseau interprets this very strictly indeed. It does not mean electing somebody to make laws on your behalf. In other words, representative democracy is not democracy at all. According to Rousseau, one person cannot represent the will of another. In a representative democracy, therefore, one would still be living according to someone else's laws and still be a slave. Rousseau's conception of democracy is that of direct democracy, where the whole citizen body gathers in the public place and makes the laws. His model here is the small city-states of Ancient Greece, where this was possible. How it could possibly apply to large modern states, like contemporary France, Rousseau does not make clear. All that is clear is the implication that large modern states cannot be legitimate.

However, direct democracy alone does not solve Rousseau's problem, since majority decisions would mean that minorities would not live according to their own laws. For this to be possible, all laws would have to be passed unanimously. From what we know of democratic politics of any kind, this would seem to be impossible. It is to solve this problem that Rousseau introduces his most famous doctrine, that of the General Will. The basic idea is that each one of us wills or desires a variety of things, but among the things that each of us desires is the good of the community in which we live. It is the aggregate of this desire for the communal good that Rousseau calls the General Will. It follows from this that if a law is passed that is in accord with the General Will, then in obeying this law we are in a sense obeying ourselves.

Conversely, since it is precisely by obeying the General Will that we obey ourselves and are therefore free, disobeying the General Will means that we deny our own freedom. This explains Rousseau's infamous and chilling remark about those who refuse to obey the law being 'forced to be free'. Rousseau is not using here the usual common-sense or 'negative' notion of freedom as simply doing what we want, but rather a 'positive' notion of freedom that insists that we are only truly free when we are obeying our 'higher selves' (in this case our desire for the common good) rather than our baser selfish instincts (when we are merely a 'slave to our passions').

There remains the problem of how to ensure that in the assembly the citizens will vote according to the General Will rather than according to their own selfish interests. Rousseau is initially quite realistic and admits that on any given occasion just one citizen in the assembly, or even none at all, are thinking of the general good, and therefore expressing the General Will rather than their own interests. He insists (Book II, Chapter 3) that the General Will is not the same as the will of all. Unfortunately, he gives us no means of telling who is thinking of the public good and who is not. This is something of a problem, but later in the book (Book IV, Chapter 2) he identifies the will of the majority with the General Will, which does not square at all with his initial account. If the will of all is not necessarily the General Will, then neither is the will of the majority.

Nevertheless, Rousseau believed that a unified collective view would emerge for two reasons. First of all he envisaged a relatively simple society of farmers and artisans with no rich or poor (though he railed against property, he never advocated its abolition), a situation that it is the duty of the sovereign to maintain. All are equal and consequently there would be few conflicts and what is good for society would be relatively simple, a situation in which it would be easy to inculcate love of the community. Second, Rousseau conceived of a political system in which there would be no political parties or pressure groups, where citizens would simply vote on laws spontaneously without debate.

This procedure may seem odd, but Rousseau did not conceive of democracy in terms of discussion or a mechanism for resolving disputes. The good society was not for him a collection of individuals pursuing their own lives and consequently having conflicting interests. He saw the state in Ancient Greek terms, as a moral community and as a corporate person with a single will. Parties and groups were divisive. Like **Plato**, whom he greatly admired, he aspired to unity. And like Ancient Sparta and the early Roman Republic, as he pictured them, he wanted a unified citizenship inspired by patriotism and civic virtue.

Rousseau's rather peculiar political system is designed to give optimum opportunity for the expression of the General Will. It is not expected that men, fresh from the state of nature, will set up such a state (women never have a political role for Rousseau, who thinks them only fit to be wives and mothers), will have the wisdom and understanding to hit upon this ideal constitution. Instead, Rousseau sees a lawgiver as providing a constitution. Critics have sometimes seen this figure as dictatorial, even totalitarian, embodying the General Will in his own person. But this was not Rousseau's intention. As so often, his model is the Ancient Greek city-states, where many were given their constitutions by lawgivers, such as Lycurgus at Sparta, who designed the constitution and then retired.

It is always the people who are sovereign (a notion introduced by Rousseau) and that authority cannot be usurped. However, the function of the sovereign is to pass laws, while the executive's function is to administer them. But this is not democratic; indeed Rousseau says (rather confusingly) that democracy is only possible for gods and not men. What he means here is that a democratic executive would be virtually impossible because, according to his idea of democracy, the whole citizen body would have to be equally involved. Besides, those making the law and those who administer it should not be the same. So long as government is strictly the agent of the sovereign people, laws express the General Will and rulers have the same sense of civic duty as in Ancient Rome, it does not really matter what form the executive takes. Even kingship is acceptable, although Rousseau's preference would seem to be for representative democracy – or 'elective aristocracy' as he calls it.

Rousseau was aware that there was no going back to the easy-going freedom of the state of nature. But he believed this could be exchanged for the higher freedom of citizenship in which the individual is merged into a unified moral community sustained by a strict civic virtue. That in turn must, Rousseau insists, be supported by a civic religion. With characteristic ambivalence, he says that while Christianity may be true, it cannot function as a civic religion because it cannot underpin civic virtue in the ways that the religions of Ancient Greece and Rome did. His Roman-like solution – outward conformity to the civic religion combined with tolerance for private belief, except for atheists – is hardly satisfactory.

Rousseau's views on many subjects caused storms of controversy at the time and intense debate ever since. Much criticism has been directed at his notion of the General Will. Even given that such a thing exists, we have seen that Rousseau gives us no sure way of determining what its dictates are. Yet identifying the General Will is vital to Rousseau's system, since he insists that only laws based on the General Will are authentic laws, which are the only ones that need to be obeyed. It would presumably be open to anyone accused of breaking the law to claim that the law did not express the General Will and was therefore not a proper law, with no sure means of proving them wrong. Yet it is only by obeying such laws that freedom, which is the whole point of the exercise, is guaranteed.

Even without these problems, the concept of the General Will is open to question. There is no guarantee that what people will agree upon is what is best for the community, even when they are all genuinely thinking about what is best for the community. Rousseau believes that if citizens vote spontaneously and without debate for the common good, thereby expressing the General Will, then all will vote for the same policy; this policy *ipso facto* will be in the community's best interests, since Rousseau insists that the General Will is always right. But this plainly does not follow. What is good for the community is not something absolute and unambiguous that can be determined if the correct procedures are followed. There can be legitimate disagreement on what is for the best, a possibility Rousseau does not allow.

Apart from these logical problems, there are severe practical ones in relation to what the implications of Rousseau's ideas might be for modern politics. How could his ideas apply to the modern states of his own day, such as France? He simply does not tell us. Indeed, since only direct democracy is legitimate, then legitimate government is impossible in the modern world.

This is closely connected with another major criticism concerning totalitarianism. In *The Origins of Totalitarian Democracy* (1952), J.L. Talmon argued that Rousseau, despite his reputation as the first modern democratic thinker, was in fact the father of modern totalitarianism. This is because the opportunity is always there for an individual or party to claim that they alone embody the General Will to which all must conform, thereby obeying their higher selves. Certainly the French Revolutionaries, who were all steeped in Rousseau (though he never advocated revolution), made such claims. Robespierre claimed to embody the will of France and declared those in conflict with that will to be 'enemies of the people' who must be eliminated. Rousseau clearly did not envisage modern totalitarianism.

Nevertheless, whatever the ambiguities of his legacy in respect of totalitarianism, there is no doubt that Rousseau is the key figure in the development of democratic thought. All previous significant thinkers, from Plato onwards, had regarded democracy with suspicion: it was usually equated with the rule of the mob, and at best could only be an element in a wider system that thereby allowed a degree of participation for the better off. It was Rousseau who developed the concept of the sovereignty of the people, and he was the first to insist upon the fitness and right of ordinary people to participate in the political system as full citizens. These were sensational claims in his day, but would eventually permeate modern political thought and practice. More generally, Rousseau profoundly changed the way we think of ourselves as human beings, considering us creatures of feeling and not just of reason. His thought is complex, subtle and original, and he is among the most influential thinkers of modern times.

Further reading

Primary sources

The Discourses and Other Early Political Writings, ed. V. Gourevitch (Cambridge: Cambridge University Press, 1997).

The Social Contract and Other Later Political Writings, ed. V. Gourevitch (Cambridge: Cambridge University Press, 1997).

Secondary sources

Cooper, L.D.: *Rousseau, Nature, and the Problem of the Good Life* (University Park, PA: Pennsylvania State University Press, 1999).

Hall, J.C.: *Rousseau: An Introduction to his Political Philosophy* (Basingstoke: Macmillan, 1972).

Hendel, W.: *Jean-Jacques Rousseau: Moralist* (New York: Library of the Liberal Arts, 1962).
Talmon, J.L.: *The Origins of Totalitarian Democracy* (London: Sphere Books, 1970).
Wokler, R.: *Rousseau* (Oxford: Oxford University Press, 2001).

IMMANUEL KANT (1724–1804)

Kant had a famously uneventful life, entirely confined to the provincial town of Königsberg in the remotest province of the Kingdom of Prussia (now Kaliningrad in Russia), where he was born in 1724 and died in 1804. Although of humble origins Kant obtained a place at the town's university, where he went on to be a lecturer and its most distinguished professor. He never married and was well known in the town for the regularity of his daily routine. Despite his isolation, Kant kept abreast of developments across Europe. He has come to be recognised as one of the greatest philosophers of modern times.

In his *Critique of Pure Reason* (1781), *Groundwork of the Metaphysics of Morals* (1785), *Critique of Practical Reason* (1788), *Critique of Judgement* (1790) and other major works, Kant made the great contributions to metaphysics, epistemology and ethics for which he is best known. He also made important contributions to other areas, including politics, but he wrote no major political treatise. His political ideas are found in various works and in various essays on related topics. Essentially they develop the social implications of his ethics and metaphysics.

As a young lecturer Kant was a great admirer of Newtonian science, and was greatly shocked at reading the sceptical philosophy of David Hume, which seemed to undermine the very foundations of science and question its claim to certainty. Hume argued that, strictly speaking, the process of cause and effect cannot be observed and that in consequence all the causal laws of science have no solid empirical foundation. In order to defend the scientific view of the world, Kant developed a revolutionary account of reality, which argued that the world is the way it is because our minds shape it that way. The world we experience is characterised by cause and effect, time and space, and so forth, because these are built into our minds to generate a view of the world that we can comprehend. What the world is really like, independent of human experience of it – what he calls 'the thing in itself' – we cannot possibly know. Kant does, however, identify this unknowable world with the world of 'noumena', which is the world of spirituality and freedom beyond the senses.

The everyday world of the senses, the world of 'phenomena', is entirely governed by causal laws and this includes the behaviour of animals and human beings. When we pursue our self-interest, Kant thinks, the relationships between our desires and what we do to satisfy them are causal ones. The fact that we use reason in this process does not crucially distinguish us from other animals. It just gives us an extra instrument that animals lack. However, human beings *are* different and special in so far as they alone can step outside of the phenomenal world of cause and effect in which they are normally bound.

Human beings can escape the world of phenomena, and partake of the world of noumena, by acting morally. That is, by acting according to one's moral duty *against* one's self-interest. It is in this way that the human being can be fully free and fully human. This is a variation on **Rousseau**'s view, which greatly influenced Kant, that what makes human beings distinctively human is their capacity for moral choice. Again like Rousseau, Kant took this capacity for moral choice as a justification for political freedom, although his conception of such freedom was very different and politically much more conventional than Rousseau's.

However, when it comes to the question of what moral choices individuals should make, Kant is firmly individualist. In his *Foundations of the Metaphysics of Morals* he argues that it is up to each individual to decide his or her own moral rules by means of what he calls the 'categorical imperative'. This is an abstract principle, which requires that we act in ways that we would want others to act in the same circumstances. The moral imperative to do what is right is, for Kant, categorical or absolute, whatever the circumstances. How we ought to act to achieve some end, however desirable, is only a 'hypothetical imperative', which for Kant is not moral at all. In practice the categorical imperative means that we should treat people as we would have them treat us. Kant believes that it means the same as always treating people as ends and never as means. He also believes that because human beings are capable of giving themselves their own moral rules, then every human being is of infinite moral worth, and as such every human being has a right to freedom and autonomy.

The political question is: what kind of government is appropriate to a society of such human beings? Kant's answer is that it must be a 'republican' government (first outlined briefly in *Critique of Pure Reason*, p.312, and developed in other essays). By 'republican' Kant means, first of all, a constitutional government, but one based upon the principle that all are entitled to maximum freedom that is compatible with the freedom of others. Kant thought such a government was necessary for all rational beings and that we have a moral duty to strive for a government of this kind.

Kant's notion of good government is in line with moderate liberal thinking in his day (although, as he was living in an authoritarian, absolutist state, his ideas are highly radical in relation to his situation). This included a range of civil liberties, a constitutional monarchy and a legislative assembly elected on a wide but not universal franchise (exclusions include women, tradesmen and servants, since they were dependent upon others for their livelihood and could not be expected to vote independently). Kant has a remarkable faith in the efficacy of this kind of government. He believes it will drastically reduce wars, crime and other horrors of the human condition. This is because he believes that unless people are free they cannot achieve their full moral stature: even the most benign paternalism stops people from morally growing up and this explains much of the evil in the world. Whenever republican government is introduced, people must become ever more mature, responsible and rational.

Kant believed that the spread of republican government would eliminate war, which he considered to be the enemy of all things good. He did not, however, believe that a republican world government was feasible. What would eventually ensure perpetual peace was a league of republican governments, by means of which all international disputes could be settled. This Kant took to be the highest political goal. It would take time, but he was in no doubt that this was humanity's ultimate destiny.

Kant's confidence that humanity was moving towards an ideal future was based on more than a general Enlightenment belief in the gradual spread of rationality and education. He also believed that human progress was guaranteed by nature. In his *Idea for a Universal History with a Cosmopolitan Purpose* (1784), Kant wrote that there was a 'hidden plan' of nature to lead man towards the perfect constitution both within states and between them, so that all the natural capacities of humanity can be developed completely. The 'plan' will be fulfilled because nature has implanted within humanity what Kant calls its 'unsocial sociability'. Human beings are naturally social beings, while at the same time their behaviour displays a strong bias towards the anti-social: they are ambitious, egocentric and aggressive. But while these lead to conflict, crime, tyranny and war, they also ultimately lead to their opposites, since the horrors of crime and civil strife force people to create orderly societies with laws and institutions, and eventually to recognise the need to live within a rational legal order based on the principles of freedom. In time, Kant believed, the horrors of war would teach humanity the same lesson, and permanent peace would be the eventual outcome.

Kant's political writings are redolent with Enlightenment optimism, yet there is a certain ambiguity in his work concerning the extent to which progress will eliminate the human capacity for evil. Perhaps today we find the pessimistic view the more convincing. More basic are questions surrounding the Kantian approach to moral philosophy, which has been greatly admired and followed down to the present day. Its critics question whether the different versions of the categorical imperative amount to the same thing, as Kant suggests. It is also highly questionable whether, if everyone were fully rational, they would all come to the same moral conclusions, as Kant seems to think. However, the most telling criticism is, as **Hegel** emphasised, that all Kant gives us is a formula with no content. Some argue that it is a formula that, with sufficient ingenuity, can be made to justify almost anything. Despite these criticisms, Kant's political ideas remain one of the most intellectually powerful, compelling and influential defences of liberal values.

Further reading

Primary sources

Critique of Pure Reason, ed. N. Kemp Smith (Basingstoke: Macmillan, 1933).
Foundations of the Metaphysics of Morals and What is Enlightenment?, ed. L.W. Beck (Indianapolis, IN: Bobbs Merrill, 1959).
Kant's Political Writings, ed. H. Reiss (Cambridge: Cambridge University Press, 1971).

Secondary sources

Caygill, H.: *A Kant Dictionary* (Oxford: Blackwell, 1995).
Gayer, P.: *The Cambridge Companion to Kant* (Cambridge: Cambridge University Press, 1992).
Saner, H.: *Kant's Political Thought* (Chicago, IL: Chicago University Press, 1973).
Williams, H.: *Kant's Political Philosophy* (Oxford: Blackwell, 1983).

EDMUND BURKE (1729–97)

Edmund Burke was born in 1729 in Dublin, Ireland, and studied at Trinity College from 1743 to 1748. He went to London to read for the bar, but, like his older contemporary **Hume**, abandoned law for a literary career. He made a point of attaching himself to the literary lions of the age; he is frequently mentioned in Boswell's *Life of Johnson*. In 1756 he published a satire called *A Vindication of Natural Society*. This was followed in 1757 by a treatise of aesthetics, called *A Philosophical Enquiry into the Origin of our Ideas of the Sublime and Beautiful*, that was admired in its day. In 1765 his literary career gave place to a political one. He was elected to the House of Commons and became Lord Rockingham's private secretary. With one short break, he remained a Member of Parliament until his death. As one of the 'Rockingham Whigs', he criticised George III's conception of monarchy in a pamphlet called *Thoughts on the Causes of the Present Discontents* (1770). From 1770 until the American Revolution, he was the London agent of the State of New York, and in two celebrated speeches ('On American Taxation', 1774, and 'On Moving his Resolutions for Conciliation with the Colonies', 1777) attributed unrest in the American colonies to British misgovernment. The same concern with colonial misgovernment led him to campaign against the activities of the East India Company, and he was largely responsible for the impeachment of Warren Hastings in 1788. His best-known political work, *Reflections on the Revolution in France*, was published in 1790. It made a considerable stir among fellow Whigs, who believed him to be betraying the principles for which he had hitherto stood, and he defended and developed his views in several subsequent publications: *An Appeal from the New to the Old Whigs* (1791), *Thoughts on French Affairs* (1791) and *Letters on a Regicide Peace* (1796–7).

It is customary to describe Burke as the founder of modern conservatism. The keynote of his thought is a mistrust of what Michael **Oakeshott** was to call 'rationalism' in politics: the belief that politics can be conducted according to *a priori* principles not rooted in previous experience and practice. It was for this belief that he chiefly criticised the French Revolutionaries. The arrangements by which human beings live are, he argues, those that long trial and experience have shown to work. They have emerged during the slow processes by which men have accommodated themselves to changing circumstances. This is true especially of the British constitution, thanks to the importance of precedent in establishing the English common law; but it is true also as a generalisation. The very existence of any long-established order tends to validate that order. The complex and organic nature of society is all we know about it, and all we need to know. There is no point in looking for the origins of society in a social contract. Society is not a contractual or voluntary association that any one generation has created. It is a vast and seamless historical partnership between those who are living, those who are dead, and those who are yet to be born. So complex an organism cannot be understood by any one individual or group, or during any single generation. To try to destroy it and build another from scratch, which is what Burke takes the French Revolutionaries to have done, is therefore presumptuous folly. Nor can the values that should govern human association be reduced to dogmatic abstractions such as the 'rights of man'. Human beings are not atoms or isolated essences. We are the products of a long and intricate history. We are created by the culture of which we are a part. It makes no sense to consider us except in relation to that culture, or to attribute to us theoretical rights that we have independently of it or in spite of it. Our manners, customs and laws – the general way of doing things that Burke calls 'prejudice' – are parts of that culture. To sweep them away in the name of speculative and untried political doctrines is to conceive human association without any of the things that make human association real.

It follows, therefore, that revolutionary change is a destructive affront to nature: a leap away from the known into the perilous unknown. If reform is to be undertaken at all, it should be brought about in a gradual and *ad hoc* fashion. It should happen in response not to the stipulations of an abstract doctrine, but to changing needs and conditions as they arise. It should be directed towards a specific problem. It should have no purpose more general than the solution of that problem. It should preserve the existing harmonies: there should always be a presumption in favour of leaving things alone. Burke, therefore, though in favour of religious toleration, is also in favour of an established Church. Again, though not a member of it himself, he is convinced that a landed aristocracy – an aristocracy of wealth, leisure and sensibility – is essential to the preservation of the complex fabric of society as he understands it. The House of Commons, too, should dissociate itself from interest and faction and the changing winds of popular opinion. Members of Parliament, he explained in his 'Address to the Electors of Bristol', are not delegates whose job it is to lobby for the interests of their constituencies. They are representatives, sent into parliament to secure the general and long-term good of the community. He advocates political parties, but only in so far as they are mechanisms for concerting and enacting the opinions of the right-minded.

Burke does not, as so many conservatives do, seek to ground his political prescriptions on a mythical ideal constitution or a Golden Age that it should be the purpose of politics to commemorate or restore. He understands that the historical origins of things are unrecoverable. His conservatism consists, in essence, of a few simple generalisations: that the present state of things is the sum total of all past developments; that it is too complex to understand; that meddling with it is therefore dangerous; and that arrangements that work well enough are best left alone. It may seem odd that Burke applauded the Glorious Revolution of 1688 and supported the American colonists' grievances against George III, yet was in 1790 so eloquent in condemning the French Revolutionaries; this apparent inconsistency illustrates the nature of his conservatism. The Glorious Revolution, even while getting rid of a king, had left the traditional institutions of government untouched. The Americans were defending the traditional right of Englishmen not to be taxed without representation. The French, by contrast, were sweeping away an immemorial order in favour of the unhistorical and contextless dogma of the 'rights of man'.

Burke is to a great degree sentimental. When he is at his most sentimental, he is at his most reactionary. He is so upset by the destruction wrought by the French Revolution that he cannot understand the injustices against which the French Revolutionaries believed themselves to be acting. Tom **Paine** wrote of him in *The Rights of Man*:

> He is not affected by the reality of distress touching his heart, but by the showy resemblance of it striking his imagination. He pities the plumage, but sees not the dying bird.

Some of his contemporaries thought him inconsistent and dishonest. He does not, after all, advocate non-parliamentary, inefficient, absolutist government in Britain, yet he rends his garments over the destruction of precisely such government in France. Mary **Wollstonecraft** was convinced that, had he been a Frenchman, Burke would have been a Revolutionary himself. Nonetheless, his 'common-sense' preference for established practices against untried theory, his defence of local and national traditions, and his advocacy of cautious and moderate reform, have remained important components of conservative sensibility more than two centuries after his death. Such luminaries of twentieth-century political thought as Karl **Popper**, Michael Oakeshott and F.A. von **Hayek** are all to some extent under his influence.

Further reading

Primary sources

Reflections on the Revolution in France, ed. C.C. O'Brien (Harmondsworth: Penguin, 1968).

Edmund Burke on Government, Politics and Society, ed. B.W. Hill (London: Fontana, 1975).

The Political Philosophy of Edmund Burke, ed. I. Hampsher-Monk (London: Longman, 1987).

Secondary sources

Dreyer, F.A.: *Burke's Politics: A Study in Whig Orthodoxy* (Waterloo, Ont.: Laurier University Press, 1982).

Freeman, M.: *Burke and the Critique of Political Radicalism* (Oxford: Blackwell, 1980).

Macpherson, C.B.: *Burke* (Oxford: Oxford University Press, 1982).

O'Gorman, F.: *Edmund Burke: His Political Philosophy* (London: Allen & Unwin, 1983).

TOM PAINE (1737–1809)

Thomas Paine, usually called Tom, was born in 1737, into a modest Quaker family in Thetford, Norfolk. He was educated at the local grammar school. His father was a corset-maker, and Tom himself was for a while apprenticed to this trade (this is the point of the famous Gillray cartoon showing Tom Paine trying to lace a reproachful Britannia into a French corset). He then tried his hand as a schoolteacher, before becoming an excise officer – first in Lincolnshire, then in Sussex. While serving as an excise officer at Lewes, he became involved in local politics and established a debating club in a local inn. Campaigning for better pay and conditions (his first publication was a pamphlet called *The Case of the Officers of Excise*) cost him his position. Encouraged by Benjamin Franklin, whom he met in London, he emigrated to America. He arrived in Philadelphia just as the colonies' dispute with Britain was reaching crisis-point, and took up radical journalism. He contributed several articles to the *Pennsylvania Magazine*, including one calling for the abolition of slavery. Paine's first important work, the anti-monarchical pamphlet *Common Sense* (1776), vigorously advocated independence. It was immensely popular – it is said to have sold 150,000 copies in 1776 – and undoubtedly helped create the climate of opinion that led to the Declaration of Independence later in the same year.

After Independence, Paine returned to Britain and in 1791 published his most famous work, *The Rights of Man*. His immediate purpose was to defend the French Revolutionaries against the strictures of Edmund **Burke** in *Reflections on the Revolution in France*;

but he also attacked hereditary government and argued for equal political rights. The book was banned and Paine indicted for seditious libel. He fled to France, where he was given a hero's welcome. He was elected as a deputy in the National Assembly and sat with the Girondin faction. Despite being a passionate opponent of hereditary monarchy, Paine voted against the execution of the king: an act that almost cost him his own life. He was imprisoned by the Jacobins and, while in prison, wrote the first part of *The Age of Reason*, an attack on organised religion. After the fall of Robespierre, Paine was reinstated as a deputy, but in 1803 returned to America. *The Age of Reason*, because of its disparagement of Christianity, had cost him much of the popularity he had enjoyed before the Revolution, but he was able to settle on a farm granted to him by the State of New York, where he spent the remaining six years of his life.

Paine's political thought may fairly be described as a straightforward radical-liberal ideology, informed throughout by European Enlightenment ideas. The past, he thinks, is the story of tyranny and ignorance. The history of humanity is characterised by superstition and uncritical acceptance of the existing order. He is particularly severe on kingship. Hereditary monarchy, he insists, is unnatural and irrational. It creates a distinction between kings and subjects that has no basis beyond the willingness of the credulous to accept it. It places men in positions of power regardless of ability and moral character. It produces and sustains conditions of inequality and injustice. Kings and their hangers-on are parasites merely. They are supported in luxury out of public taxes while thousands of their subjects live in misery. They wage wars for their own glory, which their subjects have to fight in and pay for. The revival of reason in the present age equips us to sweep the mistakes of the past away and begin afresh (this, of course, is exactly the attitude that so frightens Burke). What is needed is a rational reconstruction of society and the installation of the correct form of government to administer it.

Government is a necessary evil. We cannot do without it, but, inevitably, it infringes the right of the individual to do as he likes. The less government there is, therefore, the better. Government should confine itself to the protection of the rights of man and should not take on any more extensive functions than this. It must moreover be responsible to, and removable by, those whose government it is. There is a natural sympathy and harmony of interests among people, and the amount of government needed to regulate their relations is therefore not large. Society, says Paine, in a more radical version of **Locke**'s doctrine of popular sovereignty, is created by a social contract, and the people then have the absolute right to make and unmake governments as and when they see fit.

Predictably enough, Paine is a democrat. Because government exists to manage the affairs of the whole nation, it cannot be the property of any individual or family or faction. All men are equal. Representative democracy, based on full male suffrage, is the only rational, and therefore the only legitimate, form of government. Under such government, the people would live in peace and prosperity. It would be able to levy only such taxes as the populace thought reasonable, and the populace would not, Paine assumed, wish to finance wars. But the present political organisation of England simply entrenches privilege and inequality. The County of Yorkshire, which contains nearly two million souls, returns two county members to Parliament; so does Rutland, with a population of less than 20,000. Manchester, a town with a population of 60,000, is not allowed any parliamentary representation at all. Old Sarum, where almost no one now lives, returns two members. If democracy is really to represent the interests of citizens, it needs to be organised into sensible constituencies.

Paine is an early and eloquent exponent of public welfare measures. In *The Rights of Man* he suggests state education for the poor, old-age pensions and state employment. In his *Agrarian Justice* (1796) he advocates redistributive taxation to create a more equal society, and a complex welfare-state system. In some ways his ideas point towards a later socialism, although his firm belief in the rights of property and the benefits of commerce keep him in the broadly liberal camp. He does not appear to be aware of the difficulties involved in recommending extensive welfare provision while at the same time insisting on minimal government and taxation.

Paine was, clearly, a man of great personal integrity. While living in straitened circumstances in France, he let it be known that he did not wish to make a profit from *The Rights of Man* and that anyone who wished to reprint it could do so. As a result, some 200,000 copies of the book were sold in cheap editions between 1791 and 1793. Paine was an exceptionally able pamphleteer, able to reduce complex issues to eloquent simplicity. His importance lies less in the originality or subtlety of his thought than in the clarity with which he was able to communicate political ideas to ordinary people in an age when ordinary people were increasingly entering into politics.

Further reading

Primary source

Paine: Political Writings, ed. B. Kuklick (Cambridge: Cambridge University Press, 2000).

Secondary sources

Claeys, G.: *Thomas Paine: Social and Political Thought* (Boston, MA: Unwin Hyman, 1989).
Keane, J.: *Tom Paine: A Political Life* (Boston, MA: Little, Brown, 1995).
Philp, M.: *Paine* (Oxford: Oxford University Press, 1989).
Williamson, A.: *Thomas Paine: His Life, Work and Times* (London: Allen & Unwin, 1973).

JOHANN GOTTFRIED HERDER (1744–1803)

Herder was born in 1744 in a remote part of East Prussia where his father was a village schoolmaster. His ambition was to be a Lutheran pastor. Herder went to the University of Königsberg, where he had the good fortune to be taught by Immanuel **Kant**, who introduced him to a wide range of European thought. After several years as a pastor and schoolmaster, Herder travelled extensively in France, Holland and Germany. In Strasbourg in 1773 he met the young Goethe, with whom he collaborated on a book about German character and art. Their friendship subsequently led to Herder's appointment as Court preacher at Weimar, where he remained until his death in 1803.

Herder was one of the seminal minds of his age, contributing to a range of subjects, including philosophy, history, theology and linguistics. His early inspiration was the Enlightenment, but, while he retained some of its ideas throughout his life, he was arguably the most significant single figure in the development of the Romantic 'counter-Enlightenment' that revolutionised European thought.

Herder's most important works include *Treatise on the Origin of Language* (1772) and the monumental *Ideas for the Philosophy of the History of Mankind* (1784–91). Despite a voluminous output upon a great range of subjects, Herder did not write a major work on political theory, but his ideas are diffused among other works. Furthermore, the nature of German public life and his own position at Court made it difficult to be politically candid, so that some of Herder's more radical views are only fully expressed in his letters. Nevertheless, his political ideas were important and influential. They need to be understood against the background of his general philosophy.

As a philosopher Herder challenged Enlightenment epistemology, especially in respect of human understanding. He rejected the concentration on causal laws, universal timeless truth and universal standards in behaviour and the arts. He insisted that human affairs could not be understood by the same methods as natural sciences, but only through understanding the point of view of those participating, and in terms of the traditional practices and purposes of forms of behaviour of which their actions form a part. In other words, understanding from the 'inside' and not from the external application of causal relationships. Understanding human thought and action involved the study not of science, but of history, literature, the arts and especially language; that is, the whole historical and cultural context. All this meant understanding historical events, individuals, communities and cultures as being particular and unique.

Language was central to this understanding. A language embodies the uniqueness of a culture, expressing a whole way of life, the collective experience of a nation. Language and literature forms nations and individuals. Herder has a very modern sense of thought *consisting* of language rather than merely being expressed through language. All human actions are an expression of the self but also of the particular culture as an evolving totality that embodies a total vision of life.

Herder's political thought revolves around the assertion that the cultural nation is the true basis of the political community and of political identity. This contrasts with the Enlightenment view of the political community as a construct made up of all those who are subject to a sovereign power arising from a social contract. The state was central in Enlightenment thought and remained so in the French development of nationalist ideas after the Revolution. This was not, however, Herder's conception. He loathed the centralised state, which he saw as imposing uniformity and destroying local difference. He anticipated twentieth-century concerns about the dangers of bureaucracy and of people becoming mere cogs in the vast state machine.

He thought his conception of the cultural nation would replace Enlightenment notions of contract and sovereignty. The state was an artificial construct, whereas the nation was a product of natural growth. This was a vision of society as an organic unity. But Herder was aware that the organic metaphor was indeed a metaphor and did not in any sense infer the subordination of the part to the whole or the individual as inferior to the community.

Herder's vision of an ideal society was one without central government. He believed it possible for a political community to function effectively in a non-hierarchical, non-coercive situation where social power was diffused through different but mutually interdependent communities and sectional interests within the wider nation. This could be established after a period of transition in which the people would be educated to cope with the system. Herder was a strong advocate of freedom of expression, and thought it essential to this educative process. He believed in a more egalitarian society but not in absolute equality for all. He considered hereditary monarchy and aristocratic social leadership to be thoroughly irrational. Everyone could and should participate in the affairs of the nation. In this pluralist-anarchist society violence and coercion would no longer have a place and government would be by a form of continuously negotiated consensus.

While Herder put considerable emphasis on the centrality of tradition, he did not see a contradiction between tradition and progress, as traditionalists usually do. He thought Enlightenment ideas of progress were shallow and simplistic, but not the concept of progress as such. Human society evolved and developed as traditional practices and ways of life pursued their own internal purposes and individuals creatively applied the principles and methods they inherited. There is no overall, uniform, universal plan for humanity as a whole beyond the perpetual unfolding of human potential in a multitude of ways. This involves a new way of looking at history that is evolutionary, like the growth of an organism, where there is no question of recreating a past state of affairs. Both within national cultures and between national cultures such unfolding proceeds at different speeds and in different directions. There is no natural harmony of purposes or values. Within each national community an endless accommodation and adjustment is necessary to ensure an organic unity is maintained, and can be negotiated or imposed.

The basic units of history and the basic divisions of humanity Herder saw as national cultures, every one of which had the right to develop in its own way. He was deeply hostile to any form of imperialism or racism and was thus as much opposed to European domination of non-white races as he was to the multinational empires of Central and Eastern Europe. God favoured no race and no nation.

Herder was the most important intellectual founder of nationalism in general, but his nationalism is very different from that of revolutionary France or that which subsequently developed in Germany. In French revolutionary nationalism what constitutes the nation was rather taken for granted. All the theoretical emphasis was upon the state, as an expression of the single will of a united sovereign people. The tradition of German nationalism as it developed after

Herder combined his cultural nationalism with a glorification of the state amounting in some cases to state worship; this could hardly be further from Herder's intention.

Hegel, whom Herder influenced enormously, certainly glorified the state as morally superior to the individual and saw the Prussian state of his day as the final pinnacle of the state's development. German nationalists of the late nineteenth century took xenophobic German nationalism to extremes, insisting upon the superiority of German culture. They would gladly sacrifice the individual for the state, as well as being highly chauvinist and racist. However, Herder's most direct influence was upon a group of thinkers known as the German Romantics. The German Romantics, such as Friedrich Schlegel, Novalis and Adam Müller (with whom Herder is often linked), followed Herder's emphasis on culture and history, and the political necessity of forming a unique harmony of disparate elements. However, in sharp contrast to Herder, theirs was a backward-looking vision that idealised medieval feudalism and looked for social leadership to a traditional aristocracy, albeit one advised by scholars like themselves.

As a political thinker Herder does have limitations. He can be vague and inconclusive and his anarchist pluralism is not very convincing (although no less so than other versions of anarchism). Nevertheless, he was one of the most creative and influential minds of the age. He changed the way we understand our history and ourselves, profoundly influencing major intellectual movements, such as Romanticism, German idealism and nationalism, that have shaped the modern consciousness. His central idea of cultural nationalism, when combined with French nationalist ideas of the sovereignty of the people expressed through the national state, created the form of nationalism that has shaped much of world politics over the last two centuries.

Further reading

Primary sources

Reflections on the Philosophy of the History of Mankind (Chicago, IL: University of Chicago Press, 1968).

Herder on Social and Political Culture, ed. F.M. Barnard (Cambridge: Cambridge University Press, 1969).

Secondary sources

Barnard, F.M.: *Herder's Social and Political Thought: From Enlightenment to Nationalism* (Oxford: Oxford University Press, 1965).

Berlin, I.: *Vico and Herder* (London: Hogarth Press, 1976).
Norton, R.E.: *Herder's Aesthetics and the European Enlightenment* (Ithaca, NY: Cornell University Press, 1991).

MARY WOLLSTONECRAFT (1759–97)

Mary Wollstonecraft was born in Spitalfields, London. Her father, John Edward, was a weaver who made several unsuccessful attempts to set himself up as a farmer in various parts of the country. Mary's childhood and early adulthood were disrupted by her family's frequent migrations. In 1775, she met a young woman called Frances Blood. The two became devotedly attached, and in 1784 opened a school in Islington, at which Mary's sisters Eliza and Everina also taught. At this time, Mary began to come under the influence of the rational dissenters Richard Price and Joseph Priestley, thus entering the circle of radical nonconformists to which her future husband, William **Godwin**, also belonged. (She and William Godwin first met in 1791, though at first neither much liked the other.) In February 1785 Frances Blood married. In November of the same year she died in Mary's arms while giving birth to a child, who also died. Overcome with grief, Mary closed the school and began to throw herself into a literary career. Her first work, a pamphlet called *Thoughts on the Education of Daughters*, appeared in 1786. During 1787 and 1789 she devoted herself to translation, journalism, a novel called *Mary: a Fiction*, and a book called *The Female Reader* (which has not survived). In 1790 she produced *A Vindication of the Rights of Man*, intended to be simultaneously an answer to **Burke**'s *Reflections on the Revolution in France* and a defence of her friend Richard Price. Her most famous work, *A Vindication of the Rights of Woman*, was published in 1792. She had several unsatisfactory relationships with men, including one between 1793 and 1795 with an American businessman, Gilbert Imlay, by whom she had a daughter (named Frances, in memory of Frances Blood). Imlay's treatment of her was such that she tried on two occasions to take her own life, the second time by jumping off Putney Bridge. In March 1797 she married William Godwin, and died shortly after giving birth to their daughter, the future Mary Shelley. In 1798 Godwin published an affectionate biography of his wife – *Memoirs of the Author of a Vindication of the Rights of Woman* – the frankness of which caused much scandal.

It is upon *A Vindication of the Rights of Woman* that Mary Wollstonecraft's enduring reputation depends. In it, she applies standard liberal values and arguments to the specific case of women. She rejects the assumption that the subordinate position of women is an immutable feature of the natural order. Human beings are rational creatures. It is upon their rationality that their claim to rights of liberty and self-determination depends. But women are human beings. As human beings, they are rational creatures and, as rational creatures, they must be entitled to the same rights of liberty and self-determination as male rational creatures claim for themselves. Femaleness is not a morally relevant criterion of discrimination. Women do indeed often seem ill-fitted for roles in the world outside the family. This, however, is because they are not given the opportunity to develop their talents or character through education. They are educated, but they are educated to be adjuncts to men in a world largely conditioned by male values. They are submissive, light-minded, emotional, susceptible to flattery and so on, because they are taught to be. In modern terms, their femininity is socially conditioned. If women could be properly educated, if they could enjoy full civil rights, and if they could be legally independent of their husbands and free to exercise their talents in any capacity they chose, they would be equipped to be full members of society and fit companions for men. As things stand, however, marriage is 'legal prostitution'. Women, she adds, 'may be convenient slaves, but slavery will have its constant effect, degrading the master and the abject dependent'. The values that underwrite such slavery are institutionalised in the monarchy, the Church and the military establishment. Social justice will never be achieved, Wollstonecraft maintains, while these mechanisms of inequality remain.

Despite such flashes, *A Vindication of the Rights of Woman* nowadays looks rather tame. Mary Wollstonecraft is not a 'jobs and careers' liberal feminist of the twentieth-century type, nor does she challenge the institution of the family or women's traditional responsibilities within it. More than anything, her argument is about the enhancement of women's dignity and sense of self-worth, regardless of job or occupation. She has little doubt that only a minority of exceptional women would be able, or would want, to pursue independent careers. She believes also that the majority will find fulfilment in the roles of wife and mother. Nonetheless, a proper education, the end of legal dependence on husbands and the opportunity, even if not taken up, for non-menial occupation outside the family would give women the personal resources necessary to enable them to be effective wives and mothers, and through the exercise of reason and virtue in that role to realise their nature as human beings. These doctrines were, of course, much more radical at the time than they seem now.

It is impossible not to admire Mary Wollstonecraft's drivenness and moral courage. Inevitably, she incurred the displeasure of the contemporary male establishment. Also, she suffered the same kind of attack at conservative hands as other English radicals did in the literary panic created by the French Revolution (Burke called her 'a hyaena in petticoats'). Feminists in the early nineteenth century were reluctant to associate themselves with a woman whose life had included several love affairs, an illegitimate child and two suicide attempts. By the end of the nineteenth century, however, *A Vindication of the Rights of Woman* had achieved recognition as one of the foundation documents of feminism. When American feminists Susan B. Anthony, Elizabeth Cady Stanton and Matilda Joslyn Gage published the first volume of their landmark *History of Woman Suffrage* in 1881, they put Mary Wollstonecraft first in the list of names that appears on the dedication page.

Further reading

Primary sources

A Vindication of the Rights of Woman, ed. I. Kramnick (Harmondsworth: Penguin, 1982).

A Short Residence in Sweden (Harmondsworth: Penguin, 1987). This edition also contains William Godwin's *Memoirs of the Author of a vindication the Rights of Woman*.

Secondary sources

Kelly, G.: *Revolutionary Feminism: The Mind and Career of Mary Wollstonecraft* (Basingstoke: Macmillan, 1992).

Taylor, B.: *Eve and the New Jerusalem: Socialism and Feminism in the Nineteenth Century* (London: Virago, 1983).

Todd, J.: *Mary Wollstonecraft: A Revolutionary Life* (London: Weidenfeld & Nicolson, 2000).

Wardle, R.: *Mary Wollstonecraft: A Critical Biography* (Lincoln, KS: University of Kansas Press, 1966).

WILLIAM GODWIN (1756–1836)

William Godwin was born at Wisbech in Cambridgeshire, England. The son of a Presbyterian minister, he was himself educated for the ministry at Hoxton Presbyterian College and spent some five years as a minister in Beaconsfield, where he met the radical clergymen Richard

Price and Joseph Priestley. Between 1778 and 1783 he suffered not so much a crisis as an evaporation of faith. At the same time, his early Tory sentiments gave place to increasingly radical ones. After gravitating to London, he scraped a living with various kinds of literary work before persuading a publisher to finance him while he produced a summary of recent political philosophy. The result was the work that made his reputation: *An Enquiry Concerning Political Justice*, which came out in 1792. It was published in revised editions in 1795 and 1797. In 1794 Godwin published his most successful novel, *Caleb Williams*. In 1797 he married Mary **Wollstonecraft**, who died shortly after the birth of their daughter, also called Mary (Mary Godwin would later marry the poet Shelley and write the novel *Frankenstein*). His wife's death was a loss from which he never recovered. In a more censorious age, the fact that Mary Godwin was born only five months after her parents' marriage, coupled with the candid nature of the *Memoirs of the Author of a Vindication of the Rights of Woman* (which Godwin published in 1798), did Godwin's public standing much harm. Also, as the kind of radical writing characteristic of the 1790s fell out of fashion, so his literary reputation went into decline. Despite a large, though now mostly forgotten, output, the last thirty years of his life were marked by debt and obscurity.

In common with other radicals of his day – such as Mary Wollstonecraft and Tom **Paine** – Godwin is an incurable optimist. This is the founding principle of his political thought. He adopts without cavil the Enlightenment view of human nature as rational and perfectible through reason. Individuals are, he thinks, made what they are by environment and upbringing. The human condition is capable of being improved by the application of reason. There is no unalterable human nature that fixes our station and destiny. Godwin is, at least in most respects, a utilitarian. He believes that the only rational and proper courses of action are those that bring about the greatest happiness of the greatest number. He is convinced also that truly rational human beings will know this, and will behave accordingly. Human beings are naturally benevolent towards their fellows, and become more so as their level of rational development increases. With the spread of science and philosophy and the advance of education, therefore, there is every reason to suppose that the condition of humanity will improve and that man will become ever more capable of self-government. The need for state government will disappear; so, too, war, poverty, crime and violence will vanish under the civilising influence of reason. Godwin's belief in progress knows no bounds. In the final book of *An Enquiry*, called 'On Property', he foretells a time when human beings will achieve control even over the physical processes of ageing and fatigue: a time, in short, when human beings will achieve literal immortality.

The chief obstacle standing in the way of these things, however, is the state. The common belief – fostered, of course, by governments – is that government is necessary to successful human association; but this belief is false. Governments maintain themselves by fraud and violence, and by keeping their subjects in ignorance. There are in truth no natural distinctions between one human being and another. The processes of government, and the doctrines and dogmas by which systems of government are sustained, are what create artificial distinctions of rank. Again, government both institutionalises and induces competition, greed and conflict, which are the chief sources of the ills from which mankind suffers. It is only when the dominion of one man over another has ceased that people will be able to live a fully rational life. The abolition of all political institutions will put an end to distinctions of rank and to national feeling, and will rid humanity of the destructive passions of envy and aggression that go with these things. It will restore to men their natural equality and enable them to rebuild social life on the basis of free and equal association, governed by their reason alone.

Godwin was a radical rather than a revolutionary. Revolutions (and, for that matter, ordinary party politics), he thinks, polarise society and arouse passions that result in the eclipse of reason. Social progress is entirely dependent upon intellectual progress, which in turn comes from reflection and discussion. Government will not need to be overthrown by violent or revolutionary means. As the scope of human reason broadens and grows, the structures of subordination and superior rank upon which we now rely will simply cease to be necessary. This can come to pass only when the entire population has been brought to the level of understanding at present confined to the few. It will be a lengthy process, but Godwin never doubts the inevitability of its completion. He believes that some kind of representative assembly will be necessary as a transitional measure. Finally, however, men and women will live together in a natural society governed only by natural benevolence informed by developed human reason. Matters of public interest will be decided by public debate and discussion. Like later anarchists, Godwin believes in small face-to-face communities that will federate together on a voluntary basis for larger economic and social purposes. He believes that reason will lead people to opt for a system of voluntary communism in which all will work. Such communities will, he thinks, eventually embrace the whole world.

Many early socialists and other radicals were influenced by Godwin's writings. He also enjoyed the unusual distinction of having his ideas turned into verse by a major poet. With poems such as *Queen Mab* and *Prometheus Bound*, his son-in-law Shelley inspired generations of later radicals. Although the term itself was coined later, Godwin may fairly be described as the first modern anarchist. In this respect, he is the founder of a tradition of political thinking that has continued to the present day.

Further reading

Primary sources

An Enquiry Concerning Political Justice, ed. I. Kramnick (Harmondsworth: Penguin, 1976).

Caleb Williams, ed. D. McCracken (Oxford: Oxford University Press, 1977).

Secondary sources

Clark, J.P.: *The Philosophical Anarchism of William Godwin* (Princeton, NJ: Princeton University Press, 1977).

Marshall, P.: *William Godwin* (New Haven, CT, and London: Yale University Press, 1984).

Philp, M.: *Godwin's Political Justice* (London: Duckworth, 1986).

G.W.F. HEGEL (1770–1831)

Georg Wilhelm Friedrich Hegel was born in Stuttgart in 1770, the son of a provincial official. For a thinker who came to dominate German philosophy for much of the nineteenth century and influenced Western thought for much longer, Hegel was a remarkably late developer. He was diligent but undistinguished both at school and, later, as a theology student. He worked as a private tutor for a number of years before obtaining his first lowly university post at the age of thirty-three. It was not until five years later that he published his first major work, *The Phenomenology of Spirit* (1807), which outlined the evolution of human consciousness. It became the keystone of his whole vast system of thought, which he set out principally in the three volumes of his *Encyclopedia of the Philosophical Sciences in Outline* (1817): the *Logic*, *The Philosophy of Nature* and *The Philosophy of Mind*. Other works – such as *The Science of Logic* (1812) and *The Philosophy of Right* (1821) – elaborated particular sections in more detail. Further elaborations concerned with the philosophy of history, of aesthetics and of religion appeared after his death and were based on his lecture notes. Hegel was Professor of Philosophy at Berlin from 1818 until his death in 1831 during the great cholera epidemic that swept Europe at that time.

Hegel was a major influence upon European thought generally and had much to say about politics – set out in detail in his *Philosophy of Right*. However, he tends not to be as widely studied as perhaps he should be, especially in the English-speaking world. A major reason is Hegel's bewildering and notorious obscurity. He is the most difficult of all major thinkers to read. Usually people who write this obscurely have little to say, or if they do it does not fit together. But Hegel is a rare exception. His philosophy is vast, original and quite breathtakingly audacious. A brief sketch of the total system is necessary in order to set his political philosophy in context.

We have to begin by imagining the universe totally empty. All that exists is *Geist*, which is Mind or Spirit; not a particular mind or spirit, but mind or spirit in general (it is also God, but a very strange and peculiar notion of God). It is Mind, but is totally without consciousness – more potential mind really. It contains just one idea, the concept of being, although this idea is, so to speak, pregnant with other ideas. Out of the idea of being comes the idea of nothing, which is its opposite and in turn gives rise to a synthesis of the two ideas, the notion of becoming, from which in turn further concepts flow: one and many, substance and accident, cause and effect, time and space, and so on. In this way all the basic concepts we need to understand the world are deduced, or rather deduce themselves, according to Hegel's own special kind of logic which he calls the dialectic. In the dialectic things turn into their opposites and then into something that brings together the two opposites in a higher synthesis. (This is difficult, but it is meant to reflect the way the mind works, the way it explores ideas and reaches conclusions.)

So, having deduced the possibility of the world, the next thing that happens is that Mind (still entirely unconscious) turns itself into its opposite, which is matter. In modern cosmology we might identify this moment with the famous Big Bang. How Mind can just turn itself into its opposite like this is one of the mysteries of Hegelian metaphysics. On the other hand, it is perhaps no more mysterious than the notion of God creating the world out of nothing – or for that matter the Big Bang itself.

But if the question of *how* Mind does this is deeply mysterious, the question of why it does so is not. It is because Mind (Spirit, *Geist*) has a destiny. All that happens – the creation of matter, the emergence of organised life, the appearance of mankind and the whole of human history – all happens so that Mind can fulfil that destiny, which is for Mind to achieve self-understanding and therefore freedom.

When Mind becomes matter, Mind is, so to speak, buried in matter, and gradually emerges again over time. Organic life represents progressively higher levels of complexity and rational organisation that finally culminate in the emergence of humanity. It is with the emergence of human beings that Mind (or Spirit or God), for the first time, achieves consciousness. But it is only consciousness; it is not yet self-consciousness. Self-consciousness is only achieved over the course of human history.

Hegel sees human history as a kind of growing up of Mind, modelled on the stages of human development – babyhood, infancy, childhood, adolescence and so forth – with a succession of civilisations representing the different stages. From Ancient China, to India, to Ancient Greece, Rome, medieval Europe and on to modern Europe, each of these civilisations represents a new advance of Spirit's self-understanding. Hegel sometimes speaks of it as the World Spirit passing from civilisation to civilisation as each level of maturity is reached. It is portrayed as a painful process of struggle and self-doubt, involving different forms of alienation, which is the feeling of estrangement from the world.

In each civilisation Spirit or Mind objectifies itself, expresses itself in the forms of social life, morality, politics, science, art, religion and, above all, philosophy. All the elements of a given civilisation are united by a common theme or quality or essence: the *zeitgeist*, the spirit of the age. It is through objectifying itself in this way that Mind achieves a new level of self-understanding. It is just as when we are growing up we do things, form relationships, test ourselves, and in doing so find out who we are and what kind of people we are. Hegel believed that at the end of each civilisation a great philosopher arises who sums up the age in his thought, before the World Spirit passes to the next stage – as, for example, **Aristotle** did for the Greeks.

The entire historical/cosmological process reached its climax and conclusion, according to Hegel, in the Germany of his own day: the contemporary Prussian state was the highest possible achievement of Mind as expressed in social life, Protestantism the highest expression of religion, Romanticism the highest perfection of art – all of which, in their different ways, expressed the full maturity of Spirit. But over and above all was philosophy, the crowning achievement of any age. In this case it was *his* philosophy that summed up his age; much more than that: he saw *his* philosophy as summing up the whole process, including the whole of history, the whole development of the universe, and the whole evolution of Mind since before the universe was formed. It all culminates in Hegel's philosophy, because it is through *his* philosophy that Mind finally comes to understand itself and comes to realise that reality is its own creation, is itself (that is, an objectification of itself). Thus, only in Hegel's philosophy does Mind (or Spirit or God) become fully developed, fully self-conscious and fully free, which is its final destiny, the point and purpose of the whole process.

In Hegel's philosophy the ultimate destiny of Mind/Spirit/God is fulfilled. Mind or God is not some separate being but ourselves, each one of us is part of the whole – the collective mind – and it is only through human thought that Mind or Spirit or God can express or understand itself. In achieving self-understanding God/mankind is no longer alienated; the world is no longer a strange place, but is an objectification of Mind, which is the ultimate reality. Now that the historical process is complete, Mind is finally at home in the world and free, and the evolutionary process of human history is complete.

Hegel sees human history as the history of freedom, and the modern state – exemplified above all by contemporary Prussia – represented the final stage of humanity's development of social and political freedom. The freedoms of early nineteenth-century Prussians were extremely limited by today's standards, so it is important to see just what Hegel meant by political freedom and to grasp his understanding of the modern state.

Hegel's notion of freedom is more than our usual one of people being able, within the law, to do what they like. He also has a positive conception of freedom derived from **Rousseau** and **Kant**, who both saw freedom as essential to human nature, but identified being free with acting morally. However, Hegel disagrees with Kant's view that human beings must be free to live by whatever moral rules they choose for themselves that are consistent with the freedom of others. Morality, Hegel thought, had to have a content, and this could only come from the community and institutions that have shaped us and made us what we are. The assertion of abstract rights of man, divorced from any social context, was, he believed, responsible for the violence and terror of the French Revolution. In his more social concept of morality he is closer to Rousseau, for whom citizens are free when they conform to the General Will, which represents everyone's desire for the good of the community as a whole. Hegel has a somewhat similar view, but his version – the 'Universal Will' – largely dispenses with any democratic apparatus for expressing or recognising it. On the other hand, he goes beyond the narrow conformity that Rousseau's view implies. He has a much more complex conception of the state and what freedom amounts to.

Characteristically, Hegel also saw the development of the state and of political philosophy in evolutionary terms. He saw the early Greek city as a moral community in which the individual was subsumed. It was the moral community of the family writ large. That moral community began to be weakened with the rise of Socratic philosophy and the critical attitude that went with it. **Plato** recommended an ideal state that all should strive for, but Hegel did not think that the invention of such states, which we should then be under some moral obligation to create, was an appropriate task for philosophers. Their proper function was to penetrate and reveal the inner nature of things. Hegel argued that the significance of Plato was that he revealed the tight moral unity of the city-state that subordinated the individual. As Hegel believed was characteristically the fate of philosophers, Plato revealed the nature of a way of life that was in fact passing away.

The rise of individualism, expressed in various aspects of Roman civilisation (the rule of law), and the rise of Christianity, expressing the individual conscience, were the opposite of the close moral unity of the Greek *polis*. This growth of individualism eventually culminated in the development of civil society and the social and economic individualism represented by **Locke**, Adam Smith and Kant. The rise of commercial societies, such as Britain and Holland in the seventeenth century, saw the state conceived in terms of individuals bound together by contract: that is, in terms of civil society.

As always with Hegel, the final phase of any development sums up and holds together all previous phases in a synthesis. In particular he saw in the national state of his own day a reconciliation of the concept of the state as a moral community that prevailed in the Ancient world, with more recent concepts of the state that supported freedom and individualism. It is a synthesis of the unselfconscious moral unity of the Greek *polis* and the freedom of civil society in a higher self-conscious unity of the state where people willingly and freely embrace the obligations of citizenship and duty to the nation in both war and peace. In the willing, self-conscious acceptance of these obligations, as in the obligations of the family, freedom lies. In this way Hegel claimed to combine the negative freedom of civil society with the positive freedom of living according to the ethical and political system of which we approve, because it is rational and is part of the national community with which we identify and whose moral purposes we see as our own.

Hegel's conception of the fully developed state was, therefore, a complex dialectical synthesis of the different levels of social life: of family, civil society and the state itself. It is through participating in these different levels that the individual finds self-expression and fulfilment. The most basic level is the family in which the individual shares a common life based upon unselfish love and duty, in which one cares for others as much as oneself, and does so freely. Beyond the family we are in a quite different sphere based on quite different principles. This is civil society. Civil society is the sphere of self-assertion and the pursuit of self-interest, of competition and ambition, and of the cultivation of the self. It is the sphere of individualism, and where property is important as an extension and expression of the self.

There is an overall unity in civil society, although it is the largely unselfconscious unity of the market, which makes everyone interdependent. However, there are some conscious though partial unities. As well as individuals, civil society is inhabited by many organisations, businesses, professional bodies and corporations of various kinds that also have interests that need to be represented. These should be the basis of representation in a parliament based on function, with an upper house representing the agricultural interest and a lower house the commercial; the latter should supervise the nations' finances and be elected on a limited franchise. Finally, civil society is the sphere of personal freedom and rights that Locke and Kant emphasised. But where they were mistaken, Hegel insists, was in identifying civil society with the state. They saw the representing, reconciling and regulation of the conflicts of civil society and the maintenance of freedom as the particular sphere of the state. This is indeed where the state interacts with civil society, but the state for Hegel has a much higher and more important function.

Hegel was the first theorist to insist upon a clear distinction between civil society and the state. He saw the state as embodying the ethical will of the whole people (in fact a variation of Rousseau's General Will). He argued that unless it did represent the common good in this way, the state could make no claim upon a society of purely self-interested individuals. It is because it embodies the moral will of the community that the state can demand the support of the people in peace and in war beyond the claims of mere utility.

The moral will of the community expresses itself through the executive. Parliament is the arena in which all the competing claims and conflicts of civil society are expressed, and it is the function of the executive to harmonise these and decide what is best for all. The principal elements of the executive are, first of all, the monarch and his advisers and ministers. The monarchy symbolises the single will of the community, but the person of the king has limited real power as a constitutional monarch. Second, the professional civil service, or 'universal class', works for the community as a whole. This includes a degree of intervention in the market to provide a moderate amount of social welfare, including poverty relief and education to prevent the development of an underclass that is detached from society in general (though not to the extent of undermining the self-sufficiency and self-respect that underlies civil society). In sum, a society in which the moral will of the community, embodied in the executive, accords with our own.

The state, therefore, may be said to represent a synthesis of the moral life of the family and the freedom of civil society; without destroying either, the state expresses both at the higher level. The state guarantees the individual's freedom, while at the same time the individual owes it a moral duty. As in Rousseau, conforming one's will to the General Will means obeying one's own higher self. It is the state that protects the freedoms of civil society and provides the framework within which individuals can develop into full moral beings.

Family relations are instinctual, while the autonomy and contractual relations of civil society are conscious, although morally neutral. They are both means by which the individual achieves self-realisation. It is through the state that the final stage of that self-realisation is achieved in which the individual consciously identifies himself with a higher purpose and is thereby fully developed and fully free. Hegel saw in the state a social integration and unity at a higher level, one that embraced the differentiation and variety of modern society in a way that was not possible in the more homogeneous Greek city-state or in Rousseau's somewhat unrealistic ideal.

Hegel saw his philosophy as completing the process by reconciling the individual to the state and to history by demonstrating their underlying rationality. The modern state, Hegel insisted, was rational, as was the process of its creation through history. Part of this development was conflict between states, which, especially in the extreme form of war, was a necessary part of the state establishing its identity and unity. Beyond this Hegel foresaw no further development, such as the system of universal peace envisaged by Kant. In a sense history just goes on, while in another sense it is over. Hegel's picture of reality is highly dynamic, yet all the restless movement apparently comes to a dead stop with Hegel's philosophy. Furthermore, philosophers are supposed to sum up a world that is passing, whereas Hegel appears to be presenting a permanent truth.

The end of history is thus problematic in Hegel's own terms. There is, however, much else that is open to criticism from other points of view. The dialectic is now difficult to take seriously. It is not really a kind of logic, as Hegel claims, but a metaphysics that makes sweeping and rather vague generalisations about ultimate reality – and about both physical nature and human history – that can never be tested.

More controversially, Hegel is blamed by some (most notably Karl **Popper** in *The Open Society and its Enemies*) for contributing to state worship and the development of totalitarianism. Certainly extreme German nationalists, such as von Treitschke, and some of the theorists of Italian fascism were influenced by Hegel; nonetheless, the charge is generally unfair. Hegel offers a synthesis of positive and negative freedom involving both service to the nation and the freedoms, diversity and pluralism of civil society. Constitutional monarchy is advocated, while the populist authoritarianism of the Jacobin is firmly rejected.

Hegel is a controversial figure, though undeniably a major influence on modern thought. In addition to his influence on the right of the political spectrum, he has been a major influence upon the left. This is most obviously true of **Marx** and later Marxists, such as the Frankfurt School (see **Herbert Marcuse and the Frankfurt School**), but it is also true of anarchists, such as Proudhon, and ecologists, such as Murray Bookchin. Hegel was also a significant influence on liberalism through T.H. **Green** and others. The most recent manifestation of Hegel's influence on political thought comes in the communitarian movement with writers such as Alasdair MacIntyre and Charles Taylor.

Further reading

Primary sources

Hegel's Political Writings, ed. Z.A. Pelczynski (Oxford: Oxford University Press, 1964).

Elements of the Philosophy of Right, ed. A.B. Wood and H.B. Nisbet (Cambridge: Cambridge University Press, 1991).

Secondary sources

Avineri, S.: *Hegel's Theory of the Modern State* (Cambridge: Cambridge University Press, 1972).

Beiser, F.C. (ed.): *The Cambridge Companion to Hegel* (Cambridge: Cambridge University Press, 1993).

Burbridge, J.W.: *Historical Dictionary of Hegelian Philosophy* (London: Scarecrow, 2001).
Patten, A.: *Hegel's Idea of Freedom* (Oxford: Oxford University Press, 1999).
Pelczynski, Z.A.: *Hegel's Political Philosophy: Problems and Perspectives* (Cambridge: Cambridge University Press, 1971).
Taylor, C.: *Hegel and Modern Society* (Cambridge: Cambridge University Press, 1979).

JEREMY BENTHAM (1748–1832)

Jeremy Bentham was born in Houndsditch, London. He went to Westminster School at the age of seven and to Queen's College, Oxford, at the remarkable age of twelve, taking his degree in 1764. He read for the Bar at Lincoln's Inn and was called in 1767, but never practised law as a profession. He wrote extensively on a number of subjects, although he was somewhat given to undertaking ambitious projects and either leaving them unfinished or losing interest in them when finished. A number of his works were edited and seen through the press by friends and disciples. The French editions published by his friend Etienne Dumont established his literary reputation throughout continental Europe and beyond. In 1790 he produced a *Draught of a New Plan for the Organisation of the Judicial Establishment of France*, for which he was made an honorary French citizen in 1792. He also devoted a number of years to the design and unsuccessful promotion of a new model prison called the Panopticon. But he is chiefly remembered as the most notable early exponent (though not strictly the founder) of utilitarianism: the doctrine that assesses the rightness of acts, policies, decisions and choices in terms of their tendency to promote the happiness of the people affected by them. He seems to have been a perfectly extraordinary person: part genius, part crank, amazingly industrious, capable of inspiring intense love and loyalty in his friends. As the final gesture of a remarkable life, he directed in his will that his body be dissected for the purposes of scientific research. His mummified remains now sit in a glass case in University College, London, which he helped to found.

From the point of view of the history of political thought, the most important of Bentham's numerous works are *A Fragment on Government* (1776) and *An Introduction to the Principles of Morals and Legislation* (written in 1780 and published in 1789). The latter was his major work published during his lifetime. A collected edition of his writings called *The Works of Jeremy Bentham* was published in 1838–43 by his literary executor, John Bowring, but this edition is incomplete and unsatisfactory. Its shortcomings have become increasingly clear with the modern study of Bentham's manuscript remains, and a proper scholarly edition, *The Collected Works of Jeremy Bentham*, was begun in 1968.

Bentham has a fearsome literary style. It must be admitted also that he is not always the clearest and most logical of thinkers. It seems that his version of utilitarianism – 'classical' utilitarianism, as it is called – has three distinct elements. The most fundamental is a psychological hedonism similar to that favoured by **Hobbes**. All human beings seek to maximise pleasure or happiness (Bentham tends to use the two words interchangeably) and minimise pain. At the beginning of *Introduction to the Principles of Morals and Legislation*, he asserts:

> All men are under the governance of two sovereign masters: pain and pleasure. It is for them to point out what we ought to do, as well as to determine what we shall do.

Second, utilitarianism nominates pleasure or happiness as the supreme good, in the sense that everyone seeks pleasure as an end and not as a means to some further end. Like Hobbes, Bentham thinks that 'good' and 'bad' are simply the terms we use to designate the things that cause us – or we expect to cause us – pleasure or pain. Moreover, all pleasure is equally good: we are to make no distinction between types of pleasure. What we seek, Bentham thinks, is not the highest quality but the greatest quantity of pleasure. 'Quantity of pleasure being equal', he says, 'pushpin is as good as poetry' (*The Rationale of Reward* 3:1). By 'pleasure' Bentham means a wide variety of things. He lists the pleasures of taste, smell and touch; of acquiring property; of knowing that we have the goodwill of others; of power; of seeing the pleasure of those for whom we care; and so forth. Third, utilitarianism becomes a theory of action as well as of value by virtue of a simple logical transition: if pleasure is the good, it follows that right action will be action that maximises pleasure and minimises pain, and wrong action the reverse. This, Bentham thinks, is the only meaning that 'right' and 'wrong' can have. Pleasure and pain are the criteria that govern what we ought to do.

But whose pleasure and whose pain? The pleasure and pain, Bentham replies, of whatever party is being considered. If the party under consideration is a single individual, then right actions are those that bear upon the pleasure or pain of that individual. If the party under consideration is a community (as, for example, when legislation is being contemplated), then the standard of right and wrong will be not the pleasure or pain of any particular individual, but of the community taken as a whole. But we must notice the sense in which, for Bentham, there can be such a 'whole'. He insists that a community is no more than the simple aggregate or sum total of the individuals who are its members. There is in Bentham no suggestion of the kind that we find in **Rousseau**, for example, that there is, over and above the individual members of a community, a corporate identity or social reality that is in some sense more or greater than the sum of the community's parts. For Bentham, there are only individuals; therefore, he maintains, in order to discover whether an action is right or wrong from the point of view of a community, we have to discover what its effect will be on the total pleasure within the aggregate of individuals who comprise the whole. We must add together all the individual pleasures or happinesses in the group or community, and the total that we arrive at will be the communal or social happiness or pleasure at which legislation ought to aim.

How is such an aggregation to be performed? In the *Introduction to the Principles of Morals and Legislation*, Bentham suggests that the rightness or wrongness of an action can in principle be determined by a 'felicific calculus' (sometimes the phrase 'hedonic calculus' is used). In the case of any two actions between which we have to choose, we should consider the pain or pleasure that each may be expected to produce along seven different 'dimensions': (1) intensity; (2) duration; (3) propinquity (nearness or remoteness in time); (4) certainty; (5) fecundity (how fruitful is it of further pleasures and pains after the initial ones?); (6) purity (does a pleasurable action have painful consequences?); and (7) extent (how many people do the pleasures and pains of an action affect?). If, when we have weighed up the likely outcome of each alternative in terms of these seven considerations, one action turns out to be more pleasurable or less painful than the other, then it is right and ought to be done (or at any rate need not be avoided or forbidden), and vice versa. Bentham accepts, of course, that ordinary people cannot apply these criteria to every action of daily life; nor is it seriously suggested that the calculation can be mathematically exact. But if legislators, in particular, keep these seven dimensions in mind, they will (Bentham thinks) be able to achieve the true aim of legislation, which is to secure (as he puts it in his *Commonplace Book*) 'the greatest happiness of the greatest number'. This famous expression, which has become known as the 'principle of utility', was not, incidentally, coined by

Bentham. It occurs first in Francis Hutcheson's *Inquiry into the Original of our Ideas of Beauty and Virtue* (1725).

Bentham's faith in the principle of utility knows no bounds. His belief in it is always closely coupled with the question of how to put it into practice. He believes that the task of the moral philosopher is to prescribe what morality and law *ought* to be, not merely to describe what they are; and he devoted much time to the application of the principle of utility to the criminal law. No act or motive, he believes, is wrong in itself. There is no such thing as abstract wrong which it is the law's business to punish. The law should not seek to regulate matters of private morality. Acts are criminal only if they adversely affect the general happiness. The purpose of punishment is deterrence rather than retribution. Punishments should be so calculated as to cause pain enough, but no more than enough, to deter the offender from re-offending, and fear enough, but no more than enough, to deter potential offenders from offending at all. In assigning punishments to crimes, therefore, it will be necessary to calculate the severity of the punishment in such a way as to counterbalance the pleasure that the criminal hopes to achieve from the crime. It will also be necessary to assign severer punishments to crimes that it is more difficult to detect. Clearly, there will be no point in punishing even harmful acts if it can be shown that they were carried out unintentionally or in sufficiently mitigating circumstances.

After about 1809, largely as a result of his friendship with James Mill, Bentham's mind turned more towards issues of political reform as distinct from ethics and jurisprudence. Somewhat after the fashion of **Burke**, Bentham has no patience with political arguments based on abstractions. He is famously scathing in his criticism of the French Revolutionary doctrine of the rights of man. Natural rights, he says in his *Anarchical Fallacies*, are 'simple nonsense'; 'natural and imprescriptible rights' are 'nonsense upon stilts'. He believes that the interests of the governed will be best secured by the establishment of explicit rights through a legal system. It is futile to claim rights that no legislator has made and that therefore cannot be enforced against anyone. To speak of such rights is like speaking of a child without a father. Bentham became increasingly convinced of the virtues of representative democracy based on universal franchise, a secret ballot and annual parliaments. He expressed this conviction in his *Plan of Parliamentary Reform* (1817). He was also a precursor of modern welfare-state ideas. He believed that legislation should provide subsistence, security, abundance and equality. In different places and at different times he is to be found arguing for sickness benefit, free education, a minimum wage, reform of the law of evidence, recruitment to the civil service by competitive examination and abolition of imprisonment for debt.

Bentham believed himself to have cleared away the obscurities of custom and superstition from the field of lawmaking, and to have placed morality and jurisprudence on an unambiguous footing. The principle of utility has, after all, a certain beguiling simplicity. When called upon to make a decision as to what to do or what law to enact, simply add up the pain and pleasure of all whom the decision will affect, and the decision virtually makes itself. The problem, of course, is that the reality is not as simple as that. Purely practical difficulties apart, the idea of happiness or pleasure itself gives trouble. Pleasures, surely, are qualities rather than quantities. They are subjective rather than objective, and not necessarily commensurable. What gives you pleasure may well not give me pleasure, and may, indeed, give me pain. It is therefore not easy to see how pleasures can be added together, even roughly, to make a 'greatest happiness'. And what of the notion of 'the greatest happiness of the greatest number'? Where choice is necessary, should we choose the 'greatest happiness' (assuming that there can be such a thing) or the 'greatest number'? Can it be right or just to sacrifice the happiness of one individual to secure the happiness of a collection of individuals? Can it be right to 'punish' the innocent in the name of deterrence? Utilitarianism seems to suggest that it can; but, as has been pointed out (by John **Rawls**, for example), this contradicts most people's intuitive beliefs about right and wrong. These problems, and the many others to which utilitarianism gives rise, have exercised its exponents for two centuries.

Further reading

Primary source

The Works of Jeremy Bentham, ed. J. Bowring (Edinburgh: William Tait, 1838–43). This edition is in the process of being supplanted by *The Collected Works of Jeremy Bentham*, ed. J.H. Burns, J.H. Dinwiddy and F. Rosen (London: Athlone Press and Oxford: Clarendon Press, 1968–).

Secondary sources

Halévy, E. (trans. M. Morris): *The Growth of Philosophic Radicalism* (London: Faber & Faber, 1928).

Hampsher-Monk, I.: *A History of Modern Political Thought* (Oxford: Blackwell, 1992).

Harrison, R.: *Bentham* (London: Routledge & Kegan Paul, 1985).

Hart, H.L.A.: *Essays on Bentham, Jurisprudence and Political Theory* (Oxford: Clarendon Press, 1982).
Manning, D.J.: *The Mind of Jeremy Bentham* (London: Longmans, Green & Co., 1968).

CHARLES FOURIER (1772–1837) AND UTOPIAN SOCIALISM

Utopian socialism was the first significant form of modern socialism. It developed in the aftermath of the French Revolution, but just as importantly it was a response to the impact of industrialisation on European society. Utopian socialism developed simultaneously in various forms in the ideas of a number of thinkers, of whom Charles Fourier may be taken as representative.

Charles Fourier was born in 1772, the son of a successful cloth merchant family from Besançon. Fourier's family lost its fortune in the Revolution, and he himself was nearly executed by the Jacobins. Thereafter he earned his living as a travelling salesman, but detested commerce, believing that making a profit by buying at one price to sell at another was fundamentally dishonest. He lived most of his adult life alone in Paris. He never read books, which he thought mostly full of nonsense, but was an avid reader of newspapers. From these and his own experience he spun all his theories and projects. In 1808 he published *Theory of the Four Movements and the General Destinies*, which set out his vision of the universe, humanity and history. He wrote a great deal more, but never changed his basic ideas.

Fourier had a theory of history in thirty-two stages ordained by God, beginning with savagery and gradually leading – via the present stage of so-called 'civilisation' and the subsequent stage of 'socialism' – to Harmony. Harmony, the highest stage, would last 70,000 years, before descending down the stages back to savagery, at which point the world would end. There was a certain amount of flexibility: the hateful present stage of 'civilisation' could be shortened, and the more desirable stages come sooner and last longer, if the world adopted Fourier's ideas for the ideal society quickly.

Fourier believed that, just as Newton had penetrated the mysteries of attraction and repulsion in physical nature in his theory of gravity, showing how all these conflicting forces could in fact create a perfect equilibrium and harmony in the universe, so he, Charles Fourier, had discovered the same principles in the human world. He would demonstrate that they could be the basis of a perfect equilibrium and harmony in society. His understanding of human nature came from a highly elaborate theory of the passions. These were God-given and, as such, their satisfaction must be natural and right. In fact, Fourier thought, if only the natural passions were given free rein, then a natural social harmony would inevitably result. Unfortunately, society throughout history had systematically denied and repressed 'natural passions'. This was never more so than in contemporary so-called 'civilisation', where moral conventions suffocated and repressed the passions, especially the sexual ones, creating perversion and endless misery. To a considerable extent, Fourier anticipated Freud and some of Freud's followers. In writings not published until long after his death, Fourier even suggested a new religion in which priests would advise individuals on sexual matters.

In 'civilisation', according to Fourier, the repression of natural instincts was compounded by the economic system. He attacked economic liberalism bitterly. Capitalism drives down wages, creating exploitation, poverty and misery. Political liberalism was a sham. Constitutionalism did nothing to check the depredations of economic liberalism and so did nothing to alleviate the suffering of the people. Liberalism was a benefit for the few but a disaster for the many.

A new society needed to be built in which people could be happy. But revolution was not the answer. Fourier detested the Jacobins: not merely for personal reasons, but because they represented methods of violence and terror, as well as authoritarianism and moral self-righteousness – all of which he abhorred. People should be genuinely free from the artificialities of 'civilisation', free to be themselves and be happy. Fourier's contempt for modern life as artificial and repressive comes from **Rousseau**, although he had none of Rousseau's puritanism or contempt for women. Fourier had little faith in government and believed that this new world would have to be built from below, in personal relationships and small communities. He was constantly looking for patrons to take up his schemes.

The basic building block of the new society would be the small community, the *phalanstère* or phalanx. Each would have a population of around 1,700 to 1,800 (based upon a calculation of the different emotional types of human being, doubled to account for both men and women, plus a few extras). There would be communal meals and common housing and services, including child-care. Apart from cases where people might be harmed, there would be complete sexual freedom and people would change partners freely. Women would be fully emancipated. Fourier was an ardent feminist, believing that in most things women were the superior sex. The phalanx would replace the family as the primary object of loyalty and affection. Social solidarity would also be maintained by a common education for all.

After sexual freedom, Fourier's second major principle for achievement of happiness for all was pleasure in work. Everyone must be found work according to their interests and aptitude. He disliked factories and thought in terms of crafts. However, he did not believe in abolishing property. Everyone in the phalanx would be properly housed, clothed and fed, but beyond that people would have different levels of investment in their community and profits would be equitably shared among capital, labour and talent. Some would own little, yet they would still be vastly better off than in any previous society.

Fourier says little about political organisation. Each phalanx would be run by a council of all members, but there is a strong suspicion that some would be more equal than others. He believed that the whole population of France, and ultimately the world, would come to live in phalanxes. Once established, they would create networks of co-operation; eventually national networks would direct volunteer armies in great civil engineering projects. Perhaps international armies would one day undertake, for example, the reclaiming of the world's deserts for fertile use. All this would by-pass existing political systems. What would happen to these, Fourier does not say.

In his day Fourier was widely regarded as mad. Certainly some of his ideas sound bizarre, such as sexual relations between stars and planets, but these can perhaps be put down to a poetic imagination. More importantly, he had too many interesting ideas to be dismissed easily. He also attracted many followers, as did the other major utopian socialists: Robert Owen in Britain and Henri de Saint-Simon in France. Owen had similar ideas of small self-sufficient communities in which ultimately all would live and co-operate, though he was more thoroughgoing than Fourier in his abolition of private property; Saint-Simon saw a new industrial society governed by a new elite of industrialists and administrators, scientists and engineers and priests and artists, who would organise society in great detail for the benefit of all.

In many ways these three thinkers were rivals with different schemes, and they certainly did not co-operate. Yet they had much in common. All three believed the old pre-1789 world was dead beyond recall and that a new world had to be created out of the chaos of the Revolutionary period, which had seen constant wars, civil strife and the social upheaval of industrialisation. They were all opposed to revolutionary methods, believing in the power of reason and example. The utopian socialists stressed harmony and community, as against the individualism and sense of alienation of the age. They were less interested in politics than in the psychology and sociology of human needs and values as the basis of new social structures that would be in keeping with human nature.

It was the *Communist Manifesto* (1848) of **Karl Marx** and Frederick Engels that airily dismissed Saint-Simon, Fourier and Owen as 'utopian socialists' – and the label stuck. What Marx meant by this was that their theories were not 'scientific' like his own, that they had no understanding of the dynamics of society and history and could not demonstrate that socialism was both necessary and inevitable; for that reason their ideas were little better than useless fantasies. Marx's view is reasonable given his beliefs, but from a non-Marxist standpoint the term 'utopian', used pejoratively, was not entirely fair. Besides, when Marx wrote in 1848 they could each be seen as rival socialisms with many followers. Later, when their influence had declined, Marx and Engels were more generous.

The utopian socialists were not the unrealistic dreamers that their designation as 'utopian' suggests. They did not simply present a picture of what a good society might look like with no thought to how it might be achieved, as had been the tradition of utopian literature over the previous three centuries. All three were practical men with practical proposals for achieving their ideal, each was sufficiently convincing to have a following and create a movement. These movements were the beginnings of socialism as a mass movement.

Interestingly, there has been a revival of interest in recent years in the utopian socialists and similar writers, such as William Morris. This is partly due to the general disillusionment with centralised state socialism, and partly owing to the growth of green ideas.

Further reading

Primary sources

The Utopian Vision of Charles Fourier: Selected Texts on Work, Love and Passionate Attraction, ed. J. Beecher and R. Bienvenu (London: Jonathan Cape, 1972).

The Theory of the Four Movements, ed. G. Stedman Jones and I. Patterson (Cambridge: Cambridge University Press, 1996).

Secondary sources

Beecher, J.: *Charles Fourier: The Visionary and his World* (Berkeley, CA: University of California, 1986).

Taylor, K.: *The Political Ideas of the Utopian Socialists* (London: Frank Cass, 1982).

KARL MARX (1818–83)

Marx was born in Trier, Germany, in 1818, the son of a successful lawyer. His family was Jewish, but had adopted Lutheranism to avoid the anti-Semitic persecution prevailing in Germany at that time. It is said this gave Marx his cynicism and hostility to religion generally. He was a brilliant scholar, who gave up his law studies for philosophy (he wrote his doctoral thesis on Ancient Greek philosophy). In Berlin, Marx came under the spell of Hegelian philosophy, which influenced his thought profoundly (see **G.W.F. Hegel**); there he joined the group known as the Young Hegelians, whose members believed that the dialectic of history had yet to achieve its final stage in the full emancipation of humanity. Among the Young Hegelians, Marx met Frederick Engels, who was to be his lifelong friend and collaborator.

Engels came from a rich Protestant family in the Rhineland, who owned cotton mills, including some in Manchester, which at that time was leading the world in industrial development. When he met Marx, Engels was already making a name for himself as a talented radical journalist. But his family wanted him to learn the family business. This he did in Manchester, at the same time as writing an outstanding account of working conditions: *The Condition of the Working Class in England* (1844). It was Engels who convinced Marx that the future lay in industrialisation, and that it was classical economics that had to be mastered to understand how that future would develop.

By this time both Marx and Engels had run into trouble with the authorities in Germany because of their radical journalism and been forced into exile, which they spent mostly in Paris, where Marx associated with French socialists and anarchists and developed his ideas. When the Europe-wide revolutions of 1848 broke out, Marx and Engels responded with the *Communist Manifesto*. Ignored at the time, this is the first outline statement of Marx's complete system, which he went on elaborating for the rest of his life. In the meantime, with the failure of the 1848 revolutions, Marx and Engels moved to England where they both settled. Engels returned to Manchester to run the family business there. Marx took up residence in London, where he worked in the British Museum on his research and lived by occasional journalism (he was Europe correspondent for a New York newspaper) and subsidies from Engels.

In 1867 Marx published the first volume of his major work, *Capital*. After Marx died in 1883, Engels published the remaining two volumes of *Capital* from the mountain of papers left by Marx, along with other works. Engels' own writings were also important: they included a book on the family, as well as popular versions of Marxism for the benefit of the working-class followers in Germany and elsewhere who were looking to Marx for inspiration. In his later years Marx became a major figure in the European working-class movement, and after his death Engels took over this role. When Engels died in 1895, there was no one to give an authoritative interpretation of Marx and the movement began to splinter.

Many of Marx's early writings are concerned with trying to work out his own position in relation to Hegel and the Young Hegelians (a large part of this work was not published during Marx's lifetime). Out of this process Marx's mature ideas began to develop. A crucial stage in the process was a document that has become known as the *Economic and Philosophic Manuscripts* or more simply the *Paris Manuscripts* of 1844 (they did not become widely available until the middle of the twentieth century). This represents Marx's first attempt to give a general view of his system. Here more than anywhere else he outlines his view of basic human nature and alienation.

In the *Paris Manuscripts* Marx sets out his theory that the human essence is labour. That is, what is distinctly human, what it is that differentiates us from the animals, is not so much reason as such, nor our moral capacity, as various previous thinkers had suggested, but the human capacity for labour. What Marx means by labour has to be understood in terms of human interaction with nature. It is using a combination of mental and physical effort to shape nature according to our needs. Proper physical labour, like craftsmanship or farming, involves intelligence and creativity. Through this labour mankind creates its own world to live in, a kind of second nature in which primary nature is humanised.

In this process human beings are creative: they fashion objects, make things grow, bend nature's processes to their needs. In the act of shaping nature to satisfy human needs, all human beings instinctively express themselves in what they produce; they objectify themselves, so that their product is an extension of their being. The natural feeling of satisfaction at creation is intensified if the products satisfy the needs of fellow human beings as well as the producer. It exemplifies and confirms the social nature of human existence. We create the world together.

However, in actually existing societies, these natural feelings are diminished or denied because of exploitation. Those who do most of the work in any given society, have the product of their labour taken away from them: it is expropriated by those with wealth and power, by those who own the means of production (the slave-owners or land-owners or factory-owners), who in any society are the ruling class. The workers receive a mere pittance; just enough to survive and reproduce. Furthermore, the very wealth that the workers have created becomes a power over them, the means to their exploitation. The world that *they* have created is hostile to them; it stunts their lives and keeps them in misery. Thus, they are alienated from their own world, from the product of their own labour.

Marx argued that under capitalism exploitation – and therefore alienation – are at their most intense. Capitalists are driven by competition to exploit their workers more and more. Labour is reduced to a mere commodity. Skill and creativity are destroyed by machinery and the division of labour, and the worker is reduced to the most miserable condition ever. At the same time the power of wealth is overwhelming. Since labour is part of the human essence, the essential self, the means to self-fulfilment as a human being, the workers can be said to be alienated from themselves. They are thereby dehumanised, only finding satisfaction in animal functions, mere physical pleasures. The human instinct to free, spontaneous creativity, not just for subsistence, is quintessentially human and what capitalism denies. Alienation is complete, and it is from this condition that humanity must be emancipated.

However, Marx completely rejected the idea that political or natural rights were the means to human emancipation, as for example the French Revolutionaries seemed to think (arguing that if the 'inalienable rights of man' could be proclaimed and enforced, then humanity would be free). This kind of freedom to enjoy life, liberty and property was, Marx thought, little more than the right of individuals to exploit other individuals. It merely sanctified their isolation and the competition of capitalist society. Genuine emancipation of humanity can only come about through communism, when private property and with it capitalism, exploitation, alienation and their consequences are all overcome and abolished. Only then will humanity be restored to its fullness, the human psyche made whole, and the individual's relationship with nature and with fellow human beings be what they ought to be in accordance with essential human nature.

At this stage in Marx's development, communism is seen as both an ideal and an inevitability. But why and how it must come about, Marx had not yet worked out. Over the next few years Marx developed his system in collaboration with Engels in works such as *The German*

Ideology (1846) and *The Poverty of Philosophy* (1847). It is complete in outline by the time of the publication of *The Communist Manifesto* in 1848.

At the heart of Marx's mature system is a theory, which he took to be thoroughly scientific, about how society works and how it changes over time. Marx believed that the most basic fact about any society is the nature of its economic organisation, its 'mode of production'. This involves two things: first, the methods of production (the type of agriculture, industry and so on) and, second, the way in which production is socially organised in terms of who owns what and who does which job. The distribution of wealth and work is the basis of the class structure. Although this structure might be quite complicated, Marx insisted that in any class system there is always a fundamental division between those who own the means of production, and thereby constitute the ruling class, and those who do the work.

For Marx, the socio-economic organisation of society – its 'substructure' or 'base' – is fundamental because not only does it make all the other aspects of society possible, it also determines the nature of all those aspects. Consequently, in any society its 'superstructure' of laws, government, education, religion, art, beliefs and values is a direct result of its social and economic organisation. It is a basic principle of Marxist theory that base determines superstructure.

The crucial link between the base and the other elements of society lies in the need of the ruling class to maintain its power. Thus the state – with its instruments of law, its police and its armed forces – exists to protect the property of the ruling class, and therefore its control of the economy. But the ruling class cannot maintain its control by force alone; it needs the active co-operation of most of the population. This is where, according to Marx, religion, education, the arts and prevailing ideas play their role. They help to maintain the position of the ruling class by teaching people to believe that the way society is organised is natural and right and should not be questioned.

The base, therefore, does not just determine the various institutions of society, but also determines the way people think. As Marx puts it in the Preface to his *A Critique of Political Economy* (1859): 'It is not the consciousness of men that determines their existence, but, on the contrary, their social existence that determines their consciousness.' Marx used the term 'ideology' to refer to ideas, beliefs and values that reflect the interests of a particular class. In any society, he argued, the dominant beliefs and values are always the beliefs and values of the ruling class, while those of the rest of society who accept them (that is, most people most of the time) are in a state of 'false consciousness'.

Ideology is also, therefore, an instrument of class domination, along with all the other elements of the superstructure.

Thus, the feudal society of the Middle Ages was based upon subsistence agriculture. The peasant class did all the work, while the nobility owned all the land. The power of the nobility was sustained by law and custom, and upheld by the king's courts and by force if necessary. The Church sanctified feudalism as part of God's order and taught the sinfulness of questioning one's allotted place. Art and literature either supported the Church view or portrayed the ruling class as chivalrous and superior.

In capitalist society the ruling class is the bourgeoisie, who control the finance, the factories and the machines upon which modern industrial production is based, and therefore have the power to exploit the industrial workers (the proletariat). The state and its instruments support the property and interests of the ruling class, and again the beliefs and values that prevail in capitalist society help to portray the existing state of affairs as natural and right. The classical *laissez-faire* liberalism of the early nineteenth century, with its principles of free markets, individual liberty, equality of opportunity and limited parliamentary democracy, is the ideology of capitalism. A society founded upon such principles is portrayed as the good society, which works for the benefit of all. But freedom, equality and democracy are all seen as a sham so long as the ruling class owns the means by which the masses earn their living. Religion also makes its contribution to the bourgeois world-view. Protestantism emphasises individuality, and (in some sects at least) views worldly success as a sign of God's grace; while at the same time, as with medieval religion, it reconciles the exploited to their sufferings by telling them that it is God's will and that their reward will be in Heaven. Art and literature celebrate such bourgeois virtues as individuality, freedom and the accumulation of property. Thus, all the elements of the superstructure operate in the interests of the ruling class and consequently are a direct reflection of the socio-economic organisation of society.

These accounts of feudal and capitalist societies pose an obvious question: how, if the ruling class is so solidly entrenched, can one type of society ever change into another? It is clear from the principle that base determines superstructure that, for Marx, it is social and economic forces that bring about historical change. Great events, such as the Reformation or the French Revolution, do not come about because of changes in people's ideas or because of the actions of great individuals. These are merely the surface manifestations of much deeper substructural changes.

Marx's theory of the basic dynamics of historical change is built around four interconnected ideas: economic development, class conflict, the dialectic and revolution. Each mode of production, Marx believed, had its own inner logic of development. Economies change and develop over time through technological innovation, new financial techniques or growing trade and prosperity. Such developments give rise to strains and contradictions within the system; a new kind of production evolves along with a new class to exploit it. Eventually, the old structure of society can no longer contain these new developments, and the new class challenges the old ruling class for supremacy. All the contradictions and conflicts can only be resolved by a revolution, since the old ruling class will cling on to its power by any means. But once the revolution is complete, the new ruling class will transform society in accordance with its own mode of production and its own ideology.

This intricate mechanism of change was supposed to explain how the various stages of human development evolved into each other, although Marx only applied it consistently to the latter part of the sequence. Before there was any settled civilisation, societies were characterised, Marx believed, by a primitive communism, where all property was the property of the tribe. When people settled down and created the first civilisation proper, something of this early communal ownership was retained in village life, although the surplus was paid as tribute to a despotic state that organised great public works to irrigate or defend the land. Marx called this the 'Asiatic' mode of production, since it had persisted in Asia while other parts of the world had moved on to later stages of development. The Asiatic mode is succeeded by the 'Classical' mode, which is an economic system based on slavery. This in turn gives way to the feudal mode, which is eventually succeeded by the capitalist or bourgeois mode.

Marx paid particular attention to the transition from feudalism to capitalism. The development of the feudal economy led to a growth in trade, and with trade came towns and, eventually, a new class of merchants: the bourgeoisie. This new class in time became so rich that it could challenge the power of the old aristocratic ruling class in a series of conflicts from the English Civil Wars to the French Revolution. As the new ruling class took over, the old medieval view of the world was replaced by new ideas that were scientific and secular; new art and literature began to flourish; new ideas of liberty and constitutional government began to be advocated.

The capitalist world is not the end of the historical process. By following the dynamic of historical development to its logical conclusion, Marx believed that the transformation of the capitalist stage into one further and final stage, communism, could be predicted. It would necessarily be the final stage since it would resolve all conflicts and contradictions yet synthesise the best in all previous societies.

In the capitalist economy the workers produce all the wealth and yet remain poor, while the capitalist's wealth grows. Using the labour theory of value, borrowed from the British classical economists, Marx explained that the workers generate value by turning raw materials into finished products, but only receive a fraction of this value back in the form of wages; the rest, what Marx called 'surplus value', goes to the capitalist as profit. Because he controls the means of production, the capitalist can buy labour cheaply, paying just enough in wages for the worker to live on, while keeping most of what that labour has earned for himself. The capitalist, therefore, exploits the workers, and the more he can exploit them the more successful he will be. According to Marx, the capitalist himself adds nothing to the process of value-creation, and so the capitalist class as such is entirely parasitic.

At the same time the capitalist, unlike the feudal lord, has to compete. He must constantly strive to better his rivals by producing more goods at lower cost, by exploiting his workers more and more, to extract ever greater quantities of surplus value. This fierce competition inevitably produces winners and losers: the stronger capitalists flourish while the weaker ones go out of business. Thus, the capitalist class grows smaller and richer, while the proletariat grows larger and more wretched.

This is the natural tendency of capitalism, although the process is not smooth or continuous, but is characterised by a regular progression of boom and slump, of rapid growth and sudden collapse of industrial production. Marx explained this 'trade cycle' in terms of what he believed was the most fundamental contradiction of capitalism: the ever greater production of goods is based on ever greater exploitation of the worker, while that same exploitation reduces the workers' ability to buy the goods produced. Consequently, there is always a tendency in capitalism to overproduce, causing a downward spiral of factory closures and reductions in spending power: a slump.

Marx believed that each successive boom would develop faster and higher, and each successive slump would be deeper and more catastrophic than the last. Eventually the slump would be so great that the impoverished working class would be forced by sheer necessity to overthrow capitalism and establish a workers' state. The capitalist system cannot be reformed, but will be driven to destruction by its own nature, by the working out of its own inner logic.

It is a peculiarity of the capitalist system, Marx thought, that it must train its future destroyer. Unlike other modes of production, industrial capitalism must concentrate its workforce (in factories and workshops) and teach it discipline and mutual dependence. In these circumstances the proletariat has the opportunity to organise and achieve a common understanding of its own experience and what needs to be done; in other words, it has the opportunity to achieve what Marx called 'class-consciousness'.

The progressive enmiseration of the proletariat forces it to see its own situation clearly, undistorted by bourgeois ideology. It will see that capitalist society cannot survive, that the proletariat can and must itself take over the means of production. In short, the working class will come to realise (assisted by intellectuals like Marx and Engels who defect to the proletarian cause) that communism is the true outlook of the working class, and the only hope for the future of humanity. Thus, when the revolution does come, the workers will understand their historical task, which is not only to seize control of the means of production and the instruments of the state, but to go on to build a communist society.

Marx believed that the communist revolution would only come when capitalism had reached the full peak of its development. Consequently, he looked to see the revolution begin in the industrially advanced West, above all in Britain (although he was less certain of this towards the end of his life). But wherever it began, it would be a worldwide revolution, because one of the unique features of capitalism was its capacity – through trade and the exploitation of colonies – to bring the whole world within its network. Marx thought that nationalism was an aspect of bourgeois ideology, whereas proletarian class-consciousness was truly international: that is, workers had more in common with fellow workers in other countries than with their own bourgeoisie. When the communist revolution began in one country, therefore, it would quickly spread to others and eventually the whole world, so that the whole of humanity would be emancipated together.

However, Marx did not believe that the communist revolution would be immediately followed by the establishment of the communist society. There would have to be a transitional period, which Marx called the 'dictatorship of the proletariat', in which the workers would be in control. The state and its instruments would still be the means by which the ruling class overtly maintains its domination, only now the ruling class would be the workers, the majority. The dictatorship of the proletariat has two tasks. The first is to preserve and extend the revolution. The second is to prepare the way for the ultimate stage of human history, the establishment of the classless, stateless communist society, the kind of society appropriate for human nature.

Marx was decidedly vague about the nature of communist society and deliberately so, insisting that communist society was not some utopian blueprint that people must aspire to but the actual society that they would build as they thought best. However, some general features can be given. It will be a world without class divisions and without private property; there will be no more poverty or wealth. It will be a world without the state, at least as we have known it, since Marx sees the state as an instrument of class oppression, so that in a classless society the state will, in Engels' phrase, 'wither away'. For the same reason there will be no more ideology, no more distorted perception: people will see the world as it really is.

It will also be a world of abundance. Capitalism has taught humanity the secrets of production, and once production is designed to meet human needs and not the need for profit there will be more than enough for all. Consequently, society can be organised on the principle of 'from each according to his ability, to each according to his need'. In other words, everyone will contribute to society according to their talents and capacities, and all will take whatever they need from the common stock. In this society every individual will be able to develop all their talents – physical, intellectual and creative – to the full.

Finally, Marx did not believe that history would come to an end in a kind of static perfection, but merely that all that oppresses and distorts human nature would be thrown off. Indeed, with humanity at last becoming master of its own destiny, genuine human history could really begin.

Marx firmly believed that the collapse of capitalism and the coming of communism were inevitable, and the whole apparatus of necessary historical stages and mechanisms of change point to a thoroughly deterministic system. On the other hand, Marx also believed (in at least some of his writings) in human free will. There is a strong case for arguing that determinism and free will are incompatible. This is a matter of fierce dispute among proponents of different varieties of Marxism. But determinist or not, Marx certainly made extensive predictions about the future course of events to which the world has resolutely refused to conform. Capitalism periodically reforms itself and continues to prosper, the middle class grows and flourishes, the working class shrinks and fragments as more and more join the middle class, and revolution becomes an ever more distant prospect. The only Marxist revolutions have been in poor and predominantly agricultural nations, and in any case have mostly failed.

Nevertheless, Marx's optimistic vision of humanity's future has had huge appeal. It has inspired many versions of Marxism with many followers down to the present day. And while its plausibility has declined steadily since the middle of the twentieth century, it continues to be a major influence on social and political thought.

Further reading

Primary sources

Capital, vol. 1, ed. F. Engels (London: Lawrence & Wishart, 1970).
Early Writings, ed. L. Colletti (Harmondsworth: Penguin, 1975).
Karl Marx: Selected Writings, ed. D. McLellan (Oxford: Oxford University Press, 1977).

Secondary sources

Avineri, S.: *The Social and Political Thought of Karl Marx* (Cambridge: Cambridge University Press, 1968).
Carver, T.: *The Cambridge Companion to Marx* (Cambridge: Cambridge University Press, 1991).
Kolakowski, L.: *Main Currents of Marxism*, vol. 1 (Oxford: Oxford University Press, 1978).
McLellan, D.: *The Thought of Karl Marx* (2nd edn; Basingstoke: Macmillan, 1980).
Wheen, F.: *Karl Marx* (London: Fourth Estate, 1999).
Wood, A.: *Karl Marx* (London and New York: Routledge & Kegan Paul, 1981).

ALEXIS DE TOCQUEVILLE (1805–59)

Alexis Charles Henri de Tocqueville was born in 1805 into an old Norman aristocratic family with strong Royalist sympathies. In 1827 he followed his father into government service under the restored Bourbon monarchy. The July Revolution of 1830 placed him in a difficult position. He believed a further Bourbon Restoration impossible, yet he did not feel able to ally himself with the Orléanist monarchy. He resolved this difficulty by an extended visit to America with a friend, Gustave de Beaumont, ostensibly to study the penal system. (In 1833 he and Beaumont published a study called *On the Penal System of the United States and its Application in France.*) He resigned from government service after his return and concentrated on writing what was to be his most famous book: *Democracy in America*.

The book was published in two parts in 1835 and 1840 and translated into English and German. It established his reputation at once. In 1836 he married an Englishwoman, Mary Mottley. After the publication of the second part of *Democracy in America*, Tocqueville was elected to the Académie française. By this time, he had entered politics. In 1839 he was elected as deputy for his home district of Valogner in Normandy, and after the February Revolution of 1848 was appointed to the commission that drew up the constitution of the Second Republic. He was elected to the new Legislative Assembly in 1849 and from June to October of that year was Minister for Foreign Affairs. His political career came to an end with Louis Napoleon's *coup d'état* of 1849, to which he was strongly opposed. At this time also, his health, never robust, began to deteriorate. He concentrated once more on his writing and produced a second major work, *L'Ancien régime et la révolution* (*The Ancien Régime and the Revolution*), in 1856. This work – an analysis of the origins of revolutionary democracy in France – was to be part of a much larger work on the French Revolution, left unfinished at Tocqueville's death.

Tocqueville may best be described as a conservative liberal. He was a passionate advocate of liberty, which he deemed essential for the fulfilment of human potential, but (like many nineteenth-century liberals) saw no necessary connection between liberty and democracy. On the contrary, he regarded democracy as a potential threat to liberty. He was consequently apprehensive about where the trend towards democracy in European politics might lead. He knew that the age of aristocratic dominance was over and that democracy in some form was inevitable. This process of decline and transformation had, he believed, been in slow progress since the Middle Ages. But what, in practice, would the consequences be of the establishment of democracy as the standard form of government in Europe? His travels in America were partly undertaken for the purpose of investigating these consequences and their implications for the future of European society and politics.

America, he thinks, offers as clear a picture as possible of the kind of egalitarian, unhierarchical social order that Europe is in the process of developing. Remarkably, he predicts that the United States and Russia will one day sway the destinies of half the globe. What lessons for Europe are to be found in the American experience? There are, he believes, two dangers. One is what his contemporary John Stuart **Mill** called 'the tyranny of the majority'. Contrary to what most people think, political despotism is to be feared less than social despotism. Democracy, as he sees it, is two things (his ambiguous use of the term is sometimes confusing): it is a representative system of government based on a wide franchise; it is also the belief that society should be organised according to a principle of equality of worth or status. No one is intrinsically the superior of anyone else. The levelling effect of democracy in the second sense promotes a culture not only of social equality, but of intellectual equality also. There are no experts, and traditional sources of authority are no longer respected: anyone's opinion is as good as anyone else's. Paradoxically, this does not create a rich diversity of opinion. Rather, it creates what later political scientists would call a mass society: a society in which what is said and thought and done tends to be determined by the weight of an uncritically accepted majority opinion. What is worse, the content of that majority opinion can be controlled or manipulated by sinister interests. The possibility, then, is that democratic equality, apparently the friend of liberty, can in practice be its foe. Democratic politics tends to be dominated by public opinion; it tends, moreover, to be a homogeneous and monolithic politics in which local or regional differences are ignored in the name of equality.

A second and related danger lies in the individualistic mentality which democracy engenders. Democratic individualism is associated with economic competition. In a democracy, where there are no advantages of birth, everyone is free to succeed – or fail. Democracies induce an overriding preoccupation with, and a large degree of anxiety about, the self and one's immediate family. In practical terms, this preoccupation manifests itself in a passion for material goods and success to the exclusion of communal or social concerns. The citizens of a democracy are inclined to feel that, for as long as there is peace, good order and economic freedom, things may safely be left to the politicians. The problem, once again, is that this mentality stifles any sense of political engagement and social responsibility and fosters remote and anonymous government. Government to which ordinary people entrust themselves without thought or interest may become a new kind of despotism that undermines not only liberty but the very desire for liberty.

The great danger that democracy poses to liberty, in short, is that, because of the understanding of equality implicit in it, it tends to favour remote and centralised government and to alienate the individual from politics. If democracy is inevitably the shape of Europe's future, it is necessary to build into it mechanisms that will counteract this centralising tendency. As well as the traditional liberal 'checks and balances', Tocqueville especially favours the intentional decentralisation of power through strong local government. While in America, he was impressed by the town-meeting system which he found in New England (a system that was not, in fact, as prevalent as he supposed). Such devolved local government both educates people politically and enables them to feel involved in the making of decisions that affect them. Its importance, therefore, lies not simply in its mechanisms, but in the socialising effect that those mechanisms have on people who participate in their operation. Tocqueville's acute and original grasp of the relationship between politics and society led him to understand that political institutions have neither interest nor significance except in relation to the social attitudes to which they give rise and by which they are informed. For the same reason he favours the growth of voluntary associations: not so much for what they will be able to do, as for the sense of involvement and purpose that they create in those who belong to them.

Tocqueville called himself a 'new kind of liberal'. He was conscious of the links between society and its form of government in an age of mass politics, and aware of the dangers as well as the opportunities presented by democratic society. His criticisms of democracy are not novel; nor, incidentally, are they based on a detailed study of American life and politics. His visit to America lasted only nine months, and his argument about the enervating effect of democracy on individual initiative had been largely anticipated by **Plato**. As we have noted, his fear of the stifling effect of majority opinion foreshadowed the same fear in J.S. Mill. Tocqueville's great strengths are an acute sense of history and a vivid awareness, based on personal experience, that the domination of European politics by the old aristocracies was a thing of the past. He was also the first major political writer to see in the 'new' world of nineteenth-century America the shape of the social and political order of the future.

Further reading

Primary sources

The Ancien Régime and the French Revolution, ed. M.W. Patterson (Oxford: Blackwell, 1947).

Democracy in America, ed. G. Lawrence, J.P. Mayer and M. Lerner (2 vols; London: Fontana, 1968).

Secondary sources

Brogan, H.: *Tocqueville* (London: Fontana, 1973).

Lively, J.: *The Social and Political Thought of Alexis de Tocqueville* (Oxford: Clarendon Press, 1965).

Manent, P.: *Tocqueville and the Nature of Democracy* (Lanham, MD: Rowman & Littlefield, 1996).

JOHN STUART MILL (1806–73)

John Stuart Mill was born in 1806 in London, the eldest son of the utilitarian social theorist and economist James Mill. The story of his remarkable childhood is known from his *Autobiography* (1870), written towards the end of his life when he knew that he was suffering from consumption. Educated at home by his father, with the assistance of Jeremy **Bentham** and Francis Place, J.S. Mill began Greek when he was three, Latin when he was eight, logic at twelve and political economy at thirteen. By 1813, when he was seven, he had studied the first six dialogues of **Plato**, from *Euthyphro* to *Theaetetus*, in the original Greek. Mill saw no one of his own age until he was fourteen. He says, in a manuscript fragment omitted from the published *Autobiography*, that

> It was one of the most unfavourable of the moral agencies which acted upon me in my boyhood, that mine was not an education of love, but of fear.

James Mill's children, he adds, 'neither loved him, nor, with any warmth of affection, anyone else'. During 1821 and 1822 he studied Roman Law with the jurist John Austin and began to read the works of **Bentham** in Dumont's French edition. In 1823 he was arrested and jailed overnight for distributing literature on birth control to working-class Londoners. At the age of nineteen, working as a clerk in the East India Company and at the same time acting as Bentham's amanuensis, Mill edited Bentham's *Rationale of Judicial Evidence* in five volumes. It is not altogether surprising that these exertions culminated in a nervous breakdown. During 1826 and 1827, Mill found himself exhausted, depressed and unable to concentrate. One of the things that helped him to recover, he tells us, was reading the poetry of Wordsworth. In 1830 he met Harriet Taylor, in whom he at once recognised a soul mate. The two enjoyed an apparently blameless friendship until 1851, when – Mrs Taylor's husband having died – they married. Harriet Taylor died in 1858. Mill sat briefly (1865–8) as MP for Westminster. His journalistic and literary career, too complex to chronicle here, embraced logic, ethics, analytic psychology, economics and politics. Those of his works that are chiefly of interest to us here are his essays *On Liberty* (1859), *Utilitarianism* and *Considerations on Representative Government* (both 1861). It is convenient to consider them out of chronological order.

Utilitarianism was first published in *Fraser's Magazine* (it came out in book form in 1862). Mill's object in writing it is to rescue the utilitarianism of Bentham and James Mill from the charge brought against it by Carlyle and others, that a philosophy which so emphasises quantitative pleasure is a doctrine worthy only of swine. After a few introductory remarks, he offers the following synopsis of utilitarianism:

> The creed which accepts as the foundation of morals, Utility, or the Greatest Happiness principle, holds that actions are right in proportion as they tend to promote happiness, wrong as they tend to produce the reverse of happiness. By happiness is intended pleasure, and the absence of pain; by unhappiness is intended pain, and the privation of pleasure.
>
> (*Utilitarianism* ch.2)

Pleasure is the supreme good, in the sense that it is not a means to any end beyond itself. Pleasure is that which everyone desires in and for itself. Since, Mill thinks, it makes no sense to use the word 'desirable' except in reference to what everybody does in fact desire, pleasure is therefore the supremely desirable end. This last point is the same nominalist one that we find in Hobbes and Bentham – that 'good', and therefore 'desirable', are the names we give to what we find pleasant – but Mill's way of making the point is notoriously ham-fisted, and he was soundly trounced for it in F.H. Bradley's *Ethical Studies* (1874) and G.E. Moore's *Principia Ethica* (1903).

For Mill as for Bentham, psychological hedonism points to both an individual and a social ethic. The desire for one's own greatest happiness is the sole motive of the individual; the greatest happiness of everyone is the criterion of social good and the object of moral action. But, Mill argues, not all pleasures are equal. Pushpin is not, after all, as good as poetry. Pleasures can be ranked as superior or inferior in moral quality, with pleasures of the mind higher, and hence more desirable, than bodily pleasures. 'It is', Mill says, 'better to be a human being dissatisfied than a pig satisfied; better to be Socrates dissatisfied than a fool satisfied' (*Utilitarianism* ch.2). Any competent judge – anyone who has experienced pleasures of both kinds – will think the same; anyone who does not think the same is not a competent judge. Mill, without quite realising it, has muddied the clear waters of Benthamite utilitarianism by developing his ethics along the same lines as the 'self-realisation' of T.H. **Green**. Human beings do not achieve the good through the pursuit of pleasure pure and simple, but by achieving for themselves 'a manner of existence which employs their higher faculties' (ch.2).

Marred as it is by fallacy and circularity, Mill's attempt to rehabilitate Bentham's utilitarianism is surprisingly inept. His argument, as it stands, is no more than an undefended assertion that some pleasures, or some kinds of pleasure, are higher than others. He does not appear to notice the difficulty involved in asserting simultaneously that pleasure itself is the highest good, but that pleasures differ in quality and not in quantity only. Mill's argument is not beyond rescue from this difficulty (one might argue, in impeccably Benthamite terms, that pleasures of the mind are more fecund, of greater duration, purer and so forth than pleasures of the body), but Mill himself makes no attempt to rescue it.

The essay *On Liberty* is accepted universally as one of the classic statements of liberal individualism. It created more of a stir during Mill's lifetime than any of his other writings. Liberty, on Mill's account of it, is what would later come to be called 'negative' liberty. The only freedom worthy of the name, he thinks, is the freedom to pursue our own good in our own way, provided that we do not impede other people's efforts to do the same. No one – neither individual nor government – has the right to restrict the speech, publication or conduct of anyone for any reason other than to prevent harm to other people; and by 'harm' Mill means substantive, measurable harm. That this 'harm' principle is a good deal easier to state than it is to apply is a problem of which Mill seems oblivious. We have no right to restrain anyone from harming himself. Purely 'self-regarding' actions as distinct from 'social' actions are of no concern to anyone except the individual whose actions they are (again, Mill seems unaware of the difficulties that this distinction involves for anyone who tries to apply it). Even if one man only were to dissent from an opinion held by everyone else, this would not be a reason for silencing him. No one can know what is true and what is false unless all ideas are allowed to be freely discussed. The censor who forbids discussion claims an infallibility that no one can have. Even our most cherished beliefs become lifeless pieties unless they are allowed to compete in the marketplace for recognition. If they are true, they have nothing to fear from competition; if they are false, it is better that we know they are. More broadly, Mill is an advocate of what he calls 'experiments in living'. All members of a community should be allowed, subject to the harm principle, to develop their individuality to the full by living without interference in whatever way they like, no matter how eccentric. Once again, Mill is less of a utilitarian than he thinks he is. He believes himself to be developing an argument about utility, but it is utility of a modified kind. He says,

> I regard utility as the ultimate appeal on all ethical questions; but it must be utility in the largest sense, grounded on the permanent interests of a man as a progressive being.
>
> (*On Liberty*, Introduction)

The end implicit in what Mill writes is not pleasure or happiness pure and simple, but the pursuit of such things as truth, intellectual clarity, personal robustness and individual self-realisation. As the obverse of this, he dislikes the possibility that ignorant and intolerant public opinion might swamp minorities and individuals by weight of numbers; that excellence might be drowned in mediocrity.

> If it were felt that the free development of individuality is one of the leading essentials of well-being; that it is not only a co-ordinate element with all that is designated by the terms civilisation, instruction, education, culture, but is itself a necessary part and condition of all these things; there would be no danger that liberty should be undervalued.
>
> (*On Liberty* ch.3)

Perhaps not; but this is a far cry from 'classical' utilitarianism.

Mill's mistrust of majorities is evident also in his essay called *Considerations on Representative Government*. He holds that representative government is the best type of government, at least for a people civilised and sophisticated enough to be able to take responsibility for its own affairs. By 'representative' government he means parliamentary government, with the executive chosen from and answerable to a representative assembly in turn chosen by and answerable to the people. Mill believes that, with a few specified exceptions – the illiterate, the criminal and those incapable of supporting themselves – every adult person, male or female, should have at least one vote. It is as irrational to exclude women from the vote as it would be to exclude some men because they have red hair. (Mill's essay on *The Subjection of Women*, written in 1869 in collaboration with his stepdaughter Helen Taylor, is an early plea for female suffrage.) Representative government is best, he thinks, because it encourages critical reflection, responsibility and participation by the ordinary citizen. 'Despotic' government, on the other hand, makes those subject to it apathetic and passive. Representative government tends to create self-reliant, alert, tough-minded individuals, and a community with such people in it is bound to be one in which order, progress and stability flourish. But representative government is also liable to infirmities and dangers. What Mill fears most is the tyranny of the majority. If government depends on the will of a mere numerical majority, mediocrity and ignorance will inevitably triumph over cultivation and enlightenment. It is also inevitable that governments will prefer policies that please the majority, whatever intrinsic merits or demerits those policies have. Mill insists, therefore, that political enfranchisement must go hand in hand with political education. It would be absurd to have a fully enfranchised electorate whose members are too ignorant to cast their vote responsibly. He believes also that there should be a system of plural voting related to educational attainment, and a scheme of public examinations for which individuals might enter in order to demonstrate that they deserve extra votes. Also, he is an early – though not the first – advocate of proportional representation as a means of securing the effective representation of minorities. The complex system which he favours was devised by a London lawyer named Thomas Hare and described by him in 1859 in a book called *A Treatise on the Election of Representatives, Parliamentary and Municipal.*

It is a testimony to his mental constitution that, after the childhood described in his *Autobiography*, the adult Mill was able to function intellectually at all. He is a complex character, educated, as he acknowledges, by methods that crippled him emotionally, yet imbued with a number of intense, abstract and not always consistent passions. He can never quite bring himself to forsake utilitarianism; nor, however, can he resist reinventing it in a way that makes 'pleasure' mean the kind of activities of which Mill approves. Mill praises unrestricted liberty, but he takes it for granted that unrestricted liberty will produce outcomes that he values rather than indiscipline and chaos. He applauds representative government and the morally invigorating effect that he supposes it would have on ordinary citizens, but he wishes to arrange matters so as to ensure the continued influence of an intellectual and moral elite. Mill's elegant prose sometimes conceals incoherence and shallowness of thought, and he was throughout his life the victim of his own excessively doctrinaire and pedantic education; but he is one of a numerous company of writers – fellow members are John **Rawls** and Robert

Nozick – whose contribution to political thought lies as much as anything in the debate and reflection that their works have tended to promote.

Further reading

Primary sources

The Collected Works of John Stuart Mill, ed. F.E.L. Priestley (London: Routledge & Kegan Paul, 1963–84).

Autobiography, ed. J. Stillinger (Oxford: Oxford University Press, 1971).

Secondary sources

Gray, J.: *Mill on Liberty: a Defence* (London: Routledge & Kegan Paul, 1983).

Halliday, R.J.: *John Stuart Mill* (London: Allen & Unwin, 1976).

Hampsher-Monk, I.: *A History of Modern Political Thought* (Oxford: Blackwell, 1992).

Robson, J.M.: *The Improvement of Mankind: The Social and Political Thought of J.S. Mill* (Toronto, Ont.: University of Toronto Press, 1968).

Ryan, A.: *J.S. Mill* (London: Routledge & Kegan Paul, 1974).

HERBERT SPENCER (1820–1903)

Herbert Spencer was born in Derby, the son of a dissenting schoolmaster. He was the only one of nine children to survive into adulthood. He was educated at home by his father, with the assistance of his uncle, Reverend Thomas Spencer. In superficial respects, his early life resembles that of John Stuart **Mill**, though Spencer's education was predominantly mathematical and technical. He toyed with the idea of Cambridge, but financial and religious difficulties supervened (these were days when no one could take a degree at Oxford or Cambridge without being a member of the Anglican Church). Between 1837 and 1848, Spencer was a railway engineer, working first for the London and Birmingham and then for the Birmingham and Gloucester railway companies. Between 1848 and 1853, he worked as a journalist, contributing in particular to the *Westminster Review* (a liberal and radical journal edited by the novelist George Eliot) and serving as assistant editor of *The Economist*. In 1853 his uncle Thomas died and left him a substantial sum, which enabled him to devote himself without distraction to a literary career. Spencer was an ambitious and prolific author. Even his autobiography runs to two volumes and some 400,000 words. In the early 1850s he conceived the remarkable idea of synthesising the whole of biology, sociology, psychology, ethics and politics into an integrated whole. This *System of Synthetic Philosophy* was published in ten volumes over a period of thirty years. From our point of view, his chief works are *Social Statics* (1850), *The Man versus the State* (1884) and *The Principles of Ethics* (1892–3). He seems to have been prone to bouts of depression, and in his later years became embroiled in a number of acrimonious controversies that undermined his failing health.

The founding principle of Spencer's philosophy, considered both generally and with regard to his political and social doctrines, is the idea of evolution: the 'principle of continuity', as he called it. The presence of fossil remains in railway cuttings first stimulated his interest in evolution. It was he and not Darwin who coined the phrase 'the survival of the fittest'. Spencer was resistant to Darwin's idea of natural selection, preferring instead the Lamarckian hypothesis that organisms acquire from their environment adaptive characteristics that are then inherited by successive generations. It is, Spencer believes, the nature of all organisms to move from a condition of homogeneity or simplicity towards heterogeneity and complexity. This movement is characteristic of nature as a whole, and societies evolve in this way as well as individuals. Social evolution is a process of development from homogenous primitive societies to complex heterogeneous ones exhibiting an increasingly complex differentiation of functions. Societies, Spencer believes, have a natural tendency to evolve from monarchical and military to industrial and co-operative forms of organisation. But societies, though in a certain sense 'organisms', are nothing more than collections of individuals seeking happiness – that is, seeking to achieve a surplus of pleasure over pain (Spencer is in this respect a utilitarian) – and co-operating with one another in order to do so. Individuals begin to co-operate in order to avoid the threat of violence and war. As they become increasingly aware of the benefits of co-operation, so also do they become aware of the individuality of others. This awareness, augmented by the natural sympathy that Spencer thinks human beings feel for one another, leads them to recognise a fundamental law (although Spencer is not wholly clear about whether it is a moral law or a maxim of prudence or a descriptive natural law) called the 'law of equal freedom'. This law states that every man has freedom to do whatever he likes, provided he does not infringe the equal freedom of anyone else to do the same. It will be noticed that, in so far as it purports to describe the development of human associations, Spencer's evolutionary theory also functions as a philosophy of history. Societies advance from militarism to industry, from primitive to advanced, from barbarism to civilisation.

The development of each individual according to the law of equal freedom will lead eventually to the complete adaptation of the human organism to its environment and hence to the happiness of all. History is progress; but because the evolutionary process is a natural one, we must not interfere with it or try to control it. Anything that artificially restricts the exercise of human freedom will necessarily impede human development. What this implies, as far as politics is concerned, is a minimal or negative state. What it implies for economics is the doctrine of *laissez-faire.* Governments should perform only the functions of protection and defence and leave the individual with the greatest possible freedom to act without interference or control. The liberty of individuals is, Spencer thinks, to be measured not by the nature of the government machinery they live under, but by the degree of restraint that it imposes on them. Anyone whose freedom is infringed by government action has a right to ignore the state. Since law is inevitably a curtailment of individuals' freedom to do all that they wish, there should be as little of it as possible. Eventually a state will be reached at which legislation will not be necessary at all, thanks to the full realisation of human capacities for co-operation and creativity. Meanwhile, to support the unemployed is to encourage idleness; education, economic regulation and the care of the sick and needy are not to be undertaken by the state; there should be no state regulation of industry, even in respect of such things as sanitary regulation and the introduction of safety devices into factories. Nothing must be done to protect the incompetent and idle from the consequences of incompetence and idleness. The industrious and successful will get what they deserve by their own efforts; the weakest must go to the wall, as is nature's way.

In the early part of his career Spencer was an advocate of land nationalisation and a universal franchise, but he abandoned these doctrines as impractical in later years, as youthful radicalism gave place to an increasingly morose and pessimistic conservatism. His 'social Darwinism', with its seemingly abhorrent implications, was one of the main stimuli of the late-nineteenth century 'new' liberalism of which T.H. **Green** is the most notable exponent.

In his day, Spencer was an enormously popular author in England, Europe and America. He was well regarded by a number of people whose opinions deserve respect, including Darwin himself, George Eliot, Thomas Carlyle and T.H. Huxley. But it is hardly to be denied that his ambitious philosophical schemes are full of inconsistencies and sometimes quite elementary mistakes. His synthetic philosophy is not unjustly described as the product of general knowledge and over-confidence. Born in newly industrialising Derby and trained in technology, he has tended to be seen as a child of the Industrial Revolution, whose project is to give theoretical respectability to the unrestricted exploitation of the weak by the 'industrious'. (It is mildly ironic that his ashes lie buried in Highgate Cemetery immediately opposite the grave of Karl **Marx**.) This may or may not be fair; but it is certainly true that we have lost the taste for, and abandoned faith in, gigantic syntheses of the kind that Spencer relished. Some exponents of libertarian or 'New Right' ideas – especially Robert **Nozick** – have thought well of him. On the whole, however, Spencer is an eminent Victorian whose work, though of historical interest, has fallen out of fashion.

Further reading

Primary sources

Social Statics (London: Routledge & Kegan Paul, 1954).
The Man versus the State, ed. E. Mack and A.J. Nock (Indianapolis, IN: Liberty Classics, 1981).
The Principles of Ethics, ed. T. Machan (Indianapolis, IN: Liberty Classics, 1982).

Secondary sources

Peel, J.D.Y.: *Herbert Spencer* (London: Heinemann, 1971).
Wiltshire, D.: *The Social and Political Thought of Herbert Spencer* (Oxford: Oxford University Press, 1978).

T.H. GREEN (1836–82)

Thomas Hill Green was born in Birkin, Yorkshire, where his father was rector. The family was descended, or so Green believed, from Oliver Cromwell. His main philosophical influences are Kant and Hegel, though his religious upbringing and beliefs were important factors in his intellectual development. Educated at Oxford, he became a fellow of Balliol College in 1860 and Professor of Moral Philosophy in 1878. He was the first Oxford don to serve on the city council. Important aspects of his philosophy were expounded in a long introduction (1874) to **Hume**'s *Treatise of Human Nature.* Most of Green's writings were published posthumously. *Lectures on the Principles of Political Obligation*, reconstructed from his notes and those of his students, appeared in 1882 and *Prolegomena to Ethics* in 1883. Also important is his 'Lecture on Liberal Legislation and Freedom of

Contract', occasioned by Gladstone's proposal to regulate contracts between landlords and tenants in Ireland.

Green's political views are best understood as a response to the main currents of social and political thought in his day: 'classical' liberalism, social Darwinism (as advocated by Herbert **Spencer**) and utilitarianism. He repudiated the idea that civil society can be conceived as a collection of self-interested atoms dedicated to the pursuit of happiness or pleasure. It is, he thinks, factually false to suggest that we find our satisfaction purely as individuals in the pursuit of private versions of the good life. The relation between individual and society is complex; the individual cannot be abstracted from the group. 'Without society, no persons; this is as true as that without persons ... there could be no such society as we know' (*Prolegomena to Ethics* 288). The sentiment is as much Aristotelian as Hegelian: man is by nature a social creature. 'The self', Green insists, 'is a social self' (ibid.). We achieve happiness and fulfilment as part of a community, and an adequate theory of citizenship has to be a theory of membership rather than of mere contractual association.

Despite its idealist inspiration, Green's apparent 'organicism' does not entail the submergence of the individual in the group. Green does not believe, as **Hegel** does, that the community is coterminous with the state. He does, however, insist that each individual is a social being whose happiness cannot be separated from that of the community of which he is a member. The basis of society is the mutual recognition by its members that all of them are ends in themselves. If – as, after all, classical liberalism itself postulates – men are moral equals, it does not make sense to suppose that there can be justice in a community that extends the right to happiness and fulfilment to some of its members while withholding it from others. Individual goods cannot claim precedence over – cannot, indeed, strictly speaking exist apart from – the good of the community. Every individual finds his own good in contributing to the common good. An implication of this is that individual rights are not, after all, sacred and indefeasible in the way that traditional liberal political theory insists. Individual rights – that is, individual claims to freedom of action – are in reality social rights: they are justified only if the community within which they are claimed acknowledges that they contribute to, or do not militate against, the common good. In claiming rights, we have also to recognise obligations to a good greater than our own.

Green does not dissent from the liberal conviction that the chief purpose of government is to maximise freedom. He agrees also that the maximisation of freedom is the minimisation of constraint. But, he contends, constraint must be construed more broadly than the mere physical restraint or coercion of one individual by another. Freedom is not simply 'negative' freedom in the sense later to be made famous by Sir Isaiah **Berlin**. Green also denies that freedom consists in the pursuit of undifferentiated pleasure. Anyone who lives in this way may appear free, but is really at the mercy of his own inclinations and desires; and to be at the mercy of anything is a kind of bondage. Freedom properly understood is rational freedom. Someone has it in so far as he seeks 'the satisfaction of himself in objects in which it should be found, and [seeks] it in them because it should be found in them' (*Principles of Political Obligation*, p.2). Green goes on to say that freedom in this 'positive' sense consists in 'the liberation of the powers of all men equally for contributions to a common good'. We are truly free, it seems, when and only when intentionally making as full a contribution as we can to the common good. In this way, we actualise or realise our own potentialities as social and moral beings. Freedom is self-realisation, and whatever stands in the way of self-realisation is a constraint in the required sense: it is a curtailment of freedom.

Green's positive understanding of freedom is at odds with the liberal-utilitarian view of law and legislation. The latter view, predicated on the negative conception of liberty and exemplified in the thought of Jeremy **Bentham**, is that, since law curtails one's freedom to do as one likes, it is a necessary evil and there should be as little of it as possible. Such a conception of law is, Green thinks, subversive of the very objectives that government should seek to promote. It 'affords a reason for resisting all positive reforms ... which involve an action of the state ... promoting conditions favourable to moral life' (*Works* II, p.345). When freedom is understood positively, he holds, it will follow that the law should seek not merely to remove obstacles to individual freedom of action, but to provide means of and opportunities for self-realisation to those who otherwise would not have them. Law cannot make people good, but it can enable them to make themselves good. Legislatures should take a positive role in the life of the community. They should, for instance, provide education and public health facilities. Without education, he observes, the individual in modern society is, in effect, as much crippled as he would be by the loss of a limb. Legislatures should also control the consumption of alcohol: Green was a keen advocate of temperance reform. Where necessary, the law should even interfere with that most sacred of liberal values, freedom of contract. In his 'Lecture on Liberal Legislation and Freedom of Contract', Green emphasises that serious infringements of liberty can in fact occur under the guise of freedom of contract. Here, he hit upon what is undoubtedly the central moral weakness of the negative definition of liberty. An Irish tenant farmer whose alternative to entering into a tenancy agreement with his landlord is starvation for himself and his family is, he pointed out, a free contractor only in the most empty and formal sense.

Green offered what one might call a humanised revision of liberalism in place of the nineteenth-century Gradgrind-and-Bounderby orthodoxies of *laissez-faire*; orthodoxies that were, in fact, beginning to wear thin well before Green's literary career began. Green emphasises that the identity and happiness of individuals is inseparable from the social whole, and that individual good cannot be considered as separate from the common good. He believes that freedom is not merely freedom from constraint, but freedom *to* be the best that one can be. He insists, although without going into great detail, that government should seek actively to promote the common good, and that where necessary it should do so by providing the means of self-realisation for those who lack them. Despite his philosophical idealism, Green remains a liberal in the sense that the freedom of the individual is his key political value. But his reappraisal of how we are to understand the individual and the individual's freedom identify him as a liberal in whose thought liberalism has begun to look forward to the idea of a socially responsible welfare state. Green's published output is very small, thanks to his early death, but his contribution to political thought is measurable also in the work of those who regarded themselves as his disciples: notably Bernard Bosanquet (1848–1923), L.T. Hobhouse (1864–1929) and J.A. Hobson (1858–1940).

Further reading

Primary sources

The Works of Thomas Hill Green, ed. R.L. Nettleship (5 vols; London: Longmans, Green & Co., 1885–8).

Lectures on the Principles of Political Obligation, reconstructed by his first editor R.L. Nettleship (London: Longmans, Green & Co., 1941).

Secondary sources

Milne, A.J.M.: *The Social Philosophy of English Idealism* (London: Allen & Unwin, 1962).

Nicholson, P.: *The Political Philosophy of the British Idealists* (Cambridge: Cambridge University Press, 1989).

Richter, M.: *The Politics of Conscience: T.H. Green and His Age* (Lanham, MD: University Press of America, 1983).

FRIEDRICH NIETZSCHE (1844–1900)

Nietzsche was born near Leipzig in 1844, the son of a Lutheran pastor. His father died when he was a child and he was brought up by his mother, sister and aunts. At school and at university he was a precocious and brilliant classical scholar, and this led to his appointment as Professor of Classical Philology at the University of Basel at the unprecedentedly young age of twenty-four.

His first book, *The Birth of Tragedy* (1872), was something of a shock to the academic community. It was not the expected scholarly treatise based on close argument and detailed evidence, but a work of sweeping generalisations about the course and the future of Western civilisation, written in vivid and unorthodox prose. Consequently, the book was severely criticised; but Nietzsche continued to write in this way for the rest of his career. In 1879 he retired from his professorship on grounds of ill-health and for the next ten years Nietzsche lived as a semi-invalid in various parts of Switzerland, France and Italy, during which time he wrote his most famous works. In 1889, at the age of forty-five, he became insane. He was brought back to Germany, where his mother and sister, Elizabeth Föster-Nietzsche, nursed him until his death in 1900.

It was about the time he sank into madness that his reputation as a philosopher began to grow. Works such as *The Gay Science* (1882), *Thus Spake Zarathustra* (1883–5), *Beyond Good and Evil* (1886) and *On the Genealogy of Morals* (1887) were increasingly recognised for their insight and intellectual power. However, his most notorious work, *The Will to Power* (published in several different versions beginning in 1901), was only put together from miscellaneous notes after his death. It is a highly unrepresentative and misleading selection that needs to be treated with caution. This was the responsibility of Elizabeth Föster-Nietzsche, who was a fervent racist and nationalist. She became a devoted follower of Hitler and sedulously promoted her brother's work as anticipating Nazi ideology. But while parts of Nietzsche's thought appear to chime with some aspects of fascist elitism and authoritarianism, Nietzsche was in fact strongly opposed to both racism and nationalism. Nevertheless, the association with Nazism clouded Nietzsche's reputation for many years after World War II. In fact Nietzsche has influenced thinkers across the political spectrum. His most recent and in some ways most direct influence has been upon the post-structuralists and postmodernists of the late twentieth century.

The Birth of Tragedy was a response to Schopenhauer's philosophy, which Nietzsche read as a student. He embraced Schopenhauer's vision of the sheer tragic awfulness of the human condition, and Schopenhauer's belief that we can gain some fleeting relief through art, which alone puts us in touch with the true nature of reality. But Nietzsche rejects Schopenhauer's Buddhist-like subjection of the will and renunciation of the world as the only means to genuine peace of mind. He looked to Ancient Greece for an alternative answer.

Nietzsche portrays Greek civilisation in *The Birth of Tragedy* as reaching a pinnacle of achievement *before* Socrates and the great age of Greek philosophy. The greatness of that civilisation lay in its art, above all tragedy. All art arose, he argued, from one of two conflicting principles, which he personified as two Greek gods: Apollo, representing beauty, order, clarity, reason and individualism; and Dionysus, representing sensuality and intoxication, the instinctual, the irrational and individual submergence in the group. Nietzsche argued that the Greeks achieved a perfect balance between these principles in their mythic drama, which enabled them to witness the true meaningless horror of human existence and yet nevertheless affirm life and live it to the full.

This genuine insight, as Nietzsche sees it, into the true nature of the human condition was undermined by the subsequent Socratic philosophy (by which Nietzsche always meant Socratic/Platonic philosophy – see **Plato**) and later by Christianity. This undermining ultimately led to what Nietzsche believed to be a crisis of contemporary civilisation, which he saw as reliant upon values that were no longer viable and as therefore trivial, empty and decadent. The philosophy of Socrates and his successors, with their promise of the power of reason to unravel every mystery and provide true values to live by, was the ruination of Greek tragedy and decisively tilted Western culture in favour of the Apollonian at the expense of the Dionysian. The facile optimism of their philosophy has proved false and civilisation is thus in crisis, having sunk into decadence and nihilism. Nietzsche's answer to this crisis – the revival of the arts led by Wagner's operas (also myth-based and combining the Apollonian and the Dionysian) – was soon abandoned, but he retained much of the analysis of civilisation in crisis. In later works he elaborated the nature of the crisis and offered new solutions.

Western civilisation is in crisis because the sources of values in Western society are failing. These are reason and religion, both of which, Nietzsche thinks, are inadequate sources of value. Since Socrates, Western culture had been seduced by the comforting but entirely erroneous belief that reason can provide the right values – values that will lead to harmony, happiness and fulfilment for all. The reality of life was conflict, suffering and a constant striving for power. Nietzsche saw the will to power as all-pervasive, characterising all that exists, but not (as with Schopenhauer) inherently evil. Although responsible for evil, it was also responsible for all that human beings strive for, including culture and philosophy. Nietzsche systematically interpreted human feelings, such as pity, gratitude and self-sacrifice in terms of stratagems for increasing power. All religions and systems of morality are interpreted in the same way.

The major source of Western values was Christianity, which Nietzsche attacks from two different directions: its morality and its metaphysics. He divided moral systems into two kinds: master moralities and slave moralities. Christianity had overthrown the aristocratic warrior-oriented master morality of the Classical world with one that arose among the lower orders. The master morality revelled in its superiority and despised what it deemed base, while the Christian morality was based upon resentment. It too aspired to dominate, but in a more subtle way, by shackling the superior and insisting that all were of equal worth. For all its emphasis on humility and goodness, it was as much an expression of the will to power as its aristocratic rival. It promoted the values of the lower orders – humility, subservience and pity – and condemned aristocratic pride as a cardinal sin. Ideologies derived from Christianity, including liberalism and socialism, are also based upon equality and pity and are equally contemptible. They are herd moralities based upon the resentment of the mass for their superiors. Furthermore, Nietzsche condemned Christianity as life-denying instead of being life-affirming (like Ancient Greek religion), although this aspect was attributed to St Paul rather than to Christ himself.

However, one of the side-effects of Christianity has been to instil in the Western mind a love of truth; one consequence of this has been the growth of science, which in turn has undermined the concept of God, belief in whom, Nietzsche insists, is no longer tenable. Not only does that take away the underlying metaphysics of Christianity, but all metaphysics and all meaning. Among other things, the concept of God underpinned the very notions of objectivity and truth, since it seemed to guarantee that in the last analysis there was a single unified universal point of view. Without God we have to recognise that there are multiple points of view, with none better than any others. This 'perspectivism' is a version of relativism and has the same limitations of self-reference (why is the claim that all truth is relative not itself only relatively true?), which Nietzsche never resolved. Nevertheless, Nietzsche sweeps away all foundations of knowledge and morality, including the unified self.

Nietzsche attacks the whole tradition of Western metaphysics as (anticipating Wittgenstein) largely based on verbal errors, where the nature of language seduces us into making unwarranted metaphysical assumptions. There is no evidence, he insists, for any metaphysical realm beyond the experience of the senses. At the same time, Western faith in science as the road to truth is also misplaced. There is no such thing as absolute objective truth; there are only interpretations. What is true is merely what is useful; that is, Nietzsche has a pragmatic view of truth. Science is a human construct that is useful without being true in any absolute sense. Nietzsche is prepared to say this of his own doctrines, although he is not consistent in this.

Nietzsche believed that, with the death of God, civilisation was in crisis and needed to be refounded on a new basis. Unless we are weak and self-deceiving (as most of us are) we must again learn to stare into the Dionysian abyss of the horror and meaninglessness of life and, like the Greeks, have the courage to live it vigorously nonetheless. In *Thus Spake Zarathustra*, his most famous but not his best book, Nietzsche insists that those capable of doing this are the men of the future. These are the minority who consist of what Nietzsche calls *Übermensch*, traditionally translated (rather melodramatically and absurdly) as 'supermen'. They alone are capable of creativity, of generating their own values unrestrained by conventional morality. This does not mean they all go round brutalising everyone: their greatest achievement will in fact be culture rather than conquest. Nevertheless, Nietzsche believes that these 'supermen' will be as distant from the present humanity as present humanity is from the animals, which is somewhat unconvincing.

After *Zarathustra* the 'superman' is not mentioned again. Some kind of higher being is still Nietzsche's ideal, but something a little less apocalyptic and exemplified in actual human beings such as Napoleon or Goethe. Even so, it is difficult to see what the role of these higher beings would be, since Nietzsche gives us little sense of how society should be organised. All we can say is that he believed they should be untrammelled by laws and customs and that they should 'transvalue values', thereby creating a new morality for a new age. But while the life of the superior specimens of humanity is not too clear, Nietzsche is perfectly clear that unless they can arise and flourish humanity is doomed. But doomed to what? Perhaps Nietzsche's view is best seen in his account in *Zarathustra* of the 'Last Man'. The Last Man is the herd-man, who wants only to be like everyone else, to be comfortable and happy and no more. It is an outlook that Nietzsche clearly feels could prevail but can only lead to mediocrity and nihilism and the denial of all that is best in human potential.

What then of politics in the narrow sense of policies and political organisation? Shortly before his final mental collapse Nietzsche admitted that he had unduly neglected politics, an omission he did not have the opportunity to rectify. However, there is much, both negative and positive, that can be inferred from his writings. Clearly for Nietzsche politics is not about progress or social justice or extending freedom or equality or human rights, these are the self-deluding ideals of democratic slave moralities. His ideals are aristocratic. Politics is about creating the conditions for human greatness. It is that greatness that alone can justify our awful existence. It would seem that (as in the Greek city-state) the mass of humanity is there to serve these higher beings. But of laws or institutional arrangements Nietzsche gives no account.

All this may seem absurd, but Nietzsche's value does not lie in specific prescriptions. It lies instead in the challenges he offers to our conventional ways of thinking, and the brilliance and insight he brought to some of our deeper problems. As such he has been widely influential among thinkers and writers of all kinds and across the political spectrum, from socialists to fascists to liberals to anarchists and even (despite his misogyny) to feminists. He has been particularly influential in recent decades among post-structuralists and postmodernists, having been the first to develop many of their themes. Perhaps the most basic and profound of these concern his reasoned rejection of any metaphysical foundations for our knowledge, beliefs and values. How we can know and live and act and create without such foundations is a problem that many struggle with today.

Further reading

Primary sources

The Will to Power, ed. W. Kaufmann (New York: Vintage Books, 1968).
Thus Spoke Zarathustra, ed. R.J. Hollingdale (Harmondsworth: Penguin, 1969).

The Gay Science, ed. W. Kaufmann (New York: Vintage, 1974).
The Birth of Tragedy, ed. R.J. Hollingdale (Harmondsworth: Penguin, 1993).
On the Genealogy of Morality, ed. K. Ansell-Pearson (Cambridge: Cambridge University Press, 1994).

Secondary sources

Ansell-Pearson, K.: *An Introduction to Nietzsche as a Political Thinker* (Cambridge: Cambridge University Press, 1994).
Bergmann, P.: *Nietzsche: The Last Antipolitical German* (Bloomington, IN: Indiana University Press, 1987).
Detwiler, B.: *Nietzsche and the Politics of Aristocratic Radicalism* (Chicago, IL: University of Chicago Press, 1990).
Higgins, K. and Magnus, B. (eds): *The Cambridge Companion to Nietzsche* (Cambridge: Cambridge University Press, 1996).
Thiele, L.P.: *Friedrich Nietzsche and the Politics of the Soul: A Study of Heroic Individualism* (Princeton, NJ: Princeton University Press, 1990).

PRINCE PETER KROPOTKIN (1842–1921) AND ANARCHISM

Prince Peter Kropotkin was born into a Russian noble family in Moscow in 1842. He was educated at the elite military academy in St Petersburg, and had the honour of becoming *page de chambre* to the Tsar. After graduating as top student, Kropotkin unexpectedly chose to join an unfashionable regiment in Siberia. There he was able to become involved in local reform and lead scientifically important explorations of eastern Russia and parts of China. His work on the structure of the mountains of northern Asia gained him an international reputation as a physical geographer. He also read widely in history and politics. After five years he resigned his commission and returned to St Petersburg to continue his education and his scientific work.

Already strongly influenced by anarchist ideas, in 1872 Kropotkin visited Switzerland and the French region of the Jura, then a hotbed of anarchist sympathy and activity. There he completed his conversion to anarchism. On his return he became involved in the revolutionary politics of the Populist movement, which believed in the transformation of Russia into a socialist society based on the traditional Russian peasant commune rather than on the Western model of industrialisation and a revolutionary proletariat. Kropotkin was imprisoned for his revolutionary activities, but after a spectacular escape in 1876 spent the next forty years in exile in Western Europe.

Initially Kropotkin continued his career as a political activist and writer in Switzerland and the Jura. But after expulsion by the Swiss and imprisonment by the French (1883–6) he settled in London to become the anarchist movement's leading theorist and publicist. Only at the end of his life, in 1917, did he return to Russia, but he was soon disillusioned with the new regime. His funeral in 1921 was attended by 20,000 anarchists, the last public demonstration of anarchist sympathies in the Soviet Union.

Kropotkin's anarchism grew out of two sources. The first was his Russian experience, particularly in Siberia among ordinary Russians capable of organising themselves far from the remote centres of power. The second was his reading of the major social anarchists, Proudhon and Bakunin.

The anarchist tradition in Western political thought is only as old as the French Revolution. The first anarchist thinker was William **Godwin**, who thought of society in terms of a collection of individuals in need of complete freedom to allow their natural rationality to flourish. The first exponent of a more social version of anarchism was the Frenchman Pierre-Joseph Proudhon (1809–65). His vision, despite his famous declaration that property was theft, was of a pre-industrial world of independent farmers and craftsmen, owning their own businesses and associating in local communities, which then federate together for mutual benefit, without the need for any higher political authority. A more integrated and thorough-going conception of communist anarchism was developed by Michael Bakunin (1814–76), who was primarily a full-time revolutionary. As a theorist he was rather spasmodic and inconsistent, and never developed a firm foundation for his thought. His vision of what an anarcho-communist society would be like is rather sketchy. All private property would be abolished and social life would be in communes that could associate together. He insisted that everyone must be educated and must work, implying a rather authoritarian element in a society supposedly devoted to absolute freedom.

Kropotkin was influenced by both of these thinkers and sought to build on their achievement. In particular he attempted to give a more systematic account of anarchist society than his predecessors and to place anarchism on more secure rational foundations. Kropotkin was a prolific writer, producing a multitude of books, articles and other materials on anarchist ideas. The fullest account of his vision of an anarchist society is to be found in *The Conquest of Bread* (1892), supplemented by *Fields, Factories and Workshops* (1899). His attempt to place anarchism on solid scientific foundations is to be found in his most famous book: *Mutual Aid* (1902).

Although he personally abhorred violence, Kropotkin thought that a violent revolution was necessary to usher in an anarchist world. Only a general uprising of the people could create the situation where the state could be abolished immediately and federations of self-governing communes take its place. Anarchists would lead and persuade but not take power. Like Proudhon and Bakunin, Kropotkin would have no truck with elite parties in possession of the truth.

The communities and productive associations that Kropotkin believed would spontaneously arise when people's natural sociability was released from the constraints imposed by the state would be completely voluntary and self-governing, and entirely without means of coercion. People would opt, he thought, to dispense with private property and to work without incentives, such as differential rewards: a system of 'free communism' he sometimes called it. The economy would be neither free-market nor planned. Kropotkin envisaged a decentralised and largely self-sufficient regional and local economy.

All would be equal, would work when they wished and take whatever they needed from the common store. There would be little or no crime because, with no more private property or exploitation, its causes would have been eliminated. But if there were those who committed criminal acts then they should be counselled rather than punished. For those who were lazy and would not work, Kropotkin admitted that a degree of social pressure through public opinion would be acceptable, but not coercion. He thought that most would in fact want to work and contribute to the well-being of themselves and others. This may sound naïve, but, Kropotkin argued, we would be foolish to simply assume that people would behave the same way as they did under capitalism.

If properly shared, work would only take up four or five hours per day. The rest of the time people would be free to develop themselves, for which purpose a multitude of associations would spring up, devoted to science or literature or any number of things people are interested in. People would thus have full scope to develop their individuality.

Much of Kropotkin's theoretical energy was devoted to giving anarchism a secure rational foundation, and as a scientist of some distinction his intention was to ground anarchist ideas in scientific observation and theory. The scientific theory here is Darwinian evolution. As with Herbert **Spencer** and other social Darwinists, Kropotkin sought to derive from biological science a sociology that would indicate a form of society that corresponded to basic human nature. In *Mutual Aid* (1902), he claimed to refute the contention that since competition was the 'way of nature', as evolutionary theory seemed to suggest, a competitive free-market society was in some sense 'natural' and desirable. Instead he sought to demonstrate, with a wide range of examples, that co-operation and social solidarity were more important than competition in the evolution of both animals and humans. Future evolution and therefore progress would be the result of greater co-operation, facilitated by the removal of the huge obstacles of capitalism and the state, thereby releasing humanity's natural sociability.

How far Kropotkin was successful in putting anarchism on a scientific footing is open to some doubt. Certainly he assembles empirical evidence that small traditional communities can flourish without central control, but he has little evidence for anything larger. As to founding a sociology on evolution, he cannot prove that co-operation must prevail over competition, or that one is more 'natural' than the other. Even if he could, he cannot say that co-operation is morally superior to competition. His last work, *Ethics*, which was unfinished at his death, was a systematic attempt to derive an ethics from biology. But the attempt involves the well-known fallacy that from fact alone we can deduce what is the morally right thing to do, and is a failure. In the end, belief that a society based on mutual aid is the optimum society in which human beings can flourish is not something that can be proven.

Kropotkin was the major theoretical figure in anarchism's heyday in the late nineteenth century and his anarchist vision became the predominant one, only rivalled by the later development of anarcho-syndicalism based on trade unionism (see **Georges Sorel**). Anarchism, in these two forms, was a serious rival to socialism for the allegiance of the European working class up to World War I. Thereafter it went into serious decline as a mass movement, although there have always been anarchist groups, normally taking their vision of an anarchist future from Kropotkin. There was something of a revival of anarchist ideas in the New Left movement of the 1960s. Today, anarchism is particularly associated with the green movement and as part of the general anti-globalisation movement. Some see it as peculiarly fitted to a postmodern age, but anarchism remains very much a minority view, and a peripheral but useful challenge to prevailing ideas.

Further reading

Primary sources

Mutual Aid (Harmondsworth: Penguin, 1939).
The Conquest of Bread and Other Writings, ed. Marshall Shatz (Cambridge: Cambridge University Press, 1995).

Secondary sources

Avrich, P.: *The Russian Anarchists* (Princeton, NJ: Princeton University Press, 1967).
Cahm, C.: *Kropotkin and the Rise of Revolutionary Anarchism 1872–1886* (Cambridge: Cambridge University Press, 1989).
Marshall, P.: *Demanding the Impossible: A History of Anarchism* (London: Fontana Press, 1993).
Miller, D.: *Anarchism* (London: Dent, 1984).
Miller, M.A.: *Kropotkin* (Chicago, IL: Chicago University Press, 1976).

GEORGES SOREL (1847–1922)

Georges Sorel was born in Cherbourg in 1847 and trained as an engineer. His contributions to theory began relatively late in life, publishing his first article at the age of thirty-nine. Six years later a small inheritance enabled him to retire from his profession as a road engineer to devote himself to study and writing. He wrote on philosophy, politics, economics and social theory, all areas in which he was largely self-taught. Sorel's best-known works, *Reflections on Violence* and *The Illusions of Progress*, were both published in 1908. Although possessed of insight and considerable originality, Sorel was both intellectually and politically restless. He detested bourgeois politics and culture, and mostly saw himself on the political left. Around the time of his retirement in 1892 he became a somewhat unorthodox Marxist, but then shifted his allegiance to anarchism at the beginning of the new century. In the years before World War I, Sorel associated with figures on the anti-parliamentary far right, before switching again when the Russian Revolution seemed to offer (falsely as it turned out) the prospect of power for genuine worker councils of which he approved. He never joined any political party, believing them all dominated by middle-class intellectuals, a group he particularly loathed. He is impossible to classify in conventional terms, and probably his most important influence was on the development of fascism. He died in 1922.

Sorel was one of a number of noted thinkers around the turn of the century – including **Nietzsche**, Max **Weber** and Oswald Spengler – who saw contemporary Western civilisation in terms of decadence and decline. Contemptuous of bourgeois culture and convinced that the state was irredeemably corrupt, he put his faith in the skilled working class. Sceptical, iconoclastic and pessimistic, he poured scorn on facile notions of progress. Sorel admired the harsher, warrior virtues of the Ancient world, the courage, fortitude, vigour, moral rectitude and patriotism he found especially in Republican Rome. He saw history as alternating between periods of vigour, when such virtues were to the fore, and periods of decadence. His hope was for a new age of vigour that would sweep away bourgeois decadence and domination. The only possible instrument for such a purpose was the working class. The question was how they could be instilled with the warrior virtues of the past.

Sorel believed that the violence of class war and revolution would purge society and restore these virtues. He looked to a revolutionary transformation of society led by the skilled working class that would be purified and transformed by the act of taking possession of the world and themselves. There are obvious parallels with **Marx**. Sorel admired and was influenced by Marx, but fully endorsed **Bernstein**'s revisionist criticisms: the baleful influence of **Hegel**, the falsity of historical materialism, the failure of predictions and the unacceptability of the dictatorship of the proletariat. However, he would not stomach Bernstein's alternative of a socialist party devoted to peaceful parliamentary means. Parties are always dominated by the group he hated most, middle-class intellectuals; this was true even of working-class parties, as Sorel's friend Roberto Michels taught with his famous 'iron law of oligarchy'. Sorel's contempt for the state and political parties turned him towards the social anarchist tradition, and particularly its most recent syndicalist manifestation.

Anarcho-syndicalism developed in the late nineteenth century, most fully in France, and was a form of anarchism that was associated with the trade unions. As such it was the only form of anarchism that had any discipline and organisation. The idea was that it was the trade unions alone that could push through a revolution, using the instrument of the general strike, and could thereafter run society through the voluntary association of trade unions, without any need for parties of middle-class politicians. These were not mass unions with professional national leaders, since most French unions at the time were small, local and based on crafts. Through them, workers would genuinely take over the economy and society. This is what attracted Sorel.

Sorel foresaw a new age of production, under the autonomous workers, and for all his socialist credentials he was not as hostile to capitalism as might be supposed. He was not against private property, but saw it as a necessary adjunct to personal independence. Furthermore, he saw in the free market a spur to vigour and enterprise, and was far more hostile to the idea of the all-providing state. He was opposed to the capitalist as exploiter of the workers, but not as bold entrepreneur. And while he rejected notions of progress as the bourgeoisification of the world, he was certainly a believer in economic and technological progress. What was to come was a world of greater production and technological sophistication.

Sorel was less concerned with the details of the society to come than with the processes of revolution and change. Rejecting facile liberal notions of progress he insisted that what motivated men was not reason but emotion, and in practical politics it was not theories that drove and inspired great movements but myth. In *Reflections on Violence* he explores what he calls 'social poetry', the myths that have inspired both religious and political movements. These are not to be confused with utopias, which he thought were the products of bourgeois intellectuals who would exploit the working class and lead it towards reformism. He cites as examples of myth the early Christian belief in the Second Coming, Mazzini's belief in a nationalist transformation of Italy and the Marxist belief in a proletarian revolution.

What had attracted Sorel to Marxism was not its much vaunted scientific credentials, which he dismissed as spurious, but the power of its central myth. No amount of theory or rational calculation, he thought, could possibly inspire men to the discipline, courage and self-sacrifice that were necessary to successfully prosecute a revolution. Only myths could do this. What Sorel meant by myth was a vision of the future in which the world is transformed by a catastrophic event. In terms of this vision men can make sense of their lives, as part of the struggle that will eventually bring victory in the final cataclysm. The certainty of victory, based entirely upon faith, is what makes these myths so powerful and compelling.

By the time Sorel formulated his theory of myth, his interest had switched from the Marxist myth of proletarian revolution to the anarcho-syndicalist myth of the general strike that would bring capitalism down, destroy the bourgeoisie and put the workers in control. The result would be, Sorel believed, a world morally transformed. A new 'ethic of production' would prevail, with workers steeled and purified by their struggle, dedicated to their work and their colleagues, and bound by a strict moral code centring on the family. Such a society would have the discipline and the energy to provide the entrepreneurial drive for innovation and improvement that a market economy needs and that the decadent bourgeoisie had lost.

In the meantime, before the general strike, the workers must not themselves become decadent by joining in with bourgeois parties or parliaments, or succumbing to bourgeois offers of improvement. The workers must maintain their purity of spirit by confrontation and violence. In this sense violence is seen as necessary to the renewal and preservation of civilisation.

On the other hand, despite his reputation and much violent and bloodthirsty language, Sorel is not the unambiguous advocate of violence he is sometimes supposed. He hated the mindless atrocities and assassinations then being perpetrated in the name of anarchist revolution, and he even hated industrial sabotage, which, with his passion for technology, he tended to regard as sacrilege. Violence was for the revolution itself, although Sorel sometimes seemed to think that the mere threat of overwhelming violence by a disciplined and morally determined proletariat would be sufficient to intimidate the middle classes into accepting a new order.

In general, the whole Sorelian theme of transfiguration through the revolutionary violence of the working masses inspired by myth was far more influential among fascists than socialists or anarchists.

Further reading

Primary sources

The Illusions of Progress, ed. J. Stanley (Los Angeles, CA: California University Press, 1969).

Reflections on Violence, ed. J. Jennings (Cambridge: Cambridge University Press, 1999).

Secondary sources

Jennings, J.: *Georges Sorel: The Character and Development of His Thought* (London: Macmillan, 1985).

Portis, L.: *Georges Sorel* (London: Pluto Press, 1980).

Stanley, J.L.: *The Sociology of Virtue: The Political and Social Theories of Georges Sorel* (Los Angeles, CA: California University Press, 1982).

EDUARD BERNSTEIN (1850–1932)

Bernstein came from a Jewish working-class background in Berlin. He left school early and worked in a bank. From the age of nineteen he was involved in socialist politics and he became an ardent Marxist. In 1878 Bismarck banned the German Social Democratic Party (SPD) and Bernstein went into exile in Switzerland. There he took over the editorship of the party's official journal, *The Social Democrat*, which he edited until 1890. He was close to other Marxist exiles in Switzerland, including Karl Kautsky, the SPD's leading theorist and chief upholder of orthodox Marxism. Bernstein made several visits to England, meeting **Marx** and Engels, and when he was deported from Switzerland in 1887 he settled in London for the next thirteen years. He became a close friend of Engels and was an executor of his will.

Bernstein was at this time a thoroughly orthodox Marxist and in 1891 he and Kautsky wrote the new Marxist programme for the SPD. He shared Engels' belief that while revolution was the ultimate goal, the party must, in the meanwhile, remain alive and vigorous by successfully representing the working class and making gains that would benefit it. However, such achievements could only be temporary. They were not good or bad in themselves, but only in so far as they contributed to the ultimate goal. It was, therefore, important for Engels that in pursuing this policy the party did not lose sight of its true revolutionary objective, which gave point and purpose to everything the party did; in his capacity as editor of the chief party organ, Bernstein strove to ensure this did not happen. It was only after the death of Engels in 1895 that Bernstein's ideas began to change.

While in Britain Bernstein also associated with the Fabians, who influenced his thinking and with whom he maintained contact after his return to Germany in 1901. In addition to the Fabians, British conditions convinced him that the single great leap from capitalism to socialism was an ideological illusion, that capitalism was simply not going to collapse under the weight of its own contradictions, and that socialism could perfectly well come about through incremental reform gained through democratic pressure. On this basis he constructed a system that modified a number of Marxism's basic ideas. He set out his new thinking in a series of articles in Kautsky's theoretical journal *The New Age*, beginning in 1896. The ideas were condemned at the party conference at Stuttgart in 1898 by Kautsky, Rosa Luxemburg and others, before Bernstein was able to return to Germany. It was Kautsky who urged Bernstein to clarify his ideas, which resulted in the book, *The Preconditions of Socialism and the Tasks of Social Democracy* (1899; previously translated as *Evolutionary Socialism*). It became the fundamental revisionist text and the centre of furious controversy, embracing the whole European social democratic movement, which became divided between two camps. A host of anti-revisionist resolutions and polemics followed, as most of the party theorists were ranged against Bernstein. However, revisionism steadily gained ground among party memberships and trade unions, where it often simply articulated pre-existing attitudes.

A year after his return to Germany, Bernstein was elected as a Reichstag deputy for Breslau, which he represented from 1902 to 1918 and from 1920 to 1928. He became progressively more outspoken in his rejection of Marxist ideas, and by 1914 had more in common with liberal reformers than with orthodox Marxists. When war broke out in 1914, Bernstein was among the few social democrats who opposed the war, and subsequently joined a breakaway party along with Kautsky. He rejoined the SPD after the war and helped draft its first programme. He was the real founder of the non-communist social democracy of the inter-war years. He died in Berlin in 1932.

The Revisionist Controversy was a profound split over theory, but Bernstein would have had little impact had there not already been developments and divisions over policy and tactics, particularly in the light of the failure of Marx's predictions. By 1900 the German workers had enjoyed considerable success over many years in improving living standards, increasing welfare and reducing the length of the working day. Inevitably in these circumstances a large section of the party leadership increasingly saw the task of the party as building on these gains and ignoring the prospect of future revolution, as socialists in Britain were successfully doing. Many local and trade union representatives had become indifferent to the ultimate goal and tacitly assumed a model of bringing in socialism gradually through reform.

The claim of Marxism, especially emphasised by the orthodox, was that it was *scientific* socialism. Bernstein argues that to treat Marx's ideas as sacrosanct and based on authority is not scientific. Time had shown that Marx and Engels had got some things wrong and as a consequence some of their basic ideas needed revision. He accepted that they were correct in pointing to the potentially fatal contradictions within capitalism and predicting on the basis of their initial analysis that capitalism would indeed eventually collapse of its own accord. But what he went on to say was that subsequent research had demonstrated that this was only a tendency that could be, and in fact had been, counteracted by other factors, without actually eliminating the contradictions. Marx and Engels had the evidence for this conclusion but ignored it. For example, in their later writings they had come to realise that economics was only the determining factor in the last analysis. This should have led them to talk more of 'tendencies' in their predictions. Instead they made their materialist theory of history ever more deterministic. This was because they remained under the spell of the Hegelian dialectic, their own version of which they erroneously took to be scientific but which often prevented them from seeing the implications of their own research.

Bernstein held the influence of **Hegel** responsible for much of what he thought wrong with Marxism. Above all he blamed Hegel's tendency to predict the course of history *a priori*, on the basis of abstract metaphysical categories that saw people merely as instruments of grand dialectical movements and paid little attention to empirical facts. It was this method that led Marx to adopt an erroneous historical determinism, and to rely on a single mode of explanation: the economic. Hegelianism also led Marx, according to Bernstein, to the notion of a dramatic qualitative leap from capitalism to socialism: hence the role of violent revolution in Marxism. In fact Bernstein sees Marx as trying to straddle two different and incompatible versions of socialism. On the one hand, there is the constructive evolutionary version developed by socialist sects and utopian writers – and by workers' organisations – with the aim of establishing a new economic system that would emancipate society. The other version was for instant socialism through the revolutionary seizure of the property of the governing and exploiting classes. This version was terroristic, conspiratorial and destructive; it was only justified if the first version was impossible, which in fact was not the case.

Bernstein rejected Marx's economics, arguing that the labour theory of value simply did not work. As a consequence, his predictions about the concentration of capital, class polarisation, enmiseration and a great revolutionary leap to socialism were quite wrong. Wealth was not being concentrated as he predicted but was spreading, with ever more property owners. Class polarisation was not happening because the development of the economy and technology was such that ever greater differentiation was occurring in all classes of society. Furthermore, a major crisis bringing about a collapse of capitalism was becoming less likely, not more so, because capitalism was becoming ever more financially sophisticated.

At the same time, the claim that the conditions of the workers could not really improve under capitalism was clearly false, and there were no grounds for anticipating an increase in the misery of the working class or an increase in class antagonism. However, the future prospects for socialism did not at all depend on these things. Socialism should be seen as a gradual process of increasing socialisation by using the increasing power and maturity of the working class through democratic means. Democracy was not just a means, but an end in itself, an essential part of the socialist ideal.

Social democracy had in reality become a parliamentary movement, and this being so all talk of the 'dictatorship of the proletariat' was redundant, along with any notion of the working class imposing socialism on the rest of society by force. The working class should be seeking a controlling voice in production to prevent monopoly and guarantee employment. These ends were more important than ownership, which could be gradually socialised in due course. A wholesale expropriation of all property in a revolution would involve terror and waste on an unacceptable scale.

Bernstein famously sought to sum up his views in the formula: 'What is generally called the ultimate goal of socialism is nothing to me; the movement is everything.' This was perhaps not the clearest or the most fortunate form of words, and it caused outrage among the orthodox. Bernstein tried to explain in several ways. In *The Preconditions of Socialism* he wrote:

> I am not concerned with what will happen in the more distant future, but with what can and ought to happen in the present, for the present and for the nearest future.
>
> (p.5)

Perhaps the best interpretation of what he meant was that socialism is not a perfect future world suddenly born in some great future revolutionary cataclysm, but is rather the process of gaining more representation, equality, democracy, welfare, security and other goods that contribute towards a more decent and just society. For Bernstein, the piecemeal constructing of a better, more equal and more just society by democratic means was not a tactic only of value in so far as it served the future revolution. It was valuable for its own sake. The end of a just and decent socialist society was not separate from the means.

Improving society through better welfare and more rights for everyone was not a tactic: it *was* socialism.

Bernstein developed a quite different conception of the politics of modern industrial society than the orthodox Marxist view that social class determined everything. Conflicting class interests were unquestionably important, but over and above these all classes had an interest in the maintenance of civilised values. It was the proper objective of politics to create a just and decent society to which all could and should subscribe. Things were wrong when one class monopolised power and used it against the interests of another that had been excluded from it. This had been the case in Germany and elsewhere, and in such circumstances it was perfectly proper for the excluded and exploited class to engage in revolutionary class struggle. But where democracy meant that all enjoyed equal civil and political rights, then such revolutionary struggle was no longer justified or necessary. The legitimate demands of workers could be achieved by the ordinary political means of persuasion and compromise in the common interest.

Democracy was a necessary condition of socialism and of a decent civilised society. The establishment of full democracy must therefore be the first priority of any socialist movement. It was democracy that was essential if politics were to transcend class and be for the common good. In *The Preconditions of Socialism* Bernstein defines democracy as 'the absence of class government'. Thus, while class conflict may certainly exist in modern society, it does not necessarily define or dominate that society as it must for the orthodox Marxist. The state is not necessarily an instrument of class rule, as Marx insisted it must be. It could equally be the instrument of civilised values, the means of eliminating exploitation and injustice and of civilising public life, which was social democracy's true ultimate objective. It was not in fact greatly different from the ultimate objective of many liberals, only a fuller and more consistent version.

Bernstein's ideas aroused a fierce debate in which every significant European social democrat of the period took part. The outcome of the conflict in the SPD was that the official commitment to revolutionary Marxism was retained, but in practical terms the party became entirely devoted to gradual reform by peaceful parliamentary means. Most other social democratic parties followed suit. After the Bolshevik Revolution of 1917 those social democrats across Europe still committed to revolution created separate communist parties. The term 'social democracy' became associated with Bernstein's conception of socialism. In 1959, at its conference at Bad Godesberg, the SPD finally abandoned any association with Marxism, completing the process that Bernstein had begun.

Further reading

Primary sources

Marxism and Social Democracy: The Revisionist Debate, 1896–98, ed. H. Tudor and J.M. Tudor (Cambridge: Cambridge University Press, 1988).

The Preconditions of Socialism, ed. H. Tudor (Cambridge: Cambridge University Press, 1993).

Selected Writings of Edward Bernstein, 1900–1921, ed. Manfred Steger (Atlantic Highlands, NJ: Humanities Press, 1996).

Secondary sources

Fletcher, R.: *Bernstein to Brandt: A Short History of German Social Democracy* (London: Arnold, 1987).

Gay, P.: *The Dilemma of Democratic Socialism: Eduard Bernstein's Challenge to Marx* (2nd edn; New York: Collier Books, 1962).

Kolakowski, L.: *Main Currents of Marxism*, vol.2 (Oxford: Oxford University Press, 1978).

Steger, M.B.: *The Quest for Evolutionary Socialism: Eduard Bernstein and Social Democracy* (Cambridge: Cambridge University Press, 1997).

MAX WEBER (1864–1920)

Max Weber was born in Erfurt in 1864, the son of a prominent lawyer and National Liberal deputy in the German parliament. He was a brilliant student across a range of subjects and later successively held professorships in economics, law and political science, although he gave up the teaching side of his academic duties after a mental breakdown in 1897. He produced major studies in a number of areas, particularly the relations between them: between law and economics in one society, religion and economics in another, and so on. Exploring these relationships led Weber towards the development of an overview of human history, particularly in respect of modernity. They also led to major developments in methodology and theory. All this established Weber's reputation as among the greatest of sociologists, although one subject label hardly does justice to his intellectual range and achievement. Weber died in 1920.

While Weber contributed much to political sociology, he wrote no explicit work of normative political theory. Nevertheless, a normative theory can be gleaned from his various writings, and his general account of the modern world has influenced many other political thinkers. He also wrote directly on the politics of contemporary Germany (and later in life stood as a parliamentary candidate) from which his more general outlook can be inferred, but he always sought to keep his prescriptions and prognostications rigorously separate from his 'scientific' conclusions.

Weber has been described as 'the bourgeois Marx' and while in fact he admired and was influenced by **Marx**, many of his conclusions profoundly challenged basic Marxist doctrines, including the nature of social and historical explanation, the role of ideas in history, and the nature of modernity.

There are key differences in basic methodology. Where Marxist social and historical explanations are in terms of the interplay of social and economic forces, Weber insists that adequate explanations must also involve the understanding of the participants. Their actions have to have meaning in themselves and often this is bound up with their general understanding of reality as a whole, their world-view. Weber goes to some lengths to analyse different kinds of thinking and forms of rationality, the kinds of reasons we have for action, the reasons that give actions meaning. Actions may be undertaken for emotional reasons or to conform to traditional patterns of behaviour, but these are less rational than actions directed to the fulfilment of some purpose (means/ends reasoning) or for the sake of some value (value reasoning). Weber was well aware that we usually do things for a mixture of such reasons, but the distinctions are clear enough and usually one predominates.

Social action must consist of meaningful behaviour within a meaningful universe, and this suggests that social and historical change will involve ideas and the ways people think. Weber sought above all to analyse the nature and development of modernity and why it occurred in the West rather than elsewhere. He believed that the analysis of religions within different civilisations was central to this task, since in all pre-modern societies, both East and West, it was largely religion that provided world-views and the general intellectual background. He investigated world religions and their relation to various aspects of society, such as economy and law, to see if there was something about Western Christianity that was peculiarly conducive to the rise of the modern world.

In probably his most famous work, *The Protestant Ethic and the Spirit of Capitalism* (1905), Weber argues that capitalism could not have come about through economic factors alone. Certain ideas of early Protestantism not found in other religions (the notion of a secular vocation and especially the Calvinist notion of worldly success being a mark of election) inadvertently set in train the process of capital accumulation that in due course became self-generating, but which would not have occurred without the initial non-economic impulse.

However, for Weber the rise of capitalism is not the central fact of modernity, which more or less explains everything else (as it is for Marxists), but is only one aspect of a wider trend that constitutes the true essence of modernity. This wider trend he calls 'rationalisation' and embraces not only economic activity but government and social organisation in general, as well as intellectual life. Again religion has an influence, Weber argues, in that Western Christianity's tendency to approve being active in the world as 'God's instrument' rather than totally withdrawing was more conducive to the development of means/ends rationality than Eastern mystical contemplation and disdain for this-worldly concerns.

What rationalisation amounts to is the rise and triumph of instrumental means/ends reasoning, where the most rational is that which is most efficient at achieving ends. That is, reasoning to fulfil purposes, rather than to pursue values. Capitalism is in this sense the most rational form of economic organisation, being free of previous religious and ethical considerations, such as the 'just price' and the immorality of usury, and able to calculate everything in money terms through market mechanisms.

The rise of means/ends rationality is by no means confined to the sphere of the economic. More importantly, Weber charts the development of rational organisation generally. That is, the development of bureaucracy, with its hierarchy of salaried officers bringing ever more aspects of society under rational control. Bureaucracy, as the most efficient form of human organisation, is central to government but has come to pervade most aspects of social life, including capitalist organisations. Unfortunately, the more impersonal and therefore 'dehumanising' rational organisation is, the more effective and efficient it is. It produces a fragmentation of the individual: what Weber called a 'parcelling out of the soul'. Through capitalism and bureaucracy, the ever growing rationalisation of social life progressively reduces the individual to a mere cog in the great Kafkaesque socio-economic machine: hence Weber's reference to the 'iron cage of modernity' (*The Protestant Ethic and the Spirit of Capitalism*, p.181). Although in capitalism there was some room for individuality and creativity, particularly for the entrepreneur, in Marxian socialism Weber saw a necessary merging of the governmental and economic bureaucracies into one mighty organisation that would crush all individuality completely, hence his strong opposition.

Rationalisation has a further dimension in the intellectual sphere. The impulse we possess to make sense of the world has led us through science and technology to a convincing picture of reality. And here again Weber stresses the role of religion. He argues that Western Christianity had absorbed the intellectual inheritance of the Greeks in philosophy and science, which provided an environment, given suitable stimulus, conducive to the generation and growth of modern science, an environment that other major religions could not have provided.

The role of religion here is particularly ironic, for our vastly extended knowledge and control of reality, and the wealth and organisation that has flowed from this, has come at a cost. It has undermined religion and all metaphysical foundations of value and ethics, and reduced them, together with the alternative form of rational action that is value-oriented, to the sphere of the irrational. Weber himself thought that religious belief was no longer rationally tenable. As a consequence, the world had become 'disenchanted'. Our impulse to understand the world as rationally meaningful has only resulted in a conception of reality that is ultimately meaningless, in the sense of being devoid of moral value.

This has serious consequences for human life, since we cannot live without values. Value reasoning has been increasingly reduced to the private sphere, regarded as a matter of personal faith that is subjective and conflicting, and thereby marginalised. On an individual level, this forces us, Weber believes, to choose our values in order to try to live a meaningful life in a meaningless universe. One possibility (important for him personally) was committing oneself to a vocation. His own vocation was science and not politics, although he attached great importance to politics as a vocation – both could give meaning to life.

What, then, of the ethical possibilities of politics? In his essay 'The Profession and Vocation of Politics' (*Political Writings*, p.309), Weber argued that, in the first place, one could satisfy one's ethical needs by identifying oneself with a cause or ideology. He believed that the actions of those who merely 'lived off' politics, who made their living from manipulating power without any fixed principles, led only into 'emptiness and absurdity'. On the other hand, one may devote oneself to a cause to such an extent that its demands are absolute, make no compromises with reality and blame the disastrous effects of policies on others. But this absolute ethics or 'ethics of conviction' was irresponsible and also potentially disastrous. The genuine vocation of politics involved dedication to a cause, but one modified by an 'ethic of responsibility', and making the pragmatic recognition that evil must sometimes be used to produce good. The acceptance of this 'ethical irrationality of the world' is what the pure ideologue cannot accept.

Weber had a somewhat bleak view of the nature of politics, which he thought was necessarily bound up with violence and never-ending struggle. Struggle between nations and within nations was inevitable and would not end in some future utopia of peace and brotherhood – it was permanent. Weber famously defined the state as an institution that has a monopoly of legitimate violence within a given territory, and in fact he believed that the politician's capacity to get things done ultimately rested upon the threat of physical violence. Politics frequently had to use morally questionable means to achieve good ends. This gave politics a morally compromised and even tragic dimension.

However, politics involved not only power but also authority, and Weber's analysis of different forms of political authority is a central feature of both his political sociology and his own normative political beliefs. He thought that there were three basic types of authority or legitimate domination: traditional, legal-rational and charismatic. The first two are by far the more common and fit in with his overall account of the rise of modernity and its central characteristic of rationalisation. Traditional authority is based on the idea of the sanctity of tradition and prevailed in pre-modern societies. Legal-rational authority is based on the authority of law and the notion that through law, society is rationally organised. This is closely related to bureaucracy and corresponds to the general rise of rationality that is central to modernity. Charismatic authority, based on devotion to a charismatic leader, is more rare, but can appear at any time and cuts across the other two. In the name of new values, the charismatic leader can institute change that overthrows tradition, but can also set aside the imperatives of legal-rational organisation.

This was Weber's 'scientific' picture of the social world and its historical development. It forms a background to his own passionately held ethical and political commitments, which – as matters of personal choice – he sought to keep rigorously separate from his scientific life.

His vocation as a scientist, committed to value-free social science, was deeply important to him on a personal level. At the same time, he was strongly committed to the cause of German nationalism, although he was not any kind of extreme nationalist. He subscribed to no belief in the necessity of all Germans belonging to the same state, nor in the intrinsic superiority of Germans or their culture; he merely believed that the culture was irreplaceable, just as other cultures were, and the state had a central duty to preserve it. He also believed that Germany, because of geography and history, was fated to play a major role in international affairs. Nationalism was a possible substitute for religion because it can give death meaning in a disenchanted universe, in the sense of offering a cause worth dying for.

More importantly, Weber was a liberal, although of an unusual kind, deeply influenced by the scepticism and pessimism of **Nietzsche**. We have already seen that Weber believed there was no rational basis for any system of values or ethics, but he was also deeply sceptical about what had been (and for many still remains) a central article of liberal faith: the ideal of progress towards a fully rational world. Indeed, Weber was more inclined to see Western civilisation as being in decline.

The ideal of an ever more rational world had been a central liberal ideal ever since the Enlightenment, yet Weber saw the progress of rationalisation as little more than a curse upon humanity. Ever more detailed social and economic organisation turned people into cogs in a vast socio-economic machine that limited their freedom and crushed their individuality. Weber expresses this in dark phrases like the 'iron cage' and (in relation to the development of a welfare state) 'the new serfdom'.

For Weber, freedom and individuality were absolute values. Following **Kant**, Weber believed that human dignity and worth were bound up with the human capacity to choose moral values and live by them. As a normative political thinker, Weber was therefore preoccupied with the question of how human freedom and individuality can be preserved in a hostile world. It was not through capitalism, for that (at least for the vast majority) was part of the problem.

Despite his Nietzschean pessimism, Weber did explore some hopeful possibilities, especially in relation to German politics. In so far as he had an answer, it lay in his support for parliamentary democracy, though not for the usual liberal reasons. It was not in terms of the people ruling themselves, for that was a fiction in the sense that ultimately it is always elites that rule. The attraction of parliamentary democracy lay precisely in the struggle between elites, which tended to generate two desirable outcomes: a political class and charismatic leaders.

Weber believed that Bismarck's rule had left Germany without a viable political class. Political power lay in the hands of the Emperor and the bureaucracy, neither of which was fit to rule. Bad decision-making was the result, and a consequent failure to maintain Germany's proper place in world affairs. By contrast, Britain had a democratic or semi-democratic system, which Weber greatly admired. Not only did it sustain a competent and confident ruling class, it also threw up charismatic leaders such as Gladstone and Lloyd George. Parliamentary democracy could be the means of both unifying the nation and providing an acceptable combination of rational-legal government and charismatic political leadership, which could be an antidote to the deadening conformity of modern rationalised society. Thereby a degree of personal liberty and creativity might just possibly be preserved.

Weber saw bureaucracy and charismatic leadership as polar opposites. Perhaps a fusion of the two might hold back the organisational juggernaut a little longer before it crushes everybody. However, Weber's solution seems less than convincing. Charismatic leadership is in its nature an ephemeral phenomenon, which no system can guarantee it will generate. More significantly, it seems more important to Weber that there be charismatic leadership than where that leadership might be leading. It is beyond question that Weber would have hated the Nazis and all they stood for (apart from anything else he was a fierce opponent of anti-Semitism), yet a more perfect example of charismatic leadership in modern times than Adolf Hitler is difficult to imagine.

But perhaps the initial problem that Weber poses is too stark and unrealistic. We do not live in a society where everything is organised to the last detail, but one where individuality flourishes: a post-industrialist 'disorganised capitalism' that Weber could hardly have foreseen. The dangers lie more in our consumerist over-fondness for creature comforts and mass entertainment, and the cultural conformity these tend to impose.

Whatever the weaknesses of Weber's prognostications and prescriptions might be, his analysis of the modern world has been immensely influential. Fear of bureaucracy has haunted much political theory, and indeed practice, in the twentieth century, from conservatives such as **Oakeshott** to New Right liberals such as **Hayek**, as well as revolutionary Marxists such as **Marcuse and the Frankfurt School**.

Further reading

Primary sources

The Protestant Ethic and the Spirit of Capitalism, ed. T. Parsons (London: George Allen & Unwin, 1968).

Political Writings, ed. P. Lassman and R. Spiers (Cambridge: Cambridge University Press, 1994).

Secondary sources

Beetham, D.: *Max Weber and the Theory of Modern Politics* (London: George Allen & Unwin, 1974).

Giddens, A.: *Politics and Sociology in the Thought of Max Weber* (Basingstoke: Macmillan, 1972).

Sayer, D.: *Capitalism and Modernity: An Excursus on Marx and Weber* (London: Routledge, 1991).

Turner, S.: *The Cambridge Companion to Weber* (Cambridge: Cambridge University Press, 2000).

VLADIMIR ILICH LENIN (1870–1924)

Vladimir Ilich Ulyanov was born in the small town of Simbirsk (later renamed Ulyanovsk), south of Moscow, in 1870. The Ulyanovs were a middle-class intellectual family, the father being a distinguished inspector of schools. When Vladimir Ilich was seventeen, the family reputation was clouded when his elder brother was hanged for involvement in a plot to assassinate the Tsar. After early expulsion from university for participating in a demonstration, Vladimir Ilich became a full-time revolutionary, adopting the name Lenin.

Thereafter all Lenin's thought and energy was directed, with extraordinary single-mindedness, towards promoting the revolution. All his voluminous writings, including the most abstractly theoretical, were written for polemical revolutionary purposes. This is true of his two most important contributions to theory: the theory of the revolutionary party and that of capitalist imperialism.

A Marxist party (see Karl **Marx**), the Russian Social Democratic Party (RSDP), was established in Russia towards the end of the nineteenth century and began to recruit among the comparatively small industrial workforce. But, unlike the German Social Democratic Party (SPD), it was not legal: it was hounded by the Tsarist police, its leaders lived in exile, and its effectiveness in organising and supporting the working class was small. This was the party that Lenin joined as a student. There was already a strong revolutionary tradition in Russia before Marxism arrived, and Lenin was already a revolutionary before he became a Marxist.

Lenin's zeal and organising ability soon made him a leading figure in the party and led to his exile. As time went on, Lenin became increasingly disillusioned with the RSDP and became convinced that its whole programme and its strategy were wrong. The leadership was fatalistic about the possibilities of revolution, believing that Russia must first pass through a long capitalist phase before it was ripe for revolution, which would in any case begin elsewhere first. Lenin disagreed and insisted that the party should work for revolution in Russia as soon as possible, irrespective of what was happening in other countries.

Lenin also disagreed with the strategy of building a mass party on the model of the German SPD. The conditions in Russia were just not the same, the party being illegal, wide open to police penetration and largely restricted to backing workers' demands for better pay and conditions. Lenin's alternative was set out in his most important work, *What Is To Be Done?* (1902). In this he argues that the working class, if left to its own devices, would only develop what he called 'trade union consciousness' and not the necessary 'revolutionary consciousness'. What the workers needed was leadership from a new type of party, which did possess the necessary revolutionary consciousness, plus the theory and tactics to go with it.

Lenin proposed, therefore, the creation of a small party of dedicated professional revolutionaries, trained in revolutionary activity and thoroughly grounded in Marxist theory. The organisation of the party would be based on the principle of 'democratic centralism'. That is, open discussion and opinion passing up through the hierarchy, but once a decision has been made at the top it must be rigidly enforced throughout the party. This new party would be the 'vanguard of the proletariat', meaning that it is not separate from the working class, but is rather its elite, the most class-conscious part of it. Lenin also insisted that whatever was done to further the revolutionary cause was justified, no matter how immoral it might seem. In other words, the end justifies the means.

Lenin's ideas split the leadership of the RSDP, and his faction broke away to form their own party that came to be called the 'Bolsheviks'. The party he left came to be known as the 'Mensheviks'. Some sympathised with Lenin's belief in working for an immediate revolution, but could not stomach his dictatorial leadership. Most notable was Leon Trotsky, who had an independent reputation as a writer and revolutionary; Trotsky returned to the Bolsheviks after the Revolution broke out.

Lenin's second major contribution to Marxist theory dealt with the problem of the failure of Marx's predictions and at the same time presented a case for why the world revolution should begin in Russia. Contrary to Marx, capitalism had not shown the slightest sign of collapsing in advanced capitalist countries; the classes were not polarising; the middle classes were growing and the working classes becoming more prosperous. In his main work on the subject, *Imperialism, the Highest Stage of Capitalism* (1916), Lenin offered a solution. The late nineteenth century was the period when the major powers competed to carve up Africa and other uncolonised parts of the world. World War I was essentially a war for colonial possessions, so that the capitalists of the winning country could extend their exploitation and profits. Lenin argued that this imperialist expansion constituted a higher stage of capitalism, which Marx could not have foreseen. Capitalism increasingly exploits the undeveloped part of the world and uses part of the profits to 'buy off' the domestic working class with a higher standard of living and state welfare. The exploited masses of the colonial world were thus the new proletariat. Consequently, the communist revolution would not necessarily take place in the advanced West.

The country that was in fact particularly ripe for revolution, Lenin argued, was Russia. It was not economically advanced, but then the workers had not been bought off, and its industry, largely financed by foreign capital, was the 'weakest link' in the chain of capitalist imperialism. A revolution in Russia would begin the process that would spread to the rest of the world and bring the whole system crashing down.

In February 1917 the Tsarist regime collapsed under the strain of World War I, and Lenin's Bolsheviks, joined by Trotsky, seized power in November (in October according to the old Russian calendar that was then still in use, hence the 'October Revolution'). The Bolshevik Party was renamed the Communist Party of the Soviet Union. Once in power, Lenin encouraged the peasants and workers to seize the land and the factories and he suppressed all opposition parties. The principles of the revolutionary party, as set out in *What Is To Be Done?*, became the principles of the governing party. They were also reinforced by Lenin's creation in 1919 of the Communist International (known as the 'Comintern'), which he dominated, insisting that all member parties adopt his doctrines and his system of party organisation, as well as recognising Soviet leadership. Despite civil war and foreign intervention, the Soviet Union had been established by the time Lenin died in 1924.

It was Lenin's particular interpretation and extensions of Marx's theory, known as Marxism–Leninism, that became the official doctrine of the Soviet Union and of all subsequent communist regimes (although sometimes with native additions, as in China). It is the version of

Marxism that we know as 'communism' and it was to be the only orthodox version until the 1960s. Its reputation as the only authentic Marxism was simply a result of Lenin's success. Marxism–Leninism is in fact a rather crude version of Marxism, relying on Marx's later works and especially Engels' popular expositions. For one thing, it is very mechanical, putting great stress on economic determinism. Democratic centralism is extended from a principle of party organisation, where it amounts to rigid control from the top, to a principle of social organisation, with party control of every significant social organisation and the suppression of any kind of opposition. This is true of all other communist regimes, producing totalitarian one-party states.

The justification of this in Marxist terms is based on Marx's theory of the 'dictatorship of the proletariat', which was seen as the temporary phase of working-class rule prior to full communism. Since, in Lenin's theory, the party *is* the proletariat, its vanguard, the party has the right to rule on behalf of the rest of the workers. Various justifications were also offered on democratic grounds. It was said that multi-party systems reflected class divisions, which did not exist in communist countries, and that the Communist Party can alone represent the interests of the people. It was because of arguments like this that communist regimes styled themselves 'people's democracies' – as distinct from liberal democracies, which were dismissed as a sham because the people had no real power.

On the other hand, while communist regimes claimed to be 'workers' states', they saw themselves as being a long way from achieving a communist society. When Lenin seized power in 1917 he was convinced that his revolution could not succeed unless the workers of other countries followed the Russian lead. This, of course, did not happen. In Marxist terms, all communist states are stuck in the transitional phase of the dictatorship of the proletariat (which Marxists, rather confusingly, sometimes refer to as 'socialism' as distinct from the final phase of 'communism') and must maintain a powerful state so long as they are surrounded by hostile capitalist states. Only when the rest of the world has its revolution and catches up, can humanity progress together towards a truly communist society.

Lenin's theory of the vanguard party still dominates wherever communist regimes remain. But at least since the 1960s, and particularly since the collapse of European communism (1989–91), it has been criticised as a distortion of Marxism by many Marxists in the West. Marx clearly taught that the whole working class needed to be educated and self-consciously ready for revolution, not merely the uncomprehending instrument of an elite who would take power on the workers' behalf. Furthermore, many now argue that the Mensheviks were right all along when they insisted that Russia was far too backward to sustain a genuine proletarian revolution. These, however, are contentious issues within Marxism.

The theory of imperialism, however, retains its appeal for all Marxists since it overcomes objections based on Marx's failed predictions. It is still widely adhered to, despite the ending of Western colonialism after World War II. The argument is that although overt political control may have gone, the Third World is still dominated and exploited by the capitalist West, only now through more subtle economic means. However, the theory lost some of its force as some countries, particularly in the Far East, flourished in the late twentieth century: the theory suggests that latter-day economic imperialism would prevent this.

The failures of communism in recent decades have diminished Lenin's reputation; nevertheless, as the founder of modern communism he remains among the most important and influential figures of the twentieth century.

Further reading

Primary source

Selected Works (London: Lawrence & Wishart, 1971).

Secondary sources

Carr, E.H.: *The Bolshevik Revolution* (3 vols; Harmondsworth: Penguin, 1966).
Gooding, J.: *Socialism in Russia: Lenin and his Legacy, 1890–1991* (Basingstoke: Palgrave, 2001).
Harding, N.: *Lenin's Political Thought* (2 vols; London: Macmillan, 1981).
—: *Leninism* (London: Macmillan, 1996).
Service, R.: *Lenin: A Biography* (London: Papermac, 2001).

BENITO MUSSOLINI (1883–1945) AND FASCISM

The intellectual standard of fascist thinking is generally agreed to be poor and it is therefore not surprising that fascism produced no outstanding thinker. Nevertheless, it is beyond question that fascism represented something new and quite distinctive in political thinking, that it had a major impact on the politics of the twentieth century, and that Benito Mussolini was the key figure in its initial development. Hitler's national socialism, the major alternative form of fascism, retains the essentials of Mussolini's fascism and supplements them with an elaborate racial theory.

Mussolini was born in 1883, the son of a blacksmith with fierce socialist views and a schoolteacher mother. After an unruly childhood and youth, he had difficulty settling down, doing various jobs including teaching. He was also a Marxist agitator and journalist advocating violent socialist action, although his Marxism was unorthodox in that he believed in the importance of will rather than economics (see Karl **Marx**). But he became disillusioned by the in-fighting among various socialists and communists at a time when Italy was in chaos and plainly in need of strong leadership. Mussolini gravitated towards a small but vociferous and influential group of extreme nationalists, who were united in advocating Italy's entry into World War I, believing that through war the nation could be purified and regenerated. They all tended to see politics in terms of a heroic elite, contemptuous of democracy and prepared to use force, that would create a new and dynamic Italy. The country was seen as divided and poor, with a weak and corrupt government, yet its glorious past meant that Italy ought to be a Great Power.

Italy did not do well in the war and there was general disappointment at Italian gains. Mussolini, after serving briefly in the army, was among those who blamed the government and demanded an end to the decadent liberalism it represented and the creation of a new, strong, united Italy. World War I confirmed for him that national feeling was a far more powerful political force than social class, a force capable of inspiring sacrifice and total commitment as an antidote to the selfish individualism of decadent liberalism. He built a fascist paramilitary organisation, the Blackshirts, and his followers fought elections, using violence and intimidation. Finally, Mussolini himself seized power after an audacious march on Rome in 1922 (which could easily have been frustrated had his enemies worked together). Opposition was then ruthlessly suppressed and Mussolini ruled Italy for the next twenty-one years.

Mussolini's ambition was to build Italy into a major world power. This meant the creation of a powerful economy as the basis for imperial expansion and European war. An alliance with Hitler, setting up the 'Rome–Berlin Axis' in 1936, seemed initially successful but eventually led to the Allied invasion of Italy and the intervention of a large German army to repel it. Mussolini was dismissed by the king and arrested in July 1943, but was rescued by German paratroops and set up as national leader in Northern Italy, which the Germans still controlled. As the Allies advanced he was seized by anti-fascist partisans and murdered in 1945.

Mussolini was not a consistent theorist, but rather adapted ideas as he went along, according to need. Nevertheless, influenced by extreme nationalists of various kinds, both left and right, and by thinkers such as **Nietzsche**, **Sorel** and the Italian theorist of elites, Vifredo Pareto, Mussolini was able to construct a fairly consistent body of belief based upon revolutionary nationalism expressed through the authoritarian state. He sought a rebirth of Italy, a revolutionary transformation of the country into a strong, united and imperialistic state, controlling all aspects of Italian life. All policies and all propaganda were directed to this end.

The term 'fascism' comes from the Italian *fascio* meaning 'bundle' or 'bound together', which had implications in Italian politics of an insurrectionary brotherhood and had been used by some ultra-nationalists before 1914. It also comes from the same Latin root as *fasces*, which was the bundle of rods with axe-head carried before the Consuls in Ancient Rome as a symbol of state authority: the bundle represented the unity of the people under the state, which was represented by the axe. Mussolini coined the term 'fascism' and used the *fasces* as a symbol of his regime. Such Roman symbolism was important to Mussolini, the implication being that he was recreating the greatness of Ancient Rome.

On the other hand, Italian fascism was not an especially backward-looking movement (much less so than Hitler's national socialism) and indeed prided itself upon its modernity. It looked above all to the future and to the creation of a new kind of society dominated by a new kind of human being, the 'new man' (fascism is resolutely sexist): young, virile, dynamic, creative, selflessly devoted to the nation and willing to sacrifice himself for its sake. Some of Mussolini's earliest supporters were a group of artists who styled themselves 'Futurists', and who called for the destruction of existing art and culture in order to make way for the new. A later supporter was Gabriele d'Annunzio who, in 1919, led the seizure of the disputed Croatian city of Fiume, which he ruled for fifteen months. He saw himself as a Nietzschean superman, a new man, both poet and man of action, and he pioneered a number of the ideas and methods that Mussolini adopted.

Italian fascist theory is to be found in the writings and speeches of Mussolini and his followers, the most notable of whom was Giovanni Gentile (1875–1944). Gentile was a distinguished philosopher who, after the seizure of power, became convinced that Mussolini was the embodiment of Italy's destiny. Gentile acted briefly as Mussolini's Minister of Education and subsequently as the Fascist Party's chief theorist. He is responsible for a strong Hegelian element in fascist thought. Together, Mussolini and Gentile wrote the best-known epitome of Italian fascist thinking, 'Fascism: Doctrines and Institutions', in the *Encyclopædia Italiano* of 1932.

Fascists glorify the state as representing the unified people, and absolute unity is the ideal. All division and diversity is anathema. Hence fascism is totally opposed to liberal democracy with its divisions of opinion, right of dissent, tolerance, pluralism and party conflict; above all, it rejects liberalism's emphasis on individualism. At the same time, the fascist system is claimed to be superior to liberal democracy and capitalism in that it caters for all groups in society and not just those to whom the system gives an advantage. Equally, fascism rejects socialism's egalitarianism and its insistence on the reality of class division and the necessity of class conflict. Both Hitler and Mussolini talked of their systems as a 'middle way' between liberalism and socialism, while transcending both.

Fascism aspires to total unity with discipline imposed and inspired from above. The individual must be subordinated to and, if necessary, sacrificed for the sake of the state. People are therefore expendable, for value lies not in the individual but only in the unified whole. This is fully understood by the great leader, to whose will the masses must be moulded.

Fascism is consciously and explicitly totalitarian, with no organisation capable of resisting the state allowed to exist. The state has complete control of the media and education, and imposes ideological uniformity. The term 'totalitarian' was coined in Italy to describe Mussolini's regime, and he adopted it and used it with pride (though Hitler ignored the word). In 1932 Mussolini wrote:

> The keystone of Fascist doctrine is the conception of the state, of its essence, of its tasks, of its ends. For Fascism the state is an absolute before which individuals and groups are relative. Individuals and groups are 'thinkable' in so far as they are within the state . . . When one says Fascism one says the state. The Fascist conception of the state is all-embracing; outside it no human or spiritual values can exist, much less have value. Thus understood, Fascism is totalitarian, and the Fascist state – a synthesis and a unit inclusive of all values – interprets, develops and potentiates the whole life of a people . . . This is

> a century of authority, a century tending to the 'right', a Fascist century.
>
> ('Fascism: Doctrines and Institutions' in *Encyclopædia Italiano*, 1932; quoted in Lyttleton, p.39)

Both Hitler and Mussolini conceived of the state as an organism and its organisation as ideally corporatist. Mussolini wrote:

> Every interest working with the precision and harmony of the human body. Every interest and every individual working is subordinated to the overriding purposes of the nation.

In Italy this meant the different aspects of the economy were represented by corporations of workers and employers (in fact dominated by fascists) who planned everything in co-operation with the state. The system is known as 'corporatism'. Mussolini borrowed the idea from the syndicalists, but instead of just workers there would be capitalists as well. In practice the workers were disciplined while the capitalists could exploit them as they wished so long as they did what the national plan required. The aim was to build up the Italian economy and make it strong and independent, although in fact it ended up corrupt and inefficient. Economic self-sufficiency was one of the preoccupations of the aggressive nationalism of the late nineteenth and early twentieth century (as distinct from the liberal belief in free trade).

Fascists also glorify leadership. Mussolini called himself 'il Duce' and Hitler 'der Führer', both meaning 'the Leader'. The Leader is the symbol of his people and their struggle. Both Mussolini's *Autobiography* and Hitler's *Mein Kampf* (meaning 'my struggle') were romanticised and mythologised versions of their authors' lives with which the people were supposed to identify and from which gain inspiration. It is the great leader alone who can understand and articulate the 'true' will of the people. The great leader has the right to hold absolute authority over his people and demand their absolute obedience; it is what Hitler called the 'leadership principle' or *Führerprinzip*. This was absolute dictatorship, but because the leader was supposed to fully express the people's will, the fascists also claimed it to be the purest democracy.

The leader is the best of his people and has proved this by having struggled to the top. This idea comes from the social Darwinism that both Mussolini and Hitler embraced. Action, struggle and violence are natural and good, hence the fascist glorification of war. Mussolini wrote:

> Fascists above all do not believe in the possibility or utility of universal peace. It therefore rejects the pacifism that masks surrender and cowardice. War alone brings all human energies to their highest tension and sets a seal of nobility on the people who have the virtue to face it . . . For Fascism the tendency to empire, that is to say the expansion of nations, is a manifestation of vitality, its contrary is a sign of decadence. Peoples who rise, or suddenly flourish again are imperialistic; peoples who die are peoples who abdicate.
>
> ('Fascism: Doctrines and Institutions' in *Encyclopædia Italiano*, 1932; quoted in Lyttleton, p.56)

Fascist values reach their highest expression in war. It is in war that the nation is most united, disciplined and possessed of a sense of purpose and national pride. War is thought to 'purify' and strengthen the people; the individual is submerged in the mass, while the opportunity is presented for individual courage and self-sacrifice for the good of the whole. In war the state is supreme and leadership responds to its greatest challenge. The people forget their difficulties and conflicts and respond to leadership with a heightened sense of national emotion and participation. Not surprisingly, fascist regimes tended to be highly militaristic.

Fascist dictators have not been remote autocrats, but demagogues appealing directly to the mass of the people. They have sought to arouse mass passion and maintain a heightened emotion of mass solidarity against those identified as enemies within and without. Control and use of the mass media (especially radio and film, but also newspapers) is a crucial element in fascism, and helps to make it a peculiarly twentieth-century phenomenon. Emotional rhetoric, especially the rhetoric of hate, played a central part, and Mussolini and Hitler were both masters of swaying mass audiences. Great emphasis was put on symbolism and ritual, with flags, uniforms, insignia, rallies and parades to excite and unify the people with a common emotion. Mass adulation of the leader was generated and sustained, in a way quite different from mere fear of a ruthless dictator. Both Mussolini and Hitler were immensely popular when at the height of their power.

Fascist ideas and methods tend to be intellectually crude; indeed, fascists despise intellectuals and sophisticated theory. Instead, they stress instinct, emotion, will and above all action. There is, therefore, a strong irrationalist element in fascism: emotion and will are the basis for action, rather than reason (Mussolini exhorted his followers to 'think with your blood'). In consequence, fascism is widely understood as a relapse into barbarism, a return to the primitive and a denial of the basic values of civilisation. On the other hand, fascism is not as incoherent as is sometimes claimed and is more than merely an *ad hoc* jumble of ideas thrown together by political opportunists.

At the height of its influence, in the years between the two world wars, there were fascist or quasi-fascist movements in most European countries, and even beyond (most notably in Argentina). This included Britain, where the British Union of Fascists, led by Sir Oswald Mosley, caused a stir but had no electoral success. The crushing defeat of the Axis Powers in World War II discredited fascism as a serious political movement. Since 1945 pure fascism has been mainly associated with racist groups on the political fringe. Only Italy maintained a small non-racist fascist party based in the south. In the 1990s it embraced democracy and achieved a degree of respectability as a partner in the right-of-centre coalitions of Silvio Berlusconi. Elsewhere, right-wing parties with a tinge of racism have had periods of electoral success in France and Germany, and more recently in Austria, Holland and other European countries. But these parties are a long way from the fascism of Hitler or Mussolini.

Further reading

Primary sources

Lyttleton, A. (ed.): *Italian Fascisms: Pareto to Gentile* (London: Jonathan Cape, 1973).

Griffin, R. (ed.): *Fascism* (Oxford: Oxford University Press, 1995).

Secondary sources

Bosworth, R.J.B.: *The Italian Dictatorship: Problems and Perspectives of Mussolini and Fascism* (London: Arnold, 1998).

—: *Mussolini* (London: Arnold, 2002).

Griffin, R.: *The Nature of Fascism* (London: Routledge, 1991).

Nolte, E.: *The Three Faces of Fascism* (London: Weidenfeld & Nicolson, 1965).

Ridley, J.: *Mussolini* (London: Constable, 1997).

MARCUS GARVEY (1887–1940) AND BLACK EMANCIPATION

For almost a century after the formal abolition of slavery African Americans were segregated, discriminated against and denied their rights as full citizens in the country of their birth. The long struggle to achieve genuine emancipation was largely unsuccessful until frustration and anger finally exploded in the mass protests, riots and black radicalism of the late 1950s and 1960s. This explosion would ultimately result in a degree of integration and recognition of rights hardly imaginable to many living in previous decades. The century and a half of black struggle produced a number of outstanding leaders whose ideas are of interest and importance. Among these is Marcus Garvey.

The effective denial of rights to the former slave population after the American Civil War (1861–5) called forth a number of political responses which can be divided into two broad categories: integrationist and separatist. The integrationist case, by far the dominant view, was based upon the demand that former slaves had a right to be treated as full citizens with full civil rights, in accordance with America's ideals as expressed in the Declaration of Independence and the Constitution. The separatist alternative at that time was represented by societies that were established to encourage black emigration back to Africa, none of which were successful.

By the turn of the century the most successful African-American leader was Booker T. Washington. He counselled blacks to postpone their demands for civil rights until, through hard work and virtuous conduct, they earned the respect and friendship of whites. This view was highly acceptable to the white population, but infuriated black activists who, along with white liberals, founded the National Association for the Advancement of Colored People (NAACP) in 1909. However, many black Americans joined up to fight for their country during World War I, believing that there would be progress on rights and integration once the war was over. In fact, in the post-war years discrimination and denial of rights were worse than ever, with the racist Klu-Klux Klan coming to the height of its power and political influence. This left many in the black community angry and disillusioned, and some turned to separatist ideas of pan-Africanism and black nationalism. It was Marcus Garvey who turned these ideas into a mass movement.

Marcus Moziah Garvey was born in Jamaica in poor circumstances in 1887. His father was a stonemason and he was the youngest of eleven children. After elementary education, Garvey was apprenticed to a printer. He pursued his craft in various parts of the Caribbean, before moving to London in 1912. There he became associated with a group of African exiles to whose anti-colonial journal he contributed. Inspired by this experience and by the ideas of black self-help he found in Booker T. Washington's autobiographical *Up From Slavery*, Garvey returned to Jamaica and in 1914 founded the Universal Negro Improvement and Conservation Association and African Communities League, better known as the Universal Negro Improvement Association (the UNIA).

The aim of the UNIA was to unite 'all the Negro peoples of the world into one great body to establish a country and Government absolutely their own' (*Philosophy and Opinions*, p.126). Its first manifesto called upon all people of Negro or African descent to work towards the rehabilitation of the race. The Association's general objectives were:

> To establish a Universal Confraternity among the race; to promote the spirit of race pride and love; to reclaim the fallen of the race; to administer to and assist the needy; to assist in civilizing the backward tribes of Africa; to strengthen the imperialism of independent African states; to establish Commissionaries or Agencies in the principal countries of the world for the protection of all Negroes, irrespective of nationality; to promote a conscientious Christian worship among the native tribes of Africa; to establish Universities, Colleges and Secondary Schools for the further education and culture of the boys and girls of the race; to conduct a world-wide commercial and industrial intercourse.
>
> (Quoted in Cronon, p.17)

There were later modifications, in particular the addition of 'to establish a central nation for the race'. The motto of the Association was 'One God! One Aim! One Destiny!' and members dedicated themselves to the 'general uplift of the Negro race'. It was all extraordinarily ambitious, but Garvey felt himself destined to lead his race.

In 1916 Garvey moved to New York and made Harlem the headquarters of the UNIA. This was a time when Southern black people were migrating to the Northern cities in large numbers, and Harlem was becoming the centre for black writers and artists and radical ideas, expressed in the 'Harlem Renaissance' or 'New Negro' movement in the 1920s. The UNIA celebrated and complemented this movement, spreading from Harlem to the rest of the USA and beyond. It claimed to have branches in forty countries across four continents and to have millions of members worldwide.

The UNIA was an umbrella organisation for black groups and developments of all kinds. It published newspapers and journals, most notably *Negro World*, which was circulated internationally. There was a paramilitary African Legion and a black church, the African Orthodox Church, complete with black God, Christ and Virgin, although other religions were welcome. There was a women's nursing organisation, the Black Cross, and a host of social and cultural societies. From 1920 the UNIA held annual conventions with delegates from around the world, which were great festivals of activity with parades and celebrations, political discussions and umpteen artistic and social events. The 1920 Convention elected Garvey as the 'Provisional President of the Republic of Africa' together with a 'cabinet' of distinguished people with grandiose titles. It was all rather fanciful and meant little in the real world. More importantly, it passed a Declaration of the Rights of the Negro Peoples of the World demanding, among other things, freedom and civil rights for all people of African descent. The UNIA also strove to create a base in Liberia, which had been created by freed slaves in the early nineteenth century and was one of the few independent black states in Africa, but the plans fell through.

One of the UNIA's major initiatives was to create an organisation, the Negro Factories Corporation, that would provide finance and practical assistance to black people setting up businesses, although in the end it was not a financial success. Garvey also had various schemes for connecting African Americans to Africa and to other black communities. The best known of these was the Black Star Steamship Company, created to take trade, travellers and migrants between Africa and communities of African descent, particularly in North America and the Caribbean. Unhappily, the company was a financial disaster, buying poor ships in bad repair and showing poor business sense. The directors were accused of fraud, although commercial incompetence was perhaps more the reality. At their trial, Garvey conducted his own defence and alienated the jury by using the opportunity to expound his ideas; he alone was convicted. After two years of appeals he went to prison in 1925, although his sentence was commuted and he was deported to Jamaica two years later. The UNIA never really recovered from Garvey's deportation, despite his many attempts to revive it. He moved to London in 1934 and died a somewhat forgotten figure in 1940.

Garvey believed in the creation of a Negro civilisation for the future, but one that black men and women had created for themselves, free of white influence. This could not be done while still under the domination of the white man. Instead, he believed that the black community had to make itself self-sufficient in all things, social, cultural and economic.

The new Negro civilisation had to arise, Garvey believed, from a pure Negro race, and he was opposed to racial mixing. It had to bind together all blacks in all countries. Two things were needed create international racial solidarity. The first was the common African inheritance. A major theme of *Black World* and other Garveyite publications was black pride in the African cultural heritage. The second thing that should bind all Negroes together was the common struggle against racial oppression. Black people in America, the Caribbean and elsewhere should help Africa to throw off colonialism, while Africans should support black struggles in America and beyond.

Garvey believed in the liberation of Africa and the creation of an all-African state, a United States of Africa, of which all black people around the world could have citizenship in addition to being citizens of their own countries. In a 1922 article, 'The True Solution to the Negro Problem', he wrote:

> we are determined to solve our own problem, by redeeming our Motherland Africa from the hands of alien exploiters and found there a government, a nation of our own, strong enough to lend protection to the members of our race scattered all over the world, and to compel the respect of the nations and races of the earth.
>
> (*Philosophy and Opinions*, pp.38–9)

Garvey is often primarily associated with the 'Back to Africa' movement, but this is misleading. He did not see the fundamental solution to black Americans' particular problems in terms of some future mass exodus to a free Africa, although undoubtedly many of his followers did think in these terms (especially in the Caribbean). He did believe that large numbers, perhaps many tens of thousands, of African Americans would emigrate to a free Africa to help build a new nation, but he knew that the whole black population of America could not return in this way. Garvey also rejected the idea of creating a separate black state carved out of the USA (which proponents called the 'Republic of New Africa'), although the idea was much discussed in the UNIA. Garvey thought more in terms of an African state that would stand up for black people all over the world, similar to the Zionist conception of a Jewish state.

Within the USA itself Garvey envisaged a parallel society, with African Americans recognised and respected as a separate nation. He supported the demands of integrationists for full citizenship, while remaining a convinced separatist. He wanted to see an end to black Americans being exploited and discriminated against, but he had no wish to see them culturally assimilated or the two races amalgamated. African Americans must develop their own society with its own institutions separate from white society and white ideas. They should be less concerned with the struggle for political rights and social equality and more with becoming as independent as possible within the white man's world. Intellectually and culturally they should connect with black people beyond the USA and contribute to international racial solidarity.

Garvey was an autocratic leader, reluctant to delegate. He admired Mussolini and Hitler in so far as they were restoring their respective nations to greatness. This, together with his insistence on racial purity and his paramilitary African Legion (mostly used for ceremonial purposes), have led some to call him a fascist. But this is hardly fair. His 'Declaration of Rights of Negro Peoples of the World' makes clear his view that all peoples have rights of self-determination and all individuals have absolute civil rights. But his high-handedness did make him many enemies. He was disliked and distrusted by integrationists, both black and white, and he had little support from better-off African Americans.

Garvey was a protean figure whose thought was many-sided and not always consistent. One particular weakness was a perhaps surprising ignorance of Africa, of which he had a somewhat romanticised view. Although fairly widely travelled, he never actually set foot on African soil and did not seem to be aware of the variety and complexity there that would have made political unity extremely difficult. Nevertheless, he built an organisation of global importance and promoted what is sometimes called Diaspora Pan-Africanism, concerned not just with African decolonisation and unification, but with the status and future of all peoples of African descent.

The UNIA was very much an organisation for ordinary black people, especially in the northern ghettos. It gave them hope and a sense of purpose and pride in their race and its heritage. It was the first black mass movement and was a precursor of future developments. Garvey also helped to inspire nationalist movements in Africa itself, movements that would eventually lead to independence for all major colonies.

The UNIA declined after Garvey was deported and, with the Great Depression, the 1930s was a bleak time for Americans generally. It was not until the 1950s that the black movement revived again on a mass scale, after another world war in which blacks again fought for their country in large numbers only to return to face the same discrimination and marginalisation as before. By this time, the Nation of Islam had become the leading black nationalist movement. It was a combination of the integrationist civil rights protests of Martin Luther King, together with the separatist protests of the Nation of Islam and more radical groups like the Black Panthers, that shook the white establishment in the 1960s and led to the subsequent progress in the recognition of black rights and dignity in American society. This movement was also in many ways an inspiration and a model for other marginalised and oppressed groups – such as women, gay people and indigenous peoples – whose struggles have helped to create a generally more tolerant and egalitarian society across the Western world today.

Although there has been immense progress in respect of black rights in America, there is still some way to go towards full African-American equality, and there is still the basic dichotomy in the black movement between integrationists and separatists. The latter are still dominated by the Nation of Islam, led by Louis Farrakhan, who demands a rich portion of American soil for a black state in compensation for America's historic crimes against its black people. Much of this echoes the black nationalism of Marcus Garvey, although in his fostering of black pride and a sense of heritage and in his demand for black solidarity, Garvey remains an inspiration for both integrationists and separatists alike.

Further reading

Primary source

Philosophy and Opinions of Marcus Garvey, compiled by A.J. Garvey (2nd edn; London: Frank Cass, 1967).

Secondary sources

Cronon, E.D.: *Black Moses: The Story of Marcus Garvey and the Universal Negro Improvement Association* (Madison, WI: University of Wisconsin Press, 1969).

Essien-Udom, E.V.: *Black Nationalism: A Search for an Identity in America* (Chicago, IL: Chicago University Press, 1972).

Stein, J.: *The World of Marcus Garvey* (Baton Rouge, LA: Louisiana State University Press, 1986).

Van Deburg, W.L.: *Modern Black Nationalism: From Marcus Garvey to Louis Farrakhan* (New York: New York University Press, 1997).

Vincent, T.G.: *Black Power and the Garvey Movement* (Berkeley, CA: Ramparts Press, 1972).

HANNAH ARENDT (1906–75)

Hannah Arendt was born into a middle-class Jewish family in Hanover in 1906. She was a brilliant student who studied philosophy under two major existentialist thinkers: Karl Jaspers and Martin Heidegger. With the rise of the Nazis, she was obliged to flee Germany, eventually reaching the USA in 1941, where she became an American citizen. For a number of years Arendt worked for Jewish organisations and in publishing, before gaining her first academic post in Chicago in 1963. Thereafter she held a number of distinguished posts in American universities until her death in 1975.

Although influenced by her existentialist mentors, this was a matter of method rather than content. It gave Arendt an approach to politics very different from the prevailing traditions of political thought. She sought to understand the nature of political experience 'from the inside' rather than construct an external 'objective' theory of how it all works. She strove to be systematic without producing a system. It made her a very individual political thinker, with a distinctive understanding of the nature of politics. This she applied to her particular themes of the nature and origins of totalitarianism and the basis of the optimum form of politics based on a proper understanding of authentic political experience.

Arendt's first major work was *The Origins of Totalitarianism* (1951), in which she was the first theorist to show the phenomenon of totalitarianism to be something quite new and peculiar to the twentieth century. Her account is a vivid reconstruction of the totalitarian experience and was much criticised for this imaginative element and its deployment of her wide understanding of literature and culture as well as her subsuming of Nazism and communism within the same category. She saw totalitarianism's essence in terms of the bureaucratisation of terror in the enforcement of an ideology. It was a controversial analysis at the time and remains so. A later book, *Eichmann in Jerusalem: A Report on the Banality of Evil* (1965), was equally controversial in that it portrayed Eichmann more as an unimaginative bureaucrat than a monster.

These accounts see totalitarianism as exhibiting what Arendt saw as a general weakness in modern political thinking. Existentialism in general sees Western philosophy, beginning with Plato, as at fault in its understanding of human existence. It attempts to view human existence objectively, from 'outside', in the same way we view nature. In nature we see vast complexity and dazzling variety, but through metaphysics and science we perceive an underlying order and clarity and system. The next step, a mistaken step, is to extend the analysis to humanity, indeed to extend the order of nature to human affairs and try to shape those affairs accordingly: that is, to identify the underlying aspect of nature that is 'human nature' and then shape society to fit that nature. Totalitarianism is an extreme version of this.

What then is the basis of a true understanding of political life? Arendt sets out her ideas in *The Human Condition* (1958), in which she offers an analysis of human activities. There are theoretical and practical activities, with politics coming under the category of the practical. Practical activity comes in a hierarchy of three broad forms: labour, work and action. What Arendt calls 'labour' is at the bottom, and includes everything to do with maintaining our physical well-being on a day-to-day basis, such as preparing food and keeping warm and earning a living. 'Work' is the making of things on a more permanent basis: the creative work of the craftsman and artist, the building of institutions, and so on.

Finally, at the top of the hierarchy is 'action', by which is meant the human capacity to publicly intervene in the world and initiate something new or change the way we do things, however slightly, through word or deed. In this way individuals participate in the public life of the community and more fully realise themselves. The highest form of this participation, and the highest form of action, is politics. The reason that Arendt grants this high status to politics is that she sees it as creating the framework that gives meaning and purpose to all the rest. However, the mistake of most theorists is, in Arendt's terms, to treat politics as a form of work. That is, in terms of designing and creating permanent structures that supposedly 'fit' human nature. Arendt sees politics in terms of a way of life by which citizens actively participate in the public affairs of the community and see that participation in communal discussion and action as a vital part of daily life. She believes that it is only in a true political community of this kind that we have genuine freedom and autonomy and we can completely realise ourselves as human beings.

Arendt's conception has some affinities with Ancient Greek political thought and practice, especially Greek citizens participating in the affairs of the city-state. These could not be recreated in the modern world. However, Arendt has another Classical model in mind, that of Classical Republicanism. This was a tradition of Western political thought that drew its inspiration more from Republican Rome, which stressed unity and patriotism and saw the 'public space' as an arena of competition to serve the public good. This tradition of thought was revived in the Renaissance and influenced thinkers like **Machiavelli**, **Harrington** and the American and French Revolutionaries, though it rather died out in the nineteenth century. Arendt believes that we need to create a fuller sense of the political life as embodied in this tradition, to be aware of its fragility and to nurture it in the future.

Arendt's thought has been criticised on a number of grounds. Not all human activities fit into her labour–work–action categories, which in any case overlap with each other. She is also ambiguous on whether politics is ideally seen as an arena of competition or of co-operation. Arendt founded no school of political theory, nor has any genuine followers, but she is nevertheless greatly admired as a political thinker for her originality and insight.

Further reading

Primary sources

The Human Condition (Chicago, IL: University of Chicago Press, 1958).
Eichmann in Jerusalem: A Report on the Banality of Evil (New York: The Viking Press, 1963).
The Origins of Totalitarianism (3rd edn; London: George Allen & Unwin, 1966).

Secondary sources

Canovan, M.: *The Political Thought of Hannah Arendt* (London: J.M. Dent, 1974).
—: *Hannah Arendt: A Reinterpretation of Her Thought* (Cambridge: Cambridge University Press, 1992).
Parekh, B.: *Hannah Arendt and the Search for a New Political Philosophy* (Basingstoke: Macmillan, 1981).
Villa, D.: *The Cambridge Companion to Hannah Arendt* (Cambridge: Cambridge University Press, 2000).

SIR ISAIAH BERLIN (1909–97)

Isaiah Mendelevich Berlin was born in Riga, Latvia. His father was a prosperous timber-merchant, but fled to Russia with his family when the Germans invaded Riga in 1915. The family moved to England in 1920, and settled in London. Enough of the family fortune had been rescued to enable the young Berlin to be sent to private schools. He went up to Corpus Christi College, Oxford, in 1928, and took a First in Greats in 1931 and in Philosophy, Politics and Economics in 1932.

He intended to read for the Bar, but was offered, and accepted, a lectureship at New College. In 1957 he succeeded G.D.H. Cole as Chichele Professor of Social and Political Theory, and in 1966 became President of Wolfson College, the new postgraduate foundation. He held this post until his retirement in 1971. Most of Berlin's writing, like that of his contemporary Michael **Oakeshott**, has been in the form of essays, collected into several volumes between 1978 and 2000. When Berlin was appointed to the Order of Merit in 1971, his friend Maurice Bowra said of him:

> Though, like our Lord and Socrates, he does not publish much, he thinks and says a great deal, and has had an enormous influence on our times.
>
> (obituary notice, *Independent*, 7 November 1997)

It is with his inaugural lecture as Chichele Professor, 'Two Concepts of Liberty', that students of political thought are most familiar. This famous *pièce d'occasion* has been anthologised several times, and is printed in his book *Four Essays on Liberty* (1969).

Berlin's early interests were in philosophy, and especially the philosophy of science. Like Sir Karl **Popper**, he was a critic of logical positivism, believing that verification is not a sufficient criterion of truth or meaning for many types of statement. After the war, influenced especially by the Russian radical Alexander Herzen, Berlin's interests shifted from philosophy to the history of ideas (he had already published a book called *Karl Marx: His Life and Environment* in 1939). Especially through the study of **Machiavelli**, Vico and **Herder**, Berlin came to hold the Romantic, anti-Enlightenment view that there is not, and cannot be, one unitary, architectonic view of the human good. This is the belief with which he is most often associated. The world in which we live, he holds, is one in which there exists an indeterminate number of different values. We have to accept, as a fact of moral epistemology, that values are often incommensurable and irreconcilable.

> If, as I believe, the ends of men are many and not all of them are in principle compatible with one another, then the possibility of conflict and of tragedy can never wholly be eliminated from human life, either personal or social. The necessity of choosing between absolute claims is ... an inescapable characteristic of the human condition.
>
> ('Two Concepts of Liberty')

This is true at the level of the individual, the culture or the nation. No rational criterion exists by which any one version of the good life can be shown to be better than any other; life has no single goal that reason can identify. The choices that, as moral beings, we have to make, are often difficult and sometimes agonising. It may be that we cannot have both liberty and equality, justice and mercy, candour and kindness. Our moral beliefs are ultimately personal and non-rational. Precisely because they are, we can never be justified in forcing them on others, no matter how passionately we hold them. The belief that any doctrine or ideology can offer a blanket solution to humanity's problems is fallacious and, because of the things so often done in the name of such solutions, pernicious.

The practical upshot of these observations is the kind of pluralism that Berlin advocates in 'Two Concepts of Liberty'. It is in this essay that he expounds his famous distinction between 'positive' and 'negative' freedom (although the terms 'positive' and 'negative' freedom were coined, not by Berlin, but by T.H. **Green**). 'Positive' freedom is freedom defined as the achievement of self-mastery or self-realisation, and self-realisation in itself is a chooseable good, if by it we mean the willing actualisation by individuals of what they perceive to be their highest potentialities. The problem, however, is the one which twentieth-century history so readily discloses: the ease with which 'self-realisation' can be defined in terms devised, and often forcibly imposed, by those convinced that there is indeed one true goal and that 'true' freedom is attained only when the collective effort of the nation, or even of the whole 'species-being' of humanity, is dedicated to its attainment. The belief that there is such a goal has, Berlin supposes, been productive of much misery. In particular, he deprecates the notion (associated with the British idealist philosopher Bernard Bosanquet) that we have a 'higher' or spiritual self and a 'lower' or empirical self, and the associated suggestion that one's higher self might be set free by coercing one's merely empirical self. Freedom properly understood must, Berlin thinks, take account of the ultimately personal and non-rational nature of moral choice. It must be 'negative' freedom: freedom to adopt and follow one's own preferences without obstruction or interference by others. 'By being free in this sense, I mean not being interfered with by others. The wider the area of non-interference, the wider my freedom.'

It is obvious from the obituary notices which appeared after his death in 1997 that Sir Isaiah Berlin (he was knighted in 1957) inspired great affection and respect in those who knew him. Much given to self-effacement, he did not regard himself as having made any great contribution to the stock of human ideas. His thought, like Karl Popper's, is very much that of someone who experienced at first-hand the world wars of the twentieth century. His work remains relatively little appreciated, partly because of the breadth of his interests, partly because so much of it took the form of essays written for various occasions and partly because of his determined refusal to be associated with any particular doctrine. The judgement of his obituarist and editor Henry Hardy is succinct and just:

> His account [of positive and negative freedom] has remained an indispensable reference point for thought about freedom ever since, and permeates all subsequent informed discussion of the subject; nevertheless, perhaps partly because of the unassertive and deliberately unsystematic nature of his ideas, and his rejection of panaceas of any kind, he did not (to his relief) in any narrow sense acquire disciples or found a school of thought.
>
> (*Independent*, 7 November 1997)

Further reading

Primary sources

Four Essays on Liberty (Oxford: Oxford University Press, 1969).
Vico and Herder (London: Hogarth Press, 1976).
Against the Current: Essays in the History of Ideas (London: Hogarth Press, 1979).
Karl Marx: His Life and Environment (London: Fontana, 1995).

Secondary sources

Galipeau, C.J.: *Isaiah Berlin's Liberalisms* (Oxford: Clarendon Press, 1994).
Gray, J.: *Isaiah Berlin* (London: HarperCollins, 1995).

FRIEDRICH VON HAYEK (1899–1992)

Friedrich August von Hayek was born in Vienna. He studied law and political science at the University of Vienna and worked after World War I with Ludwig von Mises on problems of trade cycles and related matters. His association with von Mises apparently cured him of an early tendency towards socialism. He taught at the University of Vienna between 1921 and 1931. Between 1931 and 1950 he held a chair at the London School of Economics. Hayek then became

Professor of Social and Moral Science at the University of Chicago, where he remained until 1962. He also taught at the Universities of Freiburg (1962–8) and Salzburg (1968–77). He was awarded the Nobel Prize for Economics in 1974.

Hayek is a versatile, though not always an entirely coherent, thinker. His most important work was done in technical economics, in the fields of capital, trade-cycle and monetary theory (his major papers are collected as *Individualism and Economic Order*, 1948), but he was interested also in philosophy, political theory and theoretical psychology. On taking up his appointment at Chicago, he became one of the founders of the so-called 'Chicago School': that is, the group of monetarist economists working at the University of Chicago who believed that the economic policy of governments should be as non-interventionist as possible and that manipulation of the money supply is the only acceptable and non-injurious means of economic control. Hayek's own views on these matters had been formed before World War II, largely under the influence of von Mises, and during the 1930s and 1940s he was a determined opponent of Keynesianism and welfare-state economics. Always a convinced monetarist, in the later part of his career he went so far as to advocate the denationalisation of money: that is, the establishment of public and private currencies that would compete with one another. In 1979, Hayek suggested a restriction of the money supply so drastic that it would end inflation completely, even at the cost of short-term inflation as high as 20 per cent.

Socialism is the ulterior target of much of what Hayek has to say about politics. In particular, he is a determined critic of what Sir Karl **Popper** calls 'historicism'. Hayek's political views are best described as outgrowths of his economic doctrines combined with what may be called a Burkean conservatism and large helpings of subjective preference. In much the way that **Burke** does, Hayek believes that human behaviour and the various moral, economic and political institutions to which it gives rise are too complex to be fully understood and explained. Such institutions arise spontaneously over time. They are not really created by anyone. They come about as the more or less unintended consequences of a myriad human actions and interactions. The knowledge of them that any one generation has is tacit, incomplete and non-propositional. We all live within, and contribute to, an intricate structure of law, moral tradition and rules of behaviour, but no one can comprehend it fully, nor can it be said to have been created by anyone's deliberate act. This view of the nature of social organisation leads Hayek to be very sceptical of the claims of the social sciences, including economics. The complexity and irregularity of social phenomena does not lend itself to the kind of generalising explanation that the social sciences attempt to provide. But if social scientific explanation is not possible, nor is social scientific prediction, and economic and social planning purportedly based on such prediction is a mistake. We can predict trends or patterns, and we can explain general principles, but nothing more precise is possible. Only the market itself will, by its own self-regulating processes, set prices and production levels efficiently, and attempts by governments to interfere with this self-regulation are worse than futile. Distributive justice cannot be manufactured or managed by governments, and attempts to do so can only lead to harm because they inevitably interfere with natural mechanisms. Governments, therefore, should have no regulatory economic powers and no social-welfare roles. Hayek is also hostile to all other institutions and bodies, such as trade unions, which threaten the spontaneous workings of the market.

Thus expressed, Hayek's argument is a predictable enough defence of *laissez-faire* economics. As is commonly the case with such arguments, however, he makes his economic justification of *laissez-faire* serve also as an argument about individual liberty. The greatest harm to which central economic planning tends to lead, he argues in *The Road to Serfdom* (1944), is totalitarianism. Governments whose aim is to plan the lives of their subjects end, even if unintentionally, by taking away their freedom. There is no master-plan or architectonic human good. The best kind of government defends its citizens' rights by value-neutral laws that treat everyone equally, while allowing them the maximum possible freedom from coercion. Such government will, Hayek thinks, give to each individual the best chance of satisfying their own material and other preferences and avoiding interference by anyone else. A utopian account of the classical liberal constitution that would make such freedom possible is set out in *The Constitution of Liberty* (1960), with various difficulties and elaborations discussed in a trilogy called *Law, Legislation and Liberty* (1973–8). It should be added that Hayek's insistence on minimal government is much influenced by an inveterate tendency to mistrust the motives of politicians. He believes, for example, that in managed economies politicians will buy votes by bribing the electorate with measures that will produce inflation.

It is not easy to remember, at the beginning of the twenty-first century, that for much of his life Hayek's views were unfashionable and unpopular. During the 1940s and 1950s, his ideas were eclipsed by those inspired by Keynes. Hayek came fully into his own in the 1970s and 1980s, with the emergence of the 'New Right' in Britain and America. His doctrines, at least in crude and simplified forms, were adopted with enthusiasm by the Thatcherite wing of the Conservative Party in Britain and by the United States government during the presidency of Ronald Reagan. In her book *The Path to Power* (1995), Margaret Thatcher said:

> the most powerful critique of socialist planning and the socialist state which I read [during the late 1940s], and to which I have returned so often since [is] F.A. Hayek's *The Road to Serfdom*.
>
> (p.50)

Further reading

Primary sources

The Constitution of Liberty (London: Routledge & Kegan Paul, 1960).
Individualism and Economic Order (London: Routledge & Kegan Paul, 1976).
Law, Legislation and Liberty (London: Routledge & Kegan Paul, 1982).
The Road to Serfdom (London: Routledge & Kegan Paul, 1976).

Secondary sources

Barry, N.P.: *Hayek's Social and Economic Philosophy* (London: Macmillan, 1979).
Bosanquet, N.: *After the New Right* (London: Heinemann, 1983).
Gray, J.: *Hayek on Liberty* (Oxford: Blackwell, 1984).

MOHANDAS GANDHI (1869–1948)

Mohandas Karamchand Gandhi (the sobriquet 'Mahatma' is a title of respect meaning 'great-souled') was born in Western India and went to England in 1888 to study law. After practising for some time in India, he moved to South Africa in 1893, where he was a determined opponent of the 'pass laws' and other kinds of racial discrimination. Returning to India in 1914, he became a leading figure in the cause of Indian nationalism. The immense moral authority that he acquired rested chiefly upon the austerity of life that he adopted as a way of identifying himself with the poor. As a young man, Gandhi trained himself to eliminate all moral weakness from his character and to feel only benevolence. It is said that he slept naked with women in order to test his ability to withstand sexual desire. (How he managed to persuade anyone to co-operate in this experiment is not recorded.) He founded the Non-cooperation Movement in 1920, the Civil Disobedience Movement in 1930 and the Quit India Movement in 1940. He was much distressed by the violence that broke out between Hindus and Muslims after Indian independence in 1947. Despite increasing frailty – he was by then seventy-eight – he travelled the country in various efforts to restore peace. He was shot dead by a Hindu militant.

Gandhi's fundamental belief is in *satya*, 'truth', which (with an eye to Western audiences) he also calls God. *Satya* is the ruling principle of the universe. *Satya* manifests itself in all living beings, and especially in humans, as self-consciousness or soul or spirit. *Satya* constitutes the essence of the human being. The body is merely material and, as such, unreal. The satisfaction of bodily desire is degrading inasmuch as it represents a concession to the material and inauthentic. It follows that desire for anything beyond what is necessary to sustain life is to be avoided. Western civilisation, in so far as it is centred upon the unrestricted satisfaction of material desire, suffers from a spiritual and moral shallowness that will lead to its downfall. For this reason, Gandhi thinks that Western modernisation is not a suitable model for India's future development. Her future must grow from the traditional rural and agricultural roots of her economy.

Because human beings all participate in *satya*, all are parts of a single whole. External differences – race, caste, class, religion, regional loyalties – are irrelevant. The only appropriate relation between human beings is love. Love, Gandhi says, is the law of our being, and by love he means what we might more usually call compassion: unconditional practical concern for the welfare and happiness of others. Such love implies *ahimsa*, non-violence, as a principle of social and political action. The achievement of political and moral ends through *ahimsa* is what Gandhi calls *satyagraha*, 'truth force' or non-violent action. This notion of non-violent action is the crucial part of Gandhi's political theory. But *satyagraha* is not merely passive or sullen. It is a theory of *action*. It calls for courage, strength of character and positive commitment to a righteous cause. Nor is Gandhi's doctrine of non-violence absolute or dogmatic. In some circumstances, he thinks, it might be better to choose violence than craven submission to injustice.

On Gandhi's account of the true essence or nature of humankind, the state as we usually encounter it is the antithesis of how human beings should be organised. It institutionalises violence. It commands, compels, constrains. It encourages dependence and undermines self-reliance. In a word, the state dehumanises us. Yet it is a truth of experience that, in the present world, human beings lack the capacity to govern themselves. How, then, should government be organised so as not to be inimical to the real nature and needs of its citizens? The answer is a 'minimal' state: a state that is as non-coercive as possible and that leaves citizens with the greatest possible degree of freedom to develop their potentialities with dignity and self-respect. Gandhi's ideal is of a state consisting of self-governing village communities small enough for 'love' to be a practical reality and for communal approval and disapproval to be effective moral forces without the need for routine and formalised coercion. The ends of such a state will be achieved not through threats and force, but through persuasion and consensus. Conflict will be resolved constructively, through discussion and negotiation. Crime will be regarded not as wrongdoing to be punished, but as an illness to be treated by help and understanding. Villages will elect district representatives, who will in turn elect provincial and national representatives. Decisions will normally be taken by a majority; but there will be two important antidotes to a possible tyranny of the majority: namely, proper representation of minority interests and an indefeasible right of individual civil disobedience if one is called upon to act against conscience. This right of civil disobedience cannot be taken away, Gandhi thinks, without violating the moral nature of humanity.

The state that Gandhi depicts will above all be committed to *sarvodaya*: that is, to the development or improvement of all human beings rather than a ruling class or favoured few (it must be remembered that he is writing of an India in which there is still a deeply entrenched caste system). Gandhi disapproves of private property in so far as private property involves exploitation and inequality and accords primacy to material desire, but he concedes that, since it is everywhere established, it would not be feasible to abolish it. Instead, he suggests that the rich should hold their property in trust for the community, taking from it what they need and distributing the surplus to the poor. Gandhi was realistic enough to realise that such a proposal will not work unless the state takes a far more interventionist stance; in fact he thinks the state should in principle adopt such a stance. Indeed, he came eventually to recommend concessions to practice hardly consistent with his minimalist view of the state: redistributive taxation, restrictions on the right of inheritance, and nationalisation of land and heavy industry.

Like so many people who have made a contribution to 'political thought', Gandhi is not a political 'thinker' in the strictest sense. He is a moralist and man of action whose prescriptions are rooted in a synthesis of ideas drawn from disparate sources. Gandhi is nothing if not eclectic. He is influenced by the *Bhagavad Gita*, the Sermon on the Mount, Buddhist scriptures and the writings of Emerson, Ruskin, Thoreau and Tolstoy. He is a product of a particular and distinctive period of Indian history. His lofty morality, despite a tincture of self-righteousness that some have found annoying, has commanded almost universal respect, though rather less emulation. Perhaps Gandhi's most important influence has been on the black civil rights movement led by Martin Luther King.

Further reading

Primary source

The Collected Works of Mahatma Gandhi (Ahmedabad: Navajivan, 1958).

Secondary sources

Bondurant, J.V.: *Conquest of Violence: The Gandhian Philosophy of Conflict* (Berkeley, CA: University of California Press, 1965).

Dhawan, G.: *The Political Philosophy of Mahatma Gandhi* (Ahmedabad: Navajivan, 1962).

Iyer, R.N.: *The Moral and Political Thought of Mahatma Gandhi* (Oxford: Oxford University Press, 1973).

SIR KARL POPPER (1902–94)

Karl Raimund Popper was born into a Jewish family in Vienna. His father had a successful legal practice, but the family's comfortable life was disrupted by World War I and its aftermath. Popper left school at the age of sixteen and earned a living as a manual worker; he also spent some time as an apprentice cabinet-maker. A youthful flirtation with communism came to an end when he witnessed and repudiated the violence of contemporary communist agitators. He became a student at the University of Vienna and took his Ph.D. in 1928. He married in 1930 and became a schoolteacher. Alarmed by increasing violence and anti-Semitism, Popper and his wife left Vienna in 1937, just before the *Anschluss*. From 1937 to 1945 Popper taught philosophy at Canterbury University, New Zealand. He then became Reader (1945–8) and later Professor (1948–69) at the London School of Economics. He became a British citizen in 1945 and was knighted in 1965. Despite a notably touchy and quarrelsome disposition, he was much loved by colleagues and students.

During and just after his student days, Popper came to know Rudolf Carnap, Moritz Schlick, Kurt Gödel and other members of the group of positivist philosophers known as the Vienna Circle. This association, coupled with his reading of **Kant**, kindled in Popper a lifelong interest in the philosophy of science. He became interested in two questions especially: (1) how is science to be demarcated from other activities such as metaphysics, logic, mathematics and what Popper calls 'pseudo-science'; and (b) what reason have we for supposing any scientific theory to be true? He published his thoughts in 1934, in a book called *Logik der Forschung*, translated in 1959 as *The Logic of Scientific Discovery.* When the book came out, friends of Popper sent a copy of it to Einstein, who thought well of it. (Einstein's comments are printed in an appendix to *The Logic of Scientific Discovery.*)

Popper's philosophy of science is often called 'falsificationism'. The simplest way of understanding it is to glance at the 'problem' of induction, identified long ago by David **Hume**. On the face of it, science is the activity of formulating generalisations based on a large number of observations. This activity of observation and generalisation is (to put it rather simply) what we mean by induction. We take it for granted that a generalisation based on a sufficiently large number of observed past instances is a 'law' that equips us to predict what will happen in the future. Implicit in the procedure of induction, therefore, is the assumption that nature is uniform: that the future will, or even must, resemble the past. The 'problem' of induction lies in the fact that this assumption is unwarranted. No matter how many times the sun has risen in the past, we cannot *know* that it will rise again tomorrow. Bertrand Russell, in his little book called *The Problems of Philosophy*, illustrates the point by asking us to think about a chicken who is fed every morning by the farmer until one day the farmer wrings its neck. The chicken's inductive belief that the farmer would always feed it turned out to be a mistake. It should be noted, however, that the problem is not simply that we may make mistakes in arriving at generalisations; rather, it is that the process of generalisation itself has no warrant independent of our belief in it. To answer this difficulty by saying that our most important generalisations have always held good in the past clearly will not do.

How, then, can science be 'true' in the way that most people think it is? Popper tries to answer this question by denying, in effect, that induction is the proper basis of scientific method. Science does not produce 'laws' if by 'laws' are meant positive, conclusive and universal proofs. Despite what the Vienna Circle thinks, we cannot 'verify' anything. We cannot do so because no amount of confirmation of what we currently believe can show that our beliefs will go on being true in the future. We can, however, falsify. Even a single counter-example will show that a given generalisation is false; or, more strictly, that it is in need of modification. Properly speaking, therefore, scientific enquiry is not a process of amassing evidence in support of generalisations. It is an activity of 'conjecture and refutation': of formulating hypotheses by the use of a kind of informed imagination and then setting about the task of falsifying or adjusting them. All scientific beliefs are provisional. They are provisional in the sense that our only justification for holding them is that no one has yet made any observation that falsifies them. Once such an observation is made, the hypothesis must be abandoned, or at least revised. If revised, it can be held in its revised form until the arrival of another counter-example requires abandonment or further revision. Intellectual systems such as Freudian psychology or Marxist social science, which are not falsifiable simply because they will not allow anything to count as evidence against what they postulate, are what Popper calls 'pseudo-sciences'.

There is a sense in which Popper's political thought is an outgrowth of his notion of falsifiability. His political ideas are developed in two books: *The Open Society and Its Enemies* (1945) and *The Poverty of Historicism* (1957). Both are written with considerable passion. Popper makes no claim to be engaging in any kind of value-free political theory, and he deliberately writes in a manner accessible to the educated layperson. What he means by 'historicism' is the belief that it is possible to discover 'laws' of historical development and so devise large-scale social and political plans based on the knowledge of the future which such laws are thought to confer. The execution of such plans is called holistic or revolutionary or utopian social engineering. But the belief that there are covering 'laws' of history is of course false. We cannot know what the future will be like. We do not know what discoveries will be made in the future and what effect they will have on the course of history. The very act of predicting the future may influence the future by causing people's behaviour to differ from what it otherwise would have been (the 'Œdipus effect' is Popper's felicitous name for this possibility). Any long-term policy based on a predetermined vision of the future may therefore turn out to have unintended and unforeseen consequences. What may seem to be social laws are at best trends, and no reliable prediction can be made on the basis of a trend. This critique of historicism is accompanied, and to a large extent motivated, by a belief that historicism is a recipe for tyranny because it enables minorities to impose their will on others by virtue of their supposedly superior knowledge. *The Poverty of Historicism* is dedicated to the memory 'of the countless men and women of all creeds or nations or races who fell victim to the fascist and communist belief in Inexorable Laws of Historical Destiny'.

In view, then, of the unknowable and hence unpredictable nature of the future, social reform – 'socal engineering' – must be gradual and piecemeal rather than wholesale and sweeping. In this way, the effects of changes can be monitored, and unforeseen and undesirable effects counteracted as soon as they begin to make themselves felt. But the only way of carrying out this monitoring process is by attending to the criticisms of those whom the changes affect. No one has a monopoly of understanding, and every individual is potentially the source of valid criticism. There are therefore two prerequisites of sustained good government. First, it must be possible for people to express their criticisms effectively; second, it must be possible for them to change by peaceful means a government that is acting to their detriment. A society in which these possibilities are present is what Popper calls an 'open society'. Those who claim that society can be governed according to central plans imposed by virtue of the esoteric knowledge of an elite are what Popper calls 'enemies of the open society'. He has in mind especially **Plato**, **Hegel** (for whom his contempt knows no bounds) and **Marx**.

Popper's political thought combines the kind of liberalism of which John Stuart **Mill** is a typical exponent, with the fear of change and liking for cautious reform associated with **Burke**. He is not an original political thinker, nor would he claim to be. His best philosophical work is in the philosophy of science. His political writing is, in essence, the utterance of one who experienced both world wars and whose experiences imbued him with a hatred of violence and authoritarian government. He is a kind of negative utilitarian, who believes in the power of cautious and rational change as a means of minimising avoidable suffering. Popper's reputation as a political thinker rests largely on the appeal that his ideas had for the generation of intellectuals to whom fell the task of rebuilding the academic life of Europe after World War II.

Further reading

Primary sources

The Logic of Scientific Discovery (London: Hutchinson, 1959).
The Poverty of Historicism (London: Routledge & Kegan Paul, 1961).
The Open Society and Its Enemies (London: Routledge & Kegan Paul, 1966).

Secondary sources

Albert, H.: *Treatise on Critical Reason* (Princeton, NJ: Princeton University Press, 1985).

Currie, G. and Musgrave, A. (eds): *Popper and the Human Sciences* (The Hague: Nijhoff, 1985).

Magee, B.: *Popper* (London: Fontana, 1973).

Schilpp, P.A. (ed.): *The Philosophy of Karl Popper* (La Salle, IL: Open Court, 1974).

MICHAEL OAKESHOTT (1901–90)

Michael Joseph Oakeshott read history at the University of Cambridge, where he fell under the influence of the idealist philosopher John McTaggart. He also came to admire **Hegel** and F.H. Bradley. After taking his degree in 1923, Oakeshott spent some time extending his philosophical education at the Universities of Marburg and Tübingen before returning to Cambridge in 1925, as a Fellow of Gonville and Caius College. In 1951 he became Professor of Political Science at the London School of Economics. He retired from his chair in 1968. Most of his writings, expressed in an elegant but mannered prose style partly inherited from McTaggart, are in the form of essays collected into several volumes. His only continuous book, *Experience and its Modes*, was published in 1937. Initially, it received little recognition. Its idealism was unfashionable at a time when philosophy in the English-speaking world was increasingly devoting itself to logical and linguistic analysis.

Experience and its Modes is concerned with nothing less than the elucidation of the nature of our experience of reality. It is a difficult book, which cannot really be explained in simple terms. Oakeshott begins with the characteristically Hegelian assumption that we cannot truly understand human experience other than as a totality of which the mind and the external world are subject and object. In plain English, we cannot fully understand experience unless we understand it 'as a whole' and 'for its own sake'. Everyday experience, however – the kind of experience that ordinary people ordinarily have – is partial, conditional, abstracted. It is reality experienced in a determinate 'mode', or from a particular and limited standpoint. In this sense, human experience may be 'recognised as a variety of independent worlds of discourse'. These 'independent worlds' are history, science and practical experience. History is our experience of reality *sub specie praeteritatis*, 'under the aspect of the past'; science (which Oakeshott does not regard as a sovereign or superior form of experience) is our experience of reality *sub specie quantitatis*, 'under the aspect of quantity'; practical experience is reality experienced *sub specie voluntatis*, 'under the aspect of will': that is, it is that mode of experience through which we devote ourselves to getting what we want. Oakeshott subsequently identified poetry – aesthetic experience – as a fourth 'mode'. Philosophy, Oakeshott thinks, is a form of intellectual activity that stands apart from and above any one mode of experience. Because it is not any one of them, and therefore not bound by any particular set of assumptions or presuppositions, it enables us to see and understand them all – to listen to their 'voices', as he likes to express it – in relation to experience as a whole. Education is the process of learning how to listen to these voices in conversation. This, he argues in *The Voice of Liberal Learning* (1989), is what distinguishes education from training, in which only one voice is heard.

Much of Oakeshott's career after *Experience and its Modes* was devoted to the explication of that form of practical experience which we call politics, and it is upon his various attempts to do this that his reputation as a political philosopher rests. Because so much of his work consists of essays published periodically during a long and active life, his position is not easy to summarise; nor, taken as a whole, is it without inconsistency. Any paraphrase inevitably makes his thought seem less complex and multi-faceted than it is.

Oakeshott's preferred form of political society is 'nomocratic' as distinct from 'teleocratic'. Both forms have from time to time made their appearance in the history of European states. Teleocratic societies, or *universitates*, are those that take a particular end or goal as a collective aim and in which the task of government is conceived as being the achievement of that end. Nomocratic political societies, on the other hand, do not aim at any particular goal. Their purpose is to provide a framework of value-neutral laws within which individuals can pursue their own preferred form of felicity. They are, in other words, communities of the kind that the liberal temperament is accustomed to applaud. The freedom which they make possible is the kind of freedom designated as 'negative' by T.H. **Green** and Sir Isaiah **Berlin**. But nomocratic societies are moral rather than straightforwardly prudential in nature: their members are united by a bond somewhat like that of friendship. Oakeshott also uses the terms *societas* (he is much addicted to Latin terms: often, it may be thought, to no real purpose) and 'civil association' to denote such societies.

Political activity, he thinks, inevitably takes place against a background from which it cannot be separated: a background furnished by the traditions and practices of the community whose activity it is. This background, or way of doing things, must be accepted as given. There is no point in trying to account for its origin or to imagine what life would be like without it. Its peculiar character conditions the kind of political activity which it is possible for the members of any given community to engage in. The traditions and practices of a particular community form a complex heritage that no one has made, that no one can fully understand and that it is dangerous to ignore or attempt to alter in radical ways. Oakeshott is therefore hostile to what he calls 'rationalism' in politics: that is, the attempt to conduct life according to abstract 'ideological' principles that take no account of the character of the community to which they are applied. Politics is not about collective salvation; it is not about centralised planning according to doctrinaire principles to achieve a redemptive purpose. It is (he says in his 1951 Inaugural Lecture on 'Political Education') an 'art of repair', the point of which is to keep us afloat on a 'boundless and bottomless sea' in which 'there is neither harbour for shelter nor floor for anchorage, neither starting point nor point of departure' ('Political Education', in Laslett, p.15). Political activity properly understood is the activity of pursuing the 'intimations' of the existing traditions of behaviour and attending to whatever changes and adjustments those intimations intimate. To do more than what is necessary to keep the ship afloat and functioning is to risk sinking it altogether.

Oakeshott's political thought takes its departure from a rather complex and unfamiliar metaphysic. The reader sometimes forms the impression that elegantly recondite language is being used to say something rather obvious. It is, however, easy to do injustice to so complex a thinker. It is fair to say that Oakeshott is a member of the family of whom Edmund **Burke** would be recognised by most people as the head, a family that includes Karl **Popper** and F.A. von **Hayek** (although Popper and Hayek are much more 'rationalist' than Oakeshott). Oakeshott is a conservative who mistrusts change, values custom and tradition, recognises historical complexity, and advocates a cautious and piecemeal approach to reform. He is said by those who were taught by him to have been a person of immense charm and magnetism. This no doubt goes some way towards explaining the esteem in which he is held in many early twenty-first century academic circles.

Further reading

Primary sources

Experience and its Modes (Cambridge: Cambridge University Press, 1933).
Rationalism in Politics and Other Essays (London: Methuen, 1962).
On Human Conduct (Oxford: Clarendon Press, 1975).
History and Other Essays (Oxford: Blackwell, 1983).
The Voice of Liberal Learning (New Haven, CT: Yale University Press, 1989).
"Political Education", in P. Laslett (ed), *Philosophy, Politics and Society* (Oxford: Basil Blackwell, 1963).

Secondary sources

Franco, P.: *The Political Philosophy of Michael Oakeshott* (New Haven, CT: Yale University Press, 1990).
Greenleaf, W.H.: *Oakeshott's Philosophical Politics* (London: Longman, 1966).

SIMONE DE BEAUVOIR (1908–86)
AND SECOND WAVE FEMINISM

Simone de Beauvoir was born in 1908 in Paris into a comfortable bourgeois family. She was educated at the Sorbonne in Paris, where the philosopher Jean-Paul Sartre, her lifelong intellectual companion, was a fellow student. Beauvoir taught philosophy during the 1930s at schools in Marseilles, Rouen and Paris, and from the 1940s began to publish – novels, essays, philosophy, articles, autobiography – becoming an internationally famous writer, celebrated as a thinker and feminist. She died in 1986, and was buried next to Jean-Paul Sartre in Paris's Montparnasse Cemetery.

Beauvoir's major feminist work is *The Second Sex*, a wide-ranging, existential analysis of women's situation that is possibly the most influential feminist text of the twentieth century. It was first published in France in 1949 in two volumes, under the title *Le Deuxième Sexe*, and was an immediate publishing success, not least because of its open treatment of women's sexuality. A shorter version in English appeared subsequently, in time to influence the 1960s women's movements in America and Britain.

When Simone de Beauvoir wrote *The Second Sex* in the late 1940s, much had been achieved politically by European and American feminists, and many of the legal disabilities of the past had been overcome. Women in many countries, for example, could vote and own property, and had access to higher education and to the professions. After two world wars, women also had more freedom socially and sexually. However, Beauvoir argued that despite all these gains women were not emancipated from men and remained in a subservient relationship. In *The Second Sex* she focused on women's situation, using a mix of history, anthropology, myth, ethnography, biology, literature and sociology to examine why women were effectively the inferior, the second sex: submissive, uncreative and unfree.

Philosophically, Beauvoir adopted an existentialist perspective in *The Second Sex*. Basic to her argument was the existential ethical concept that freedom is the most desirable of human conditions, particularly the freedom to choose. She adapted the existential categories developed by Sartre in *Being and Nothingness* (1943), in particular the notions of Subject and Object or Self and Other. These categories ultimately derive from the philosophy of **Hegel**, which sees the purpose of existence, for the individual and for humanity, as the achievement of self-understanding. Central to this process is defining and understanding oneself in terms of the 'other', or that which is not the self, that which is secondary, inessential and inferior. Modern and most historical societies, Beauvoir argued, objectified woman as Other and man as Self. Humanity had been defined as male and the human condition as masculine, with woman defined always in relation to man. The source of woman's subservience and enslavement, she suggested, lay in woman's 'otherness' in relation to man. Only man had the freedom to choose, to set himself up as essential and Subject, while woman as a consequence became inessential and Object.

The Second Sex is a massive text, dealing with a multitude of topics. It explores biological, psychoanalytic and Marxist explanations of women's destiny; reviews the history of relations between the sexes from primitive forms of society to modern times; and looks at the sexuality of women and its relationship with women's 'otherness'. Beauvoir also looks at myths relating to woman, particularly those relating to motherhood; considers the representation of women in male authors' novels; and reviews the evolution of contemporary women's situation from formative years to woman as wife and mother. The special situation of lesbians, independent women and career women is considered, and Beauvoir analyses at length the role of prostitutes, a role she saw as one where women might, in certain circumstances, use 'otherness' to exploit men.

In analysing why women were Other, Beauvoir rejected explanations of women's subordination offered by theories of biological determinism. Biologically, because women have a reproductive and rearing role, Beauvoir conceded it is difficult for women to be free.

But she argued that a woman need not be defined by her womb; it was possible for a woman to have a life beyond her reproductive function. Freud and psychoanalytical theories also did not provide satisfactory explanations of women's 'otherness'. Women's physiology and lack of a penis did not mean that women were inferior or envious of men, or suffered from a castration complex. The 'prestige of the penis', Beauvoir argued, was an aspect of power relations and the 'sovereignty of the father'. Beauvoir was also sceptical of the Marxist view that in a capitalist society everything, including women's oppression, derived from economic relations and the hegemony of the ruling class, and that with the advent of socialism the subordinate position of women would be transformed. Despite being a firm socialist, she saw women's situation not as a consequence of private property and capitalism, but due to male dominance over the female Other.

Central to *The Second Sex* was an examination of women's situation as wives and mothers. Women did not dispute male sovereignty in marriage because of their economic dependency and their reproductive function. Though Beauvoir recognised that the traditional form of marriage was in a period of transition, she maintained that within the institution of marriage women remained subordinate, secondary and parasitic, and that equality in marriage would remain an illusion as long as men retained economic responsibility. Beauvoir felt that women of talent were lost to humanity because they were engulfed in the repetitive routines of housework. She had a particular horror of cleaning, and said that 'few tasks are more like the torture of Sisyphus' than housework.

Motherhood, Beauvoir appreciated, might be for many women a supreme and happy stage in their life history, and in maternity women might be said to fulfil their destiny, but she maintained all women did not enjoy maternity and that pregnancy and motherhood were variously experienced. Some women enjoyed pregnancy, but for others the experience was one of nausea, discomfort or painful trauma. Beauvoir was sceptical of the sacred character of motherhood, and pointed out that it was only married mothers that were glorified, unwed mothers were usually considered disreputable. She recognised that some women found their whole existence justified in fecundity, but Beauvoir considered the notion that having babies made women into full, free human beings to be illusory. She thought that good mother love was a conscious attitude, a moral free choice, and not an instinct, and that there was such a thing as a bad mother. A mother's attitude depended on her total situation, and though circumstances had to be unfavourable not to be enriched by a child, Beauvoir suggested perils in motherhood, such as the mother as slave to the child and as left behind as the child transcends mother love. Beauvoir thought that to be a good mother a woman had to be well balanced, with interests and a life beyond child-rearing. She thought women who undertook paid work outside the home might be the best mothers.

Beauvoir saw the difficulties for women of reconciling work and maternity, and the 'slave labour' nature of women's work outside the home. She saw clearly that child-care outside the home was needed, and she had a very robust attitude for a French woman of her time towards contraception and abortion, and their role in permitting women to have the freedom to choose maternity or not. She advocated contraception, legal abortion, easy divorce and, indeed, artificial insemination, so that women might maximise their freedoms and choices. Paid employment outside the home, provided it was not exploitative, was a vital means to women's independence. But such things in themselves would not be enough to change women's situation. Attitudes and understanding must also change.

Beauvoir saw women's 'femininity' as supporting male sovereignty and insisted that there was no ready-made essence of femininity – it was a myth. Civilisation, not biology, had constructed the feminine. *The Second Sex* is not an assault on masculinity, but it can be said to be about femininity as a social construct, and a major theme is women's submission in their formative years to the feminine gender role, and the limitations and burdens of that role within the male-dominated power structures of the family. For Beauvoir, femininity was artificially shaped by custom and fashion, and imposed from without. She described how women learned to assume the female gender, and summarised her view in what is probably her most famous and widely quoted sentence: 'One is not born but rather becomes a woman' (*The Second Sex*, p.295).

Beauvoir concluded that there was no eternal hostility, no battle of the sexes between man and woman. Sexuality was not destiny, a woman's ovaries did not 'condemn her to live her life for ever on her knees' (p.736). There was no eternal feminine, there was no eternal masculine. 'New' woman needed an accompanying infrastructure of moral, social, cultural and attitude changes, as well as economic opportunity. Men and women should recognise each other as equals. 'New' woman needed equilibrium, a free exchange between sexes. They should be in perfect equality. Though she thought a range of relations was possible between men and women, Beauvoir's ideal was the balanced couple; a couple not living as a closed cell, but each integrated individually into society. Such a couple would display 'equality in difference, and difference in equality' (p.740) by mutually recognising each other as Subject. Thus, the slavery of half the human race would be abolished and the human couple would find its true form.

A new women's movement – sometimes called 'second wave feminism' or 'women's liberation' – began to develop during the 1960s, then grew explosively from the end of the decade. The major texts of the period, such as Betty Friedan's *The Feminine Mystique* (1963), Kate Millet's *Sexual Politics* (1970), Germaine Greer's *The Female Eunuch* (1970) and Shulamith Firestone's *The Dialectic of Sex* (1970), all owe a good deal to *The Second Sex*, in which Beauvoir anticipated many of their themes.

Since this initial phase, feminism has fragmented into a multitude of forms with many varieties – liberal, liberal socialist and radical feminism; psychoanalytical feminism; female supremacism; New Right feminism; eco- and anarcho-feminism; post-structuralist feminism and post-feminism, among others – and inevitably Beauvoir has been criticised by some. She has been accused of failing to celebrate women's nurturing and caring role, and of having little sympathy with women's reproductive function. It is said that she wanted women to be more like men. But despite such criticisms *The Second Sex* is widely recognised as the seminal text of the women's movement of the late twentieth and early twenty-first centuries.

Further reading

Primary source

The Second Sex, ed. H.M. Parshley (London: Vintage, 1997).

Secondary sources

Bryson, V.: *Feminist Political Theory: An Introduction* (Basingstoke: Macmillan, 1992).

Crosland, M.: *Simone de Beauvoir: The Woman and her Work* (London: Heinemann, 1992).

Gamble, S.: *The Routledge Companion to Feminism and Postfeminism* (London and New York: Routledge, 2001).

Okley, J.: *Simone de Beauvoir: A Re-Reading* (London: Virago, 1986).

Tong, R.: *Feminist Thought: A Comprehensive Introduction* (London and New York: Routledge, 1992).

HERBERT MARCUSE (1898–1979) AND THE FRANKFURT SCHOOL

Herbert Marcuse was born into a prosperous Jewish family in Berlin in 1898. After service in World War I, his early involvement with revolutionary politics ended with the failure of the Communist Revolution in Germany in 1919. Marcuse then studied for a doctorate in literature and spent a number of years in publishing, before turning to the study of philosophy under Husserl and Heidegger. He then joined the Frankfurt Institute of Social Research in 1933. With the rise of the Nazis in the same year, he left Germany and followed the Institute to America. During the war, Marcuse worked for American Intelligence and for a while for the State Department (later a cause of embarrassment among his student followers). He resumed his academic career in America in the early 1950s and his subsequent writings helped to inspire the New Left and radical student movements there, for which he became something of an international figurehead. Their failure was a great disappointment and led to a progressive decline in Marcuse's standing as a thinker.

For most of his career Marcuse was associated with the Frankfurt School, which was founded as the Institute of Social Research by a group of young middle-class intellectuals in 1923. Although officially part of Frankfurt University, the Institute was funded by the wealthy family of one of its founders, which gave it a good deal of independence. The Institute was devoted to interdisciplinary social research from a broadly Marxist point of view (see Karl **Marx**), seeking to integrate empirical and theoretical work. However, it was only after Max Horkheimer became Director in 1930 that it began to develop the distinctive voice of the Frankfurt School. After leaving Germany in 1933, the Institute was refounded at Columbia University in New York, where it remained until its return to Germany around 1950, along with such leading figures as Horkheimer and Theodor Adorno. Marcuse remained in America.

The distinctive outlook of the Frankfurt School grew out of disillusionment with the official 'orthodox' Marxism of social democratic parties such as the German SPD and the Marxism–Leninism of the Soviets. Both were considered too rigidly mechanical and scientistic, and too prone to reduce everything to economic determinism (Marcuse later attacked Marxism–Leninism, in his book *Soviet Marxism: A Critical Analysis*, 1958, for generating a monstrous totalitarianism). What was thought to be missing was an understanding of individuals and their experience of domination. Various attempts were made, using non-Marxist ideas, to solve the problem. Before joining the School, Marcuse had attempted to fuse Marxism and existentialism. However, the solution turned out to be provided by Marx himself. In 1932 Marx's recently discovered *Paris Manuscripts* were published for the first time. This document revealed a more humanistic Marx, concerned with alienation and domination, and the possibilities of liberation. The Frankfurt School argued that it represented a truer Marx, before positivism and economic determinism began to distort his work. Marcuse wrote the first major review of the *Paris Manuscripts* and his first book, *Reason and Revolution* (1941), stressed the Hegelian and non-positivist roots of Marxism.

This new Marxism became the basis of the Frankfurt School's outlook and programme, which they termed 'critical theory'; it was formulated by Horkheimer in a series of articles in 1937. He rejected any claim that theory could be objective and value-free, and such theories as purported to be so merely supported the *status quo*. All theory had to be from a certain point of view and critical theory's stance was from the point of view of humanity in need of liberation, which in practice meant using dialectical reasoning to analyse the forms of human domination with a view to revealing the possibilities of liberation. It also involved seeing virtually all other forms of theory or knowledge as favouring the existing system of domination. The School was committed to a revolutionary transformation of society by means of changing consciousness, rather than awaiting capitalism's collapse through the working out of its own contradictions.

Positivism was the particular bugbear of the Frankfurt School. Positivist philosophy claimed for science a monopoly of knowledge, thereby marginalising any reasoning to do with values and moral purposes. The School insisted that the essence of science was not the pursuit of knowledge but the domination of nature. Science and positivist philosophy tended to reduce everything in nature, including human beings, to objects governed by mathematical relationships. This tendency was reinforced by capitalism, which tended to reduce everything, including human attributes, to commodities with the common measure of value in money terms. Ultimately this would lead to the destruction of individuality and civilisation, and to the triumph of totalitarianism. Furthermore, since scientific reasoning was only concerned with observed regularities, all science served to reinforce the *status quo* and close off any discussion of how the world could be better.

Positivism was also held responsible for the permeation of society by the kind of instrumental reasoning that technology represented, as strictly concerned with the most efficient means of control and manipulation. Their fears were strongly influenced by those of Max **Weber**, who saw the rationalisation and bureaucratisation of society as dominating social and economic life to such an extent as to threaten to crush all freedom and individuality, a process he referred to as the 'iron cage of modernity'. Unlike Weber, however, the Frankfurt School saw capitalism as at the root of the process, forever extending its control of society.

This analysis of science and positivism culminated in *Dialectic of Enlightenment* (1947), by Horkheimer and Adorno, in which they argued that the eighteenth-century Enlightenment's aspiration to create a world of universal freedom and happiness through reason had in fact resulted in its opposite: a world dominated by totalitarian oppression. Inevitably, the rise of the Nazis was a major subject for the Frankfurt School, with several accounts of the 'authoritarian personality' and related themes; the School initially saw it as a necessary consequence of the development of capitalism. Humanity was there to be dominated and manipulated, which taken to its logical conclusion led to fascism.

However, even if the overt oppression of fascism had been defeated, the prosperous West nevertheless kept the working class in comfortable slavery, deprived of the will to change the world. So complete did this seem to be becoming in the post-war world, that Horkheimer and Adorno despaired of any possibility of revolution. Of the leading Frankfurt School figures, only Marcuse was able to find renewed revolutionary hope in new theoretical developments and fresh sources of activism.

Marcuse turned first to psychoanalysis. In *Eros and Civilization* (1955), he attempted to fuse Marxism with Freudian ideas – indeed, Freud rather eclipses Marx in the book. Using Freud was not new to the Frankfurt School (Eric Fromm and others had used Freudian ideas, especially in trying to demonstrate the social psychology of fascism), but nothing as thoroughgoing as Marcuse's attempted absorption had been attempted. What Marcuse sought to do was to rewrite Freud's theory of the relationship between civilisation and sexual repression. Freud had argued, in *Civilization and its Discontents* and elsewhere, that the powerful instinctual drives that human beings possess, especially the sexual, have to be repressed in order that civilisation – institutions, businesses, states and empires, high art – can be created. Sexual energy has to be rechannelled to make it available for other purposes. The greater the level of civilisation, the greater the level of repression there must be. Thus, civilisation comes at a heavy price in terms of widespread individual unhappiness and a high incidence of mental illness. Freud's bleak conclusion was that there was no answer to this relationship between civilisation and unhappiness. Repression was an inescapable accompaniment of any kind of advanced human society. Marcuse, however, disagreed.

Marcuse argued that the need to redirect sexual energy to build civilisation was only true of times of scarcity, including most of human history, but that in a time of abundance, like the present in the West, the repression was no longer necessary. It becomes 'surplus repression' (echoing Marx's 'surplus value'), which is used to maintain the existing socio-economic system rather than creating more civilisation. Because this repression was inessential, it was a form of repression that could be exposed, resisted and overthrown.

Marcuse was a strong advocate of violent revolution to create an ideal society, which he characterised in terms of an 'eroticised' society. This did not mean, as was frequently claimed, a utopia of endless sexual gratification. Marcuse associated the erotic with all that was free, joyful and life-enhancing, including play, the arts and philosophy, as well as sexual freedom. Such a world Marcuse regarded as genuinely fulfilling the Enlightenment ideal of a rational world in which all are free and happy. Whatever society fell short of this ideal and whatever was an obstacle to it, Marcuse regarded as correspondingly irrational.

In his most famous and influential work, *One Dimensional Man* (1964), Marcuse attacked both advanced capitalist and advanced communist societies. In particular, he analysed the way the individual under post-war capitalism was subject to more subtle forms of oppression: a new totalitarianism, based upon technology and mass culture, that distracted the workers with consumer goods and cheap mass entertainment, removing any impulse to revolution and even the desire to reflect upon experience in any critical way. The result is the shallow 'one-dimensional' person typical of modern society.

One Dimensional Man is a pessimistic book, although Marcuse does not despair in the manner of Horkheimer and Adorno. The working class is thus removed as a revolutionary subject, but there are other possibilities. Marcuse puts his hope in those who have yet to be processed and brainwashed by the system (students in particular) and in those excluded or marginalised by the system (women, blacks, gays and the poor). These would be the source of new revolutionary thought and action. *One Dimensional Man* made Marcuse an international figure, putting him in the thick of the New Left movement, advising radical groups all over the world and turning out a stream of books and articles attacking all aspects of modern society and encouraging radical movements.

However, much to Marcuse's disappointment, the revolutionary fervour of the 1960s rather fizzled out in the 1970s; Marcuse devoted his last works to aesthetics and his view that art expresses human striving for freedom and happiness. Being such a high-profile revolutionary thinker and activist, Marcuse was subject to much criticism from all directions. Much of it applies to the Frankfurt School as a whole. More orthodox Marxists complained of their abandonment of central doctrines, the substitution of psychology and cultural criticism for political economy, their despair of the revolutionary potential of the working class, the importation of alien theories, and so on. Marxists and non-Marxists alike objected to the use of Freud, especially by Marcuse, as arbitrary and unconvincing.

Marcuse and the rest of his Frankfurt School colleagues are criticised on all sides for their treatment of science. To suggest, as Marcuse does, that all science, not merely its technological application, together with formal logic, are fundamentally repressive and supportive of the *status quo* hardly bears examination. For logic, science and technology, he offers alternatives that do not stand up. Marcuse never tells us what his alternative science and technology might look like, while the reliance upon dialectic as a superior sort of logic is arbitrary and self-serving. Similarly, Marcuse demands a wholesale destruction of contemporary society with no very clear idea of what to put in its place.

Marcuse and the Frankfurt School were important in the revival of Marxism and the radical tradition in general, expanding its horizons to include changes in modern capitalist society and provide fresh focus on culture. Since his death in 1979 Marcuse has become a somewhat neglected figure. However, there remains a considerable body of unpublished work, which may be the basis of revived interest in due course. In the meanwhile, the Frankfurt School continued with a new generation of thinkers, the most notable of whom has been **Jürgen Habermas**.

Further reading

Primary sources

Reason and Revolution (New York: Oxford University Press, 1941).
Eros and Civilization (Boston, MA: The Beacon Press, 1955).
One Dimensional Man: The Ideology of Industrial Society (London: Routledge & Kegan Paul, 1964).
Soviet Marxism: A Critical Analysis (Harmondsworth: Penguin, 1971).

Secondary sources

Geoghegan, V.: *Reason and Eros: The Social Theory of Herbert Marcuse* (London: Pluto Press, 1981).

Held, D.: *Introduction to Critical Theory: Horkheimer to Habermas* (London: Hutchinson, 1980).

Kellner, D.: *Herbert Marcuse and the Crisis of Marxism* (Basingstoke: Macmillan, 1984).

Reitz, C.: *Art, Alienation and the Humanities: A Critical Engagement with Herbert Marcuse* (New York: New York University Press, 2000).

MICHEL FOUCAULT (1926–84)

Paul-Michel Foucault was born in Poitiers in 1926, the son of a wealthy surgeon. He had a somewhat troubled youth and attempted suicide several times, but went on to study philosophy, psychology and psychopathology. After working for a period with the mentally ill, he taught at a number of universities in France and abroad, culminating in his appointment to the illustrious Collège de France in 1970, choosing the title of Professor of the History of Systems of Thought.

Like most post-war French intellectuals, Foucault began as a Marxist (see Karl **Marx**), being briefly a member of the Communist Party. Disillusioned, he was strongly influenced in the 1950s by the philosophy of **Nietzsche** and by French structuralism. Structuralism was an intellectual movement that developed within linguistics and then spread to anthropology, literary studies and a variety of other disciplines. It saw human activity, social organisation and, above all, language as governed by deep internal structures, complex sets of rules, which unconsciously work to severely constrain what human beings can think and do. On this view, our natural assumptions about our freedom to think and act and confer meaning are illusory. This anti-humanist stance was retained when structuralism evolved into the more fluid and ambiguous post-structuralism. Anti-humanism was endorsed by Foucault throughout his work and only modified a little towards the end of his life.

Foucault's first major publications – *Madness and Civilization* (1961), *The Birth of the Clinic* (1963), *The Order of Things: The Archeology of the Human Sciences* (1966) and *The Archeology of Knowledge* (1969) – could be said to be broadly structuralist (although he rejected the structuralist label, as he did all labels). Subsequently, his themes and approach became more Nietzschean, stressing the role of power in society and in knowledge, as in works such as *Discipline and Punish: The Birth of the Prison* (1975) and his massive *History of Sexuality* (three volumes of which were published, beginning in 1976, out of a projected six). In the 1970s Foucault became a major inspiration for radicals, campaigning on behalf of oppressed individuals and groups of various kinds. He was especially interested in sexual identity. In later years he spent much time in America, exploring the experimental gay scene in California. He died of AIDS-related illness in 1984.

In his early writings, Foucault seeks to explain the origins of our modern conceptions of madness, of clinical medicine and of the modern conception of 'man' generated by the new social sciences. He develops the concept of 'discursive formation', by which he means the complex of concepts and arguments and techniques and technologies relating to a particular practice, and how these in fact create not only the knowledge of a subject but the object of study itself. Thus, the modern conception of madness was created along with the creation of psychiatry in the early nineteenth century. This was not, as is generally assumed, the result of improved science and greater humanity, but of the wider needs of society for increased discipline.

The new conceptualisations, including that of 'man', are therefore arbitrary and could be otherwise. Just as psychiatry defines and therefore creates the madness it studies and treats, the human and social sciences create and help to control 'man', in the sense of establishing what is 'normal', what are the rules and norms of normal human functioning and how we understand ourselves. This is the point of Foucault's notorious remark towards the end of *The Order of Things*:

> As the archeology of our thought easily shows, man is an invention of recent date. And one perhaps nearing its end.
>
> (p.387)

What he means by this is that the way we presently tend to understand ourselves can change and perhaps soon will. He may also have in mind the triumph of structuralism, which would fatally undermine current notions of what is human – a view he held at the time, but subsequently abandoned.

These studies of modern forms of thinking are set against a background of a series of 'epistemes', which are broad frameworks that have changed over time from the Renaissance to the Classical period (*c.*1750–1800) to the modern. These frameworks provide basic assumptions that underpin particular disciplines and practices at a given period. Foucault's epistemes and discursive formations bear a close resemblance to the 'paradigms' described in Thomas Kuhn's

Structure of Scientific Revolutions (1962), which are similar structures of theory and practice that define 'normal science' for long periods. Like these scientific paradigms, epistemes and discursive formations are arbitrary and do not follow each other in a rational and progressive way that scientists, and the rest of us, generally assume. Foucault's use of the term 'archeology' rather than 'history' is meant to emphasise the disjunction and discontinuities of historical change in the way we understand the various aspects of reality, especially ourselves. Foucault wanted to emphasise that these pictures are not necessary but contingent and therefore changeable.

After 1970 Foucault abandoned the somewhat rigid and deterministic framework of epistemes and made discursive formations more flexible and, at the same time, more arbitrary by concentrating upon the concept of power and how power and knowledge are deeply interwoven. It is a move signalled by his use (following Nietzsche) of the term 'genealogy' rather than 'archeology' to describe his method. Genealogy studies the way in which what we count as knowledge and the content of discourse is the outcome of power struggles between groups whose views then count as universally valid truth and knowledge. Power is an integral part of the production of truth and there is a 'politics of truth' in any society whose outcome determines what is deemed true and by what procedures it is legitimately arrived at.

This is expressed above all in what many regarded as Foucault's most important work, *Discipline and Punish* (1973), in which he analyses the origin of the modern prison in the early nineteenth century. The reason for this development, he insists, was nothing to do with greater rationality or humanity, but with the need of an industrialising society for more efficient techniques of social control, with schedules of activity and systems of surveillance, culminating in Jeremy Bentham's all-seeing 'Panopticon' prison design, with its central tower from which all prisoners can be observed, where those subject to it internalise the system and become docile bodies. The prison, Foucault believes, became the model for all kinds of disciplinary systems in schools, factories, asylums and so on. 'Panopticism' characterises modern society, where all are scrutinised and made to conform to standards of 'normality'.

Through the social sciences the modern individual, or 'subject', is created in the sense of defined and given a sense of what is normal. In creating disciplined citizens the social sciences determine the nature of the modern state, which uses its knowledge of these sciences, rather than force or custom, to control society.

Disciplinary power thus pervades the whole modern society. However, Foucault's analysis of power is a subtle one. Power in society can be creative as well as oppressive, disciplines can enable as well as oppress. In modern societies, particularly in democracies, nobody 'owns' power: it moves and flows among different groups and institutions. It inheres in the system rather than in individuals. Society cannot function without it. Nevertheless, individuals are shaped, manipulated, restricted and oppressed by webs of power relations of which they understand little.

Foucault's history of sexuality also gives a picture of the individual hopelessly entangled in a web of power relations, although in this work there is another major theme (especially in volumes two and three, published in the year of Foucault's death): namely, the creation of the subject and how the subject can resist. If there is always power, there is always the possibility of resistance.

The modern subject is created by the human sciences and the systems of disciplines associated with them, and thus the systems of socialisation and social expectation that shape us. But the picture they create of what it is to be human and behave in appropriate ways can be challenged. We can intervene in the process and shape ourselves, although not in the sense of discovering our 'true humanity'. There is no such true humanity to discover; we would only be conforming to some constructed image generated by the system and thereby submitting to the system's disciplinary power. Instead, we must understand the processes involved and be creative in the construction and reconstruction of our individual selves. Therein lies the possibility of freedom.

Foucault has been the subject of criticism from many quarters. Some have criticised his historical methods, arguing that his interpretations are based on sweeping generalisations that rely on selective use and over-interpretation of evidence. Others have pointed to ambiguities in Foucault regarding the truth of theories that claim that truth is relative or that posit thought as socially determined without being determined themselves.

Criticisms have also come from the left. Although an inspiration for radicals in the 1970s, Foucault ultimately disappointed. He gives no indication of what a better world might be like, and so no reason for changing the present one on any more than a local level. Furthermore, given the oppressiveness of modern society as he portrayed it, Foucault's account of the possibilities of resistance seems very feeble. Limited local action and shaping one's life as a work of art hardly answer to the case. **Habermas** has been among those who have criticised Foucault's ideas as ultimately conservative, since they suggest that radical change is impossible.

But despite undoubted weaknesses, Foucault's ideas have been highly influential across the social sciences, especially his concepts of discourse, the operations of power, the relationships between power and knowledge, and – perhaps above all – his perception that what we consider fixed in our concepts and practices (especially reliance on social sciences) could always be different. Through genealogical research we understand the historicity and contingency of our understanding of ourselves and the possibility of freedom.

Further reading

Primary sources

The Archeology of Knowledge (London: Tavistock Publications, 1969).
Discipline and Punish: The Birth of the Prison (Harmondsworth: Penguin, 1977).
Politics, Philosophy, Culture: Interviews and Other Writings 1977–84, ed. L.D. Kritzman (London: Routledge, 1988).

Secondary sources

Gutting, G. (ed.): *The Cambridge Companion to Foucault* (Cambridge: Cambridge University Press, 1994).
O'Farrel, C.: *Foucault: Historian or Philosopher?* (Basingstoke: Macmillan, 1990).
Poster, M.: *Foucault, Marxism and History* (Cambridge: Polity Press, 1984).
Simons, J.: *Foucault and the Political* (London: Routledge, 1995).

JOHN RAWLS (1921–2002)

John Rawls was born in Baltimore, Maryland. He went to Princeton in 1939, taking his degree in 1943. After military service during World War II, he taught at Cornell University, the Massachusetts Institute of Technology and, finally, at Harvard, where he was a Professor of Philosophy for almost forty years. He became John Cowles University Professor at Harvard in 1976. He published numerous articles and reviews. His articles tended to be preliminary exercises leading to two large and influential books: *A Theory of Justice* (1971) and *Political Liberalism* (1993). He died on 27 November 2002.

A Theory of Justice is Rawls's major contribution to political theory. The notion of justice that he develops in it is often referred to as 'justice as fairness' ('Justice as Fairness' was the title given to a preliminary article published in the *Philosophical Review* in 1958 and reprinted in several anthologies since). In a certain sense, Rawls's argument is a rehabilitation of the old explanatory device of the social contract. Unlike the social contractarians of the seventeenth century, however, Rawls does not make the device part of a theory of obligation. Rather, he employs it in an attempt to establish what he thinks are rationally necessary principles of social justice. His chief purpose in doing so is to avoid what he regards as the major drawback of utilitarian or consequentialist thinking: namely, that such thinking can sanction the sacrifice or neglect of individual interests for the sake of a 'greater good'. This, he believes, is contrary to our intuitive beliefs about right and wrong. The system of social justice that he envisages will, as a matter of principle, exclude no one from its benefits. Rawls's underlying conviction is that a just or fair political order is one that provides similar opportunities for everyone to live a happy and fulfilled life.

Rawls's procedure is to invite us to engage in a thought-experiment. We are to imagine a group of individuals placed in what he calls an 'original position' – that is, in the Rawlsian equivalent of the seventeenth-century 'state of nature'. Their project is to devise the kind of society into which, on leaving this original position, they might wish to move. But the 'original position' is located behind a 'veil of ignorance': it is characterised by the lack of knowledge possessed by the people in it. They know that it will be useful to them to have what he calls 'primary goods': rights and liberties, opportunities and powers, income and wealth, and the bases of self-respect; and it is assumed that everyone is self-interested enough to want as much of these goods as possible. They do not, however, know anything about their own talents or abilities; nor do they know what position they will occupy in the society that they are to create. In such circumstances – in circumstances, that is, such that self-interested people are required to make decisions without knowing how those decisions will affect them – what principles of 'justice' will they devise for the society into which they are to move? They will, Rawls suggests, arrive at general principles that would leave the least advantaged member of the future society no worse off than any one of them would wish to be if they were to turn out actually to be the least-advantaged member.

There will be two such principles:

1 Each person is to have an equal right to the most extensive liberty compatible with a similar liberty for others.
2 Social and economic inequalities are to be arranged so that they are both (a) to the greatest benefit of the least advantaged, and (b)

attached to positions and offices open to all under conditions of fair equality of opportunity.

Rawls's two principles are, he thinks, rationally necessary and universal in the sense that any human being capable of thinking at all will arrive at them as a matter of natural reason. We can, he suggests, test them and, if necessary, modify them by a method called 'reflective equilibrium': that is, we can act on them, see if they satisfy our basic requirements of a system of social justice and, to the extent that they do not satisfy our basic requirements, alter them. They are, in other words, capable of fine-tuning. But anyone who knows what it is to behave fairly will assent to them in a general way. They are to that extent reminiscent of the 'laws of nature' that the older social contractarians invoked. The liberty of which the first principle speaks is 'negative' liberty in the familiar liberal sense – that is, freedom from restriction or coercion. This liberty will encompass a range of basic rights, such as freedom of conscience and movement, freedom of religion, freedom of speech, freedom of assembly and so on. The second principle – Rawls calls it the 'difference' principle – is intended to overcome the drawback that arises when negative freedom is interpreted in a strictly libertarian way: that is, the possibility that one might be destitute, homeless, starving and so on, yet still be technically free in the sense of unconstrained or uncompelled by anyone. The 'difference' principle is a principle of distributive justice. Under the system that Rawls proposes, even the worst-off members of society will have at least sufficient resources to enable their freedom not to be totally without value in practice. What Rawls's system implies is a welfare state in which the poor are provided with a minimum acceptable standard of living out of taxes paid by the rich. Rawls does not object in principle to there being a difference between rich and poor. He assumes a competitive market economy in which economic inequalities will function as incentives to the wealth creation that makes redistributive or progressive taxation possible. The practical limit to redistributive taxation is the point at which such taxation becomes a disincentive to wealth creation.

A Theory of Justice has been subjected to a great deal of analysis and criticism. Perhaps the major objection to which it is vulnerable is that its main argument is a question-begging one. The people in the 'original position' are the usual stereotypes of liberal political theory: rational, risk-averse, utility-maximising individualists. They are assumed to have exactly the characteristics – acquisitiveness, competitiveness, self-interest, caution – that will lead them to formulate the principles of justice at which Rawls wishes to arrive. If one were to imagine an original position full of gamblers or altruists, the kind of society that might be inferred from the anticipated behaviour of such people would be quite different. His theory of justice is to that extent a liberal democratic theory disguised as an abstract and universal one.

This is a point that Rawls came to accept in his later writing. In his second book, *Political Liberalism*, he presents a somewhat modified version of 'justice as fairness'. His purpose now is not to formulate a theory that purports to be universal and abstract, but to show how his theory is amenable specifically to the needs and aspirations of modern liberal democracies. A liberal democracy – a political society such that citizens are free to live their own lives in their own way under the protection of the law – is, Rawls assumes, the kind of society in which any reasonable person would want to live. But modern liberal democracies are strikingly pluralistic in nature. Pluralism or heterogeneity is inevitable precisely because the liberties that liberal democracies exist to protect find expression in a wide range of different moral, religious and philosophical beliefs. How, then, can the life of such a society be ordered in such a way as to minimise conflict between different views without prejudice to freedom? Rawls's contention is that the institutions and procedures of government should rest upon his conception of 'justice as fairness': justice, that is, as described by slightly modified versions of the two principles stated in *A Theory of Justice*. Justice as fairness minimises the possibility of conflict because it secures the interests of all, while remaining neutral with respect to any one conception of the good life. As such, it is capable of acceptance by all human beings who are rational in any normally recognisable sense of the term, no matter how divergent their other beliefs may be. Justice as fairness is, as Rawls expresses it, capable of being the object of an 'overlapping consensus'. It is therefore capable of forming the basis of a reasonable, humane, well-ordered society in which all citizens can participate at the level of 'public reason', while pursuing their own private versions of the good life in conditions of economic security and personal freedom: a society in which, moreover, tolerance and understanding of others can grow. *Political Liberalism* has not, it must be added, achieved the same degree of critical acclaim accorded to *A Theory of Justice*.

Rawls is a major figure – perhaps *the* major figure – in the Anglo-American political theory of the twentieth century. His courage and intellectual ambition are not in doubt, even to his severest critics – and he has been widely criticised, by those on both the left and right wings of the political spectrum. At a time when philosophy in the English-speaking world was still almost entirely committed to the analysis of language, Rawls persisted in trying to do old-fashioned, prescriptive, deductive system-building. It may be felt that he failed, especially by those who still believe that such an enterprise must fail of necessity, but his work is to be valued not so much for its substantive achievement as for the debate that his attempt at a theory of justice stimulated.

Further reading

Primary sources

A Theory of Justice (Cambridge, MA: Harvard University Press, 1971).
Political Liberalism (New York: Columbia University Press, 1993).

Secondary sources

Daniels, N. (ed.): *Reading Rawls* (New York: Basic Books, 1975).
Sandel, M.: *Liberalism and the Limits of Justice* (Cambridge: Cambridge University Press, 1982).
Wolff, R.P.: *Understanding Rawls* (Princeton, NJ: Princeton University Press, 1977).

ARNE NAESS (1912–) AND ECOLOGISM

Concern for the environment began to appear as a political issue in the 1930s when a number of policies directed at preserving the countryside began to emerge in several European countries. It was after World War II and especially after a series of massive environmental problems were identified in the 1960s – such as the threat of atomic weapons and other nuclear pollution, acid rain and many other problems that seemed to threaten the survival of the planet as we know it – that the environmental movement began to grow.

Arne Naess was born in Norway in 1912 and pursued an academic career, becoming Professor of Philosophy in Oslo in 1939. In his spare time he developed an international reputation as a mountain climber. It was only after he retired from his university post in 1970 that Naess developed the theoretical position for which he has become famous. This is the position known as 'deep ecology' or 'deep green'. Naess set out the principles of deep ecology in a lecture in Bucharest in

September 1972 (summarised in a subsequent article, 'The Shallow and the Deep, Long-Range Ecological Movement', 1973). In this lecture, Naess made the distinction between 'shallow ecology' in the form of mere environmentalism, which he characterised in terms of preserving the environment for humanity's purposes, and genuine or 'deep ecology', which was concerned with the whole of the biosphere, including humanity. Ultimately, Naess thought, shallow ecology is concerned with the well-being of people in rich Western countries; what was needed was a move away from anthropocentric values and towards 'biocentric' values, which focused upon all life and the total environment.

The lecture sought to lay down basic principles of deep ecology, by means of which humanity can again begin to live in harmony with nature. They begin with the principle of 'biospherical egalitarianism', which means that all species have an equal right to flourish, including species of no use to human beings. From this flow other, related principles that encourage ecological diversity and the values of living together as opposed to competition and domination. There are also principles of sustainability, having to do with the avoidance of pollution and resource depletion. However, what is crucial is the application of these principles to human behaviour and society.

Naess assumes that his principles apply equally to society as to nature. The principle of diversity includes diversity of human cultures, and points to the necessity of decentralisation and local autonomy. Equality of species includes equality between societies and within societies. Naess seems to assume that one implies the other, which is open to serious question. Nevertheless, deep ecology is meant to be fully consistent with modern notions of human rights, democracy and social justice, as well as with principles of non-violence (Naess is an admirer of **Gandhi**). However, perhaps the more important point is that these principles imply not just the introduction of environmentally responsible policies and not just an ending of the ideal of economic growth, but a complete abandonment of industrial society.

Allowing all species to flourish includes the prevention of one species crowding out others, which is what the human species has been busily doing. Population reduction is therefore essential. Naess has since argued that the optimum human population of the world is around 100 million: that is, less than a quarter of 1 per cent of its present size. This is based on the idea that a century or more ago there was a much greater variety of human ways of life based upon different environments, a situation to which we should return, and 100 million he feels to be the optimum level of world population for sustaining such a variety.

However, Naess will have no truck with coercive methods, which he deems incompatible with ecosophical values, and recognises that the achievement of such a population may take hundreds of years.

The ideal of a diversity of human cultures, as was evident in the past, comes from a conception of human culture and economy growing out of a close relationship between the form of society, economy and culture and the particular physical environment – climate, vegetation, geology and so forth – in which they flourish. Regions of continents are seen as natural units for such self-sufficient ways of life, hence the term 'bioregionalism'. Naess and others who have developed this conception recognise that a variety of social and political forms would result from such a development; however, there is potential for a conflict with basic ecosophical values. Societies might 'naturally' emerge that are characterised by social hierarchy, male domination and even slavery, which would be directly contrary to the modern social and political values that Naess and most greens subscribe to.

In a later article ('Identification as a Source of Deep Ecological Attitudes', 1985), Naess links his deep green outlook with notions of human self-realisation. That is, an ever widening circle of identification that begins with family and ultimately embraces the whole of nature, and recognises at each stage the intrinsic value of those or that with which we identify and their basic right to live and flourish. Naess calls his whole ecological philosophy 'Ecosophy T'. The 'T' is quite arbitrary (it apparently refers to 'Tvergastein', the name of his Norwegian mountain hut) to suggest that it is only one of many possible 'ecosophies', which Naess welcomes as contributions to the wider movement. Certainly many varieties of ecologism have developed, some of which have been fused with other systems of thought including forms of socialism, conservatism, anarchism, feminism, Christianity and others.

It is often complained that deep green thought in general lacks intellectual rigour, that the values that it asserts, such as 'biocentric equality' and variety for its own sake, are vague and inconsistent, and that the jump from nature to human society is often not warranted. As a professional philosopher Naess recognises the force of these points, both in relation to his own ecological outlook and to others, but he rather sidesteps the issue by claiming that what ecologists are concerned about is wisdom rather than science.

However, despite the philosophical weaknesses and the sheer variety of different forms of green thinking, Naess is widely recognised as a father figure and leading philosopher of the ecology movement, a movement that grew rapidly into a significant strand of political thinking in the late twentieth century and may well grow in importance in the future.

Further reading

Primary sources

'The Shallow and the Deep, Long-Range Ecological Movement', *Inquiry* 16 (Spring 1973), pp.95–100.

'Identification as a Source of Deep Ecological Attitudes', in M. Tobias (ed.), *Deep Ecology* (Santa Monica, CA: IMT Productions, 1985).

Ecology, Community and Lifestyle (Cambridge: Cambridge University Press, 1989).

Secondary sources

Deval, B. and Sessions, G.: *Deep Ecology: Living as if Nature Mattered* (Salt Lake City, UT: Peregrine Smith Books, 1985).

Dobson, A.: *Green Political Thought* (3rd edn; London and New York: Routledge, 2000).

Mathews, F.: *The Ecological Self* (London and New York: Routledge, 1991).

Witosz, N. and Brennan, A.: *Philosophical Dialogues: Arne Naess and the Progress of Ecophilosophy* (Savage, MD: Rowman & Littlefield, 1999).

ROBERT NOZICK (1938–2002)

Robert Nozick was educated at Columbia University and Princeton, taking his Ph.D. at the latter university in 1963. He taught at Princeton, Harvard and Rockefeller Universities, before becoming Arthur Kingsley Porter Professor of Philosophy at Harvard in 1969. In 1998 he became Joseph Pellegrino University Professor at Harvard. Nozick's political ideas are set forth in the book that made his name as a philosopher: *Anarchy, State and Utopia* (1974). Political theory was only one of Nozick's interests and, as it turned out, a transient one. In his later work, as expressed in *Philosophical Explanations* (1981), *The Examined Life* (1990) and *The Nature of Rationality* (1993) he concentrated on the nature of the self, free will, ethics and epistemology. *Socratic Puzzles* (1997) is an eclectic volume of articles, reviews and fiction. His last book, *Invariancies in the Structure of the Objective World*, came out in 2001.

Anarchy, State and Utopia is one of several attempts made in the second half of the twentieth century to reaffirm the values and beliefs of 'classical' liberalism. As such, it quickly became one of the key texts of the so-called 'New Right'. Its central premise is, in effect, a traditional

Lockean doctrine of inalienable 'natural' rights. Nozick is impatient of the kind of metaphysics that depicts societies or communities as something greater than the sum of their parts. Societies consist simply of individuals, each of whom is assumed to be endowed by nature with rights that no government may infringe or abrogate without their bearer's consent. One consequence of the inviolability and moral supremacy of the individual is that for Nozick, as for **Rawls**, utilitarian arguments, inasmuch as such arguments can justify the infringement of some person's rights for the sake of a supposedly greater good, are inadmissible in any process of political decision-making. Another consequence is that the only kind of state that is rationally justifiable is a 'minimal' state, equipped with just enough power to perform the functions of protection and defence: a state, that is, that will impinge upon the rights of its subjects as little as possible.

Nozick's semi-anarchist theory of government is intended as a response to the welfare-state position of John Rawls's *A Theory of Justice*. Nozick illustrates his position by what is, in effect, a modernised version of Locke's social-contract argument. Individuals living in a state of nature would inevitably encounter what Locke had called the 'inconveniences' of that state. They would find themselves in need of protection against crime, invasion and breach of contract. They would, Nozick suggests, meet this need by co-operating with one another to form 'mutual protection agencies': 'mutual' in the sense that each individual would secure protection for himself by making some of his own time and effort available for the protection of all. Sooner or later, it would occur to the participants in this arrangement that paying specialists to protect them would be easier and safer than doing it themselves. At this point, the mutual protection agencies would become commercial protection agencies, paid for by the contributions of those in whose interests they functioned. They would be impeccably liberal creations of self-interest and private enterprise. But not all such agencies would be equally efficient. By the operation of what may fairly be described as market forces, weaker agencies would be taken over by stronger ones until a 'dominant' protection agency would emerge. Eventually, virtually everyone would opt to join this dominant protection agency, and so it would acquire a legitimate monopoly on the use of coercive force within given territorial boundaries: it would, in other words, come to answer to the traditional definition of a state. The point of this chain of reasoning is to show that a state might emerge as a result of a 'hidden hand' process involving nothing more than the free consent of rational individuals acting in their own interests, but that such a state would be entitled to do no more than perform the protective functions for which it was originally set up. It would have no right, for example, to make welfare or social-security provision available to some of its citizens by taxing others.

Nozick believes himself to be writing in defence of liberty, but, in practice, he makes no appreciable distinction between the individual's right to liberty and the individual's right to property. This move – the creation of an effective synonymy between liberty and unrestricted property rights – is a frequent feature of classical and neo-classical liberalism. Nozick's minimal-state argument is linked with, and reinforced by, an uncompromisingly libertarian stand on the question of justice. Justice, he thinks, is in its essence procedural rather than distributive. Property rights arise in two ways. Initially, they arise when property is acquired by a legitimate act of its first proprietor: that is, when someone peacefully appropriates something not already owned by someone else. Subsequent rights arise when property is transferred from one proprietor to another by some such established legitimate process as sale or bequest. These two conditions, legitimate acquisition or legitimate transfer, are what create property rights, and any distribution of property that does not infringe them is *ipso facto* just. It follows – especially since no utilitarian consideration can trump individual rights – that no one can have any other kind of claim against the property of another, no matter how great actual inequalities of distribution may become. If the poor are to be assisted by the rich, this must come about through acts of private benevolence. It cannot rightly come about through social-welfare mechanisms provided by the state and paid for out of taxation. Redistributive taxation, Nozick asserts, is in effect forced labour exacted upon those of whom it is required; as, indeed, is any taxation levied for purposes other than protection and defence.

Nozick, like Rawls, came upon the scene at a time when English-speaking philosophers had long been convinced that political philosophy has nothing substantive to contribute to our understanding of practical life: that it can do no more than analyse and clarify the language in which political arguments are conducted. To many in the 1970s, this view had, rightly or wrongly, come to seem arid and played out. To that extent, Nozick and Rawls were in some quarters welcomed as a breath of fresh air. Whether Nozick is actually saying anything remarkable or novel is a moot point. At heart, he is an old-fashioned *laissez-faire* liberal who really does no more than state the tenets of the old faith in new and often quirky forms. But, again as in the case of Rawls, his contribution lies more in the debate that his arguments have fuelled than in the originality or success of the arguments themselves.

Further reading

Primary source

Anarchy, State and Utopia (Oxford: Blackwell, 1974).

Secondary sources

Paul, J.: *Reading Nozick* (Oxford: Blackwell, 1982).
Wolff, J.: *Robert Nozick* (Oxford: Blackwell/Polity Press, 1991).

JÜRGEN HABERMAS (1929–)

Jürgen Habermas was born in Düsseldorf in 1929 and has spent his career in German universities. Between 1956 and 1959 he was research assistant to Theodor Adorno, one of the major figures of the Frankfurt School (see **Herbert Marcuse and the Frankfurt School**). He subsequently taught philosophy at Heidelberg and in 1964 became Professor of Philosophy and Sociology at the University of Frankfurt. After a period at the Max Planck Institute at Starnberg, Habermas returned to his Frankfurt chair in 1982, where he remained until his retirement in 1994.

Habermas's first major work was *The Structural Transformation of the Public Sphere* (1962), but it was the publication of *Knowledge and Human Interests* in 1968 that established him as the leading figure of a new generation of Frankfurt School theorists; his reputation was reinforced by his *Legitimation Crisis* of 1973. However, in the 1970s his thought started to move in a new direction, which culminated in his most important work: *The Theory of Communicative Action* (1981). This and later works took him progressively further from the Frankfurt School and its Marxist inspiration.

Habermas has been an enormously prolific and highly eclectic theorist. Unfortunately his writings are obscure, extremely abstract and difficult. He is nevertheless a thinker of considerable range and originality. Furthermore, despite a number of changes of tack, there is an underlying theme and direction to his work. The leading Frankfurt School theorists, especially Horkheimer, Adorno and Marcuse, had all concluded that the aspiration of the Enlightenment to the creation of a society of freedom and happiness through reason had gone seriously wrong and that 'reason' as embodied in science and rational organisation had turned into monsters that had come to enslave humanity in what Max Weber had called the 'iron cage' of modernity. With the resurgence of capitalism following World War II,

Horkheimer and Adorno, and eventually Marcuse, came to despair of the possibility of breaking the grip of modern capitalism and bureaucracy. But at no stage was the Enlightenment aspiration questioned as the ideal that should be striven for, if at all possible. For all his changes of doctrine, Habermas has consistently sought to refashion the Frankfurt School's account of reason to show that a free and rational society is indeed a possibility.

In his earlier writings, Habermas attempts to rework the approach of the Frankfurt School theorists, coming to rather different conclusions. He shares much of their suspicion of the dominance of scientific rationality, but thinks their rejection of science goes too far and cuts them off too much from **Marx**'s legacy. Habermas attacks Marcuse's belief that science and technology are inherently ideological. Science and technology are legitimate human projects; it is the illegitimate extension of scientific/technological rationality into other spheres that has to be resisted. Furthermore, Habermas maintains that Marx was right in insisting on the necessity of understanding the workings of society the better to uncover the nature of domination and the possibilities of advance. Habermas believes that social science, even positivist social science, can be productive of social knowledge, provided its conclusions are properly understood within a wider context of critical theory. He has in fact been voraciously eclectic, taking ideas from Weber, symbolic interactionism, developmental psychology, linguistic philosophy, hermeneutics, psychoanalysis, ethnomethodology, even structural functionalism – and much else besides.

One of Habermas's themes is the rise and decline of the public sphere, which he sees as developing in France, Britain and America in the eighteenth century, when, through newspapers and pamphlets, an educated public discussed the great political issues of the day and created a genuine public opinion. But this was when the middle class was in its progressive phase, challenging traditional authority and traditional beliefs in the name of reason. With the subsequent triumph of the middle class, and their capitalist system, newspapers became commercialised and interested in other things, the state proceeded to underpin and ultimately manage the economy, political parties became merely rival teams of administrators of the same system, and public opinion was replaced by public opinion polls with their simplified and undiscussed expressions of preference. Thus the public sphere has been diminished with ever more technocratic management and people making ever fewer decisions on matters affecting their lives. This technocratic management, based on supposedly value-free social science, is a new form of ideological legitimation of the state. Merely maintaining the system becomes the central value in itself, the ultimate logic of which, Habermas thinks, is society run by computers.

Modern government, he argues, has sought to treat problems of a political and moral nature as technical ones that require the application of technique to solve them. This has the effect of diminishing the public sphere, the sphere of public debate over values, and thereby allows governments to dodge issues that would call their own powers into question. But this only makes them vulnerable to crises of legitimacy when they cannot solve the problems they have labelled as merely technical, and when the necessity of supporting the economy is revealed as manifestly supporting the interests of one class as against another, thereby falsifying the claim of government to be based on freedom, equality and justice.

Establishing the proper role of knowledge in human affairs is the function of Habermas's theory of 'cognitive interests' or 'knowledge constitutive interests' set out in *Knowledge and Human Interests*. All knowledge is the outcome of the process of people creating and recreating themselves through labour – that is, humanity pursuing its basic human interests – and there is a necessary relationship between the form of knowledge and the uses to which it can be put. There are three basic interests that must be pursued: first, making things; second, communicating; and, third, self-knowledge and self-determination. These are the basic activities human beings must engage in to survive and develop and create their world. Each type of activity is pursued via a characteristic type of thinking, which in turn creates the possibility of three bodies of systematic knowledge: empirical-analytic, historical-hermeneutic, and critical. Human advance is bound up with the refinement and extension of these basic forms of thinking, each with its own inner logic of development in disciplines and in institutions and practices.

However, the unequal distribution of power in society causes distortion and misdirection. This is particularly so in modern capitalist society, where everything is treated as a commodity, people are objects of technical manipulation and our understanding is corrupted by ideology. The answer is some kind of socialist transformation, although there is no indication as to how this might come about.

In the 1970s Habermas moved towards developing a more complex epistemology, and towards ethics. Marx is somewhat obscure about the source of ethical values and the Frankfurt School were sceptical of finding any rational basis, but Habermas became quite sure that he had found a clear source of value strong enough to provide a solid moral foundation for critical theory. This source, he believes, lies in the very nature of language.

The argument is roughly this. Whenever we speak, communicate or argue – and especially when we debate some important matter – certain assumptions are, in the nature of things, being made. We trust each other to be telling the truth and to be basing assertions on what can be verified; we assume that, through discussion, the best argument will prevail; and so on. The aim of all discussion is to arrive at a consensus where it is accepted that the true facts, the correct moral evaluation or the best course of action has been established on the basis of good reasoning. This does not always happen and yet, without assumptions such as these, meaningful communication would not be possible. Habermas wishes to argue that such effective communication is systematically distorted by the prevailing power relations in society. As a consequence, ideology pervades our thinking and our language in such a way as to prevent us understanding our true position. Language is also a medium for domination and social power, serving to legitimate relations of organised force, and as such it is ideological. This is similar to the feminist argument that women's oppression is reflected in and reinforced by our ordinary forms of speech.

We thus have an ideal of communication at its best: involving mutual trust and consensus, based on the best arguments, and undistorted by oppression, domination or constraint. It follows that the ideal conditions for communication necessarily involve the moral ideals of freedom, justice and respect for truth, and ultimately a society in which the ideal conditions of communication are the norm. Such a society would have to be without domination and inequality: that is, a socialist society.

Habermas, therefore, believes that the nature of language provides the basis for a true universal ethics and the good society for humanity as such. This theory owes nothing to Marx, or the Frankfurt School, but perhaps something to **Karl Popper**. It is in many ways similar to Popper's view that the ideal conditions for science, such as free criticism, are the basis of an 'open society', which is the good society; while a 'closed' society, where criticism is artificially limited, is necessarily a bad society.

There is an implication that the ideal conditions for communication, and the society that goes with them, are in some sense 'natural' and the *telos*, or ultimate destination, of human development. This is reinforced by Habermas's use of developmental psychology as an alternative to what he sees as Marx's discredited historical materialism.

He has used Piaget's stages of the cognitive development and Kohlberg's stages of the moral development of the child as models for human evolution. Thus, humanity grows in both scientific and technical knowledge, and also in social and moral understanding, and in consequence grows in the capacity for self-understanding, autonomy and freedom. Just as the child develops to maturity, so does humanity; but just as the child's growth can be stunted, so also can humanity's – as it has in modernity, with its managed capitalism and technocratic consciousness. The task of critical theory is to demonstrate this and to reveal whatever potentiality there may be for overcoming it.

These ideas are further developed in Habermas's *Theory of Communicative Action*. This is an even more ambitious attempt to analyse the nature of rationality and of rationalisation (the embodiment of reason in institutions and practices) and their role in modern life. However, the main dichotomy, between technical rationality and communicative rationality, remains. Only now Habermas offers a more refined account of different kinds of rationalisation developing in different ways in different areas. It is an analysis that he believes provides a proper foundation for a critical sociology: one that reveals the conflicts and dangers, and also the potentialities, of modern social development.

This new critical sociology attempts to synthesise sociological theories (such as structural functionalism) that explain social life in terms of interacting structures with 'action' or 'life-world' theories that explain society in terms of the actions of free, autonomous individuals, 'negotiating' social existence and creating it as they go along (such as symbolic interactionism). Each of the two traditional sociological positions represents a necessary feature of society, and they correspond to the two basic kinds of rationality. Structural or 'systemic' thinking is technical-rational reason, while life-world thinking is communicative reason. Both may be necessary, but a good society depends on the right balance. What is wrong with the modern world is that systemic thinking has developed, and continues to develop, at the expense of communicative, life-world thinking; in Habermas's phrase, systemic rationalisation is engaged in a 'colonisation of the life-world'. Thus, the Weberian 'iron cage' still threatens (see Max **Weber**). Its advance is bound up with the development of late capitalism. Systemic rationalisation means ever greater rational organisation of everything; ever more bureaucracy and ever greater classification of social problems as technical problems, all of which masks a sophisticated system of social control, domination and repression.

However, Habermas does not despair, as his Frankfurt School predecessors were prone to do. He believes that at all levels, even our mundane daily activities, we can encourage the extension of communicative action and help to embody it in institutions and practices, thereby fighting a rearguard action against the advance of systemic rationalisation. Furthermore, Habermas is heartened by the development of social movements – such as the greens, the women's movement, the gay movement, anti-nuclear protests and so on – as representing communicative action fighting back against the tide of technical rationalisation. Even the New Right, which Habermas takes to be a mistaken and dangerous doctrine, nevertheless stands for a communicative reaction against the ever spreading system.

Since the 1980s Habermas has mellowed further, seemingly dropping his opposition to capitalism as such and concentrating on elaborating his communicative ethics and the conditions for effective democracy: that is, improving the quality of deliberation to create a form of 'discursive' democracy that provides a better balance than at present between the rights of the individual and those of the community. It could be argued that, in *Between Facts and Norms* (1992), he implies that capitalism in some form is a necessary foundation of a modern democracy. This suggests a final social democratic position that seeks to fulfil liberal ideals of individualism and democracy that can only be fully realised when a fuller citizenship, based on greater equality, dominates a genuine public sphere.

Habermas's firm commitment to the creation of a fully rational society has put him in conflict with one of the most influential intellectual movements of recent decades: namely, postmodernism. Postmodernists (such as **Jean-François Lyotard**) have interpreted 'modernity' as the outcome of the 'Enlightenment Project' but, unlike the early Frankfurt School thinkers who thought it had all gone wrong, they deem the Enlightenment Project to have been misconceived in the first place and to have now totally failed; consequently, we are now living in 'postmodernity'. Habermas, who has spent most of his career trying to refound on a more satisfactory philosophical footing the promise of a free society based upon reason, regards modernity as an 'unfinished project'. It is thus not surprising that he is hostile to postmodern reasoning and has been one of its most consistent critics.

Habermas has had many critics of his own. The vagueness and obscurity of much of his vast output offends many. More seriously, it is questioned whether it is indeed possible to conjure a universal ethics out of the conditions of language. Nevertheless, despite changes of mind on many issues, Habermas has been one of the most productive and influential political thinkers of the late twentieth century.

Further reading

Primary sources

Knowledge and Human Interests (London: Heinemann, 1972).
The Theory of Communicative Action, vol 1: *Reason and the Rationalisation of Society* (London: Heinemann, 1984).
The Theory of Communicative Action, vol 2: *Lifeworld and System* (London: Heinemann, 1987).
Between Facts and Norms (Cambridge: Polity Press, 1996).

Secondary sources

Colhoun, C. (ed.): *Habermas and the Public Sphere* (Cambridge, MA: MIT Press, 1992).
Outhwaite, W.: *Habermas: A Critical Introduction* (Cambridge: Polity Press, 1994).
Ramussen, D.M.: *Reading Habermas* (Oxford: Basil Blackwell, 1991).
White, S.K.: *The Recent Work of Jürgen Habermas: Reason, Justice and Modernity* (Cambridge: Cambridge University Press, 1988).
— (ed.): *The Cambridge Companion to Habermas* (Cambridge: Cambridge University Press, 1995).

JEAN-FRANÇOIS LYOTARD (1924–98)

Jean-François Lyotard was born in Versailles in 1924 and came from a modest background. After graduating from the Sorbonne he spent ten years teaching philosophy in schools, beginning in Algeria, where he became a political radical. Thereafter he taught as a lecturer and professor of philosophy in various institutions in the Paris area. As a young academic he joined the revolutionary Trotskyite group associated with the journal *Socialism or Barbarism* and was later active in the student revolt of 1968. His chief concern at this time was to synthesise Marxism and psychoanalysis, but he became disillusioned by both doctrines after 1968. Nevertheless, he sought to retain his uncompromising radicalism. He explored the subversive nature of avant-garde art using his own account of instinctual drives in his book *Libidinal Economy* (1974), but subsequently became more interested in the analysis of language, influenced by Wittgenstein and by post-structuralists such as his friend Jacques Derrida.

Lyotard became widely known with the publication of his *The Postmodern Condition: A Report on Knowledge* (in French in 1979, translated into English in 1984). This arose from a commission from the University of Quebec to produce a report on the state of knowledge in developed countries that might guide future university policy. The subsequent book came to be regarded by many as marking the beginning of the postmodernist movement. The terms 'postmodern' and 'postmodernism' were in fact already in use, especially in the arts, but it was this book that gave it wider currency as representing a comprehensive social and cultural theory. Postmodernism as a general theory of contemporary society and culture thereafter developed rapidly in a number of directions, although Lyotard came in time to question the modern/postmodern distinction. Nevertheless, he continued to be regarded as a major figure in the overall movement and, in books such as *The Differend* (1983) and many articles, he contributed to postmodern theory and to a postmodern conception of politics. He retired in 1987 and died in 1998.

The Postmodern Condition argues that the nature and status of knowledge has changed. The industrial age – characterised by mass production, scientific research and Enlightenment ideals of rationality and progress – is over. We are now living in a new situation, which Lyotard terms 'postmodern', where information technology predominates and the stress is upon efficiency and other pragmatic values. Science has evolved and fragmented into incommensurable areas and scientists no longer all speak the same language. Furthermore, in spite of the apparently objective nature of scientific explanation and procedure, science is in fact underpinned by a series of grand stories or 'metanarratives' that justify its existence. These are modern beliefs in progress that see reason (particularly in its scientific manifestation) as promising happiness, prosperity and freedom. Lyotard claims that we now no longer believe in these underlying justifications. Science has become just one set of language games among others.

Indeed, loss of faith in metanarratives generally is what characterises the new age in which we now live. Lyotard introduces what is still one of the most influential definitions of the postmodern as involving an 'incredulity towards metanarratives'. By 'metanarratives' or 'grand narratives' Lyotard means the overarching stories that we use to justify activities, institutions, values and cultural forms. They include ideologies, religions, notions of progress, the efficacy of psychoanalysis or benefits of capitalism, and other broad assumptions that underpin much of what we think and do. We now tend to think of them as language games valid only to those who participate in them and irreconcilable with each other. We have lost our faith in universal beliefs and theories.

The Postmodern Condition is perhaps the best-known primary postmodern text at least partly because of its relative lucidity. Most later texts are extremely difficult and obscure – including those by Lyotard himself. His notion of how we are now living in a postmodern age has been refined and extended by many postmodern theorists, who have developed the thesis in many and often conflicting directions. What is common in their outlook is seeing modernity in terms of what is called the 'Enlightenment Project', which aspired to create a more rational world with freedom, prosperity and happiness for all. This rationality was deemed to be manifested in science and technology, capitalism, the liberal state and in more efficient organisation of society generally, although there are alternative versions of the Enlightenment Project expressed in socialism, Marxism, anarchism and other modern ideologies.

The actual outcomes of the Enlightenment Project have included industrialisation, urbanisation and societies divided by class and class conflict. Great wealth has been created, but also mass poverty. There has been greater freedom, but also world wars and totalitarianism. There have also been great scientific advances, but they are accompanied by threats of nuclear annihilation and environmental destruction that threaten the whole of humanity. These horrors have undermined our faith in reason, science and progress. Furthermore, the writings of various thinkers like Derrida and **Foucault** have questioned our faith in reason and our capacity for independent reasoning. As a result, the Enlightenment Project has become discredited and has collapsed, and our loss of faith in universal theories is one symptom of this.

There is, however, more to postmodernity than intellectual disillusionment. Industrial class-based society has given way to a post-industrial, consumer-driven, media-dominated, globalised society in which social class and (to some extent) national and other identities are gone – or at least less secure than before. Who and what we are has become much more a matter of choice than in the past. This applies to political and other identities, which are now chosen in a more consumerist way. The new age we have now entered, so postmodernists argue, is an age of fragmentation, loss of identity and multiple points of view. The politics of industrial modernity centred around class-based parties with universal ideologies. The mass parties still exist, but as hollowed-out versions that are less dedicated to socialism or conservatism or other ideologies. They have to chase votes, since they no longer have the mass memberships and automatic voting support of old. The electorate is now more volatile and consumerist. The postmodern account of politics is largely based upon the growth of new social movements and the new political agenda associated with them: the politics of identity and lifestyle, such as sexual politics; the politics of small-scale nationalism and regionalism; and the politics of particular issues, such as the environment.

Although Lyotard came to doubt the extent of the break with modernity, his later writings develop his own version of what is generally recognised as postmodern theory, which derives from Wittgenstein's account of language. That is, language develops naturally along with human practices and forms of life to form a vast network of relatively discrete 'language games', each with its own concepts and rules. Where practices or forms of life clash, the respective language games are incommensurable and there is no higher language that can embrace both – no 'meta-language' that can automatically resolve differences.

Lyotard is implacably hostile to any kind of metanarrative or grand theory that informs political practice, no matter how seemingly benign. These range from full-scale ideologies, such as Marxism, socialism, nationalism, liberalism, fascism and so on, to smaller-scale theories of social engineering or economic policy. All are condemned in equal measure as totalitarian. Lyotard believes that such is the creativity and variety of human social life that no meta-language or metanarrative or grand theory can possibly do it justice. More importantly, any attempt to impose any of these on a society must of necessity involve oppression, injustice and the marginalisation of those who do not conform, with an inevitable diminution of variety and creativity.

This kind of postmodern analysis has resulted, to some degree, in a greater sensitivity to the needs of minorities in liberal democracies, with policies arising from multiculturalism, as well as modifications of liberal theory. However, Lyotard pursues the argument much further. He is fiercely hostile to any kind of general consensus, however 'reasonable' it might appear to be, on the same grounds of the oppressiveness of exclusion and the diminution of variety and creativity. Notions of compromise are firmly rejected along with those of reasonableness. Lyotard sometimes talks as though philosophy can have a role in elucidating differences between colliding language games (between, say, the outlook of employers and workers in a capitalist system), but there seems to be no question of philosophy being the basis of any kind of resolution.

Lyotard's politics is a politics of endless conflict and protest, with seemingly no possibility of constructive agreement – one might even say no possibility of politics at all. He is so extreme and indiscriminate in his rejection of theory and consensus as bad, while any kind of variety and difference is necessarily good, that it is difficult to see how any kind of productive politics is possible. As with other postmodernist or post-structuralist thinkers, like Derrida or Foucault or Baudrillard, a politics of protest on behalf of the marginalised and powerless may be of value, but Lyotard's seems too extreme in practical terms, even though the theoretical underpinnings are of considerable interest.

As to the postmodern outlook in general, it is open to a number of criticisms. One is that there is far too much continuity and overlap with modernity to make postmodernity a genuinely new age; this is a criticism in which Lyotard himself saw some force. Postmodern accounts of modernity are also far too restrictive: to define modernity in terms of the Enlightenment Project is to caricature modernity. Furthermore, postmodernism's relativism and rejection of notions of universal truth undermine its own claims. As to the rejection of metanarratives and grand theory, the whole postmodern account – including Lyotard's contributions – is in itself a metanarrative, and a theory that is at least as grand as any it rejects.

Nevertheless, postmodern theory – and Lyotard's version of it – is interesting and suggestive, challenging and significant.

Further reading

Primary sources

The Postmodern Condition: A Report on Knowledge (Manchester: Manchester University Press, 1984).

Political Writings, ed. B. Readings and K.P. Geiman (London: UCL Press, 1993).

Secondary sources

Lyon, D.: *Postmodernity* (2nd edn; Buckingham: Open University Press, 1999).

Sim, S.: *The Routledge Companion to Postmodernism* (London: Routledge, 2001).

White, S.K.: *Political Theory and Postmodernism* (Cambridge: Cambridge University Press, 1991).

Williams, J.: *Lyotard: Towards a Postmodern Philosophy* (Cambridge: Polity Press, 1998).

GLOSSARY

anarchism Anarchism is the view that social relations can and should be organised without coercive government or, indeed, any formal structures of authority that might restrict spontaneous human action and association. Implicit in anarchism is the belief that human beings are by nature benign and co-operative, and that government, as restrictive of individual freedom, is intrinsically an evil. Anarchism is almost by definition a revolutionary ideology. Reform from above is, *ipso facto*, reform initiated or covertly directed by those in authority, and therefore not real reform. True social change must involve the replacement, by violent means if necessary, of the state.

aristocracy Aristocracy comes from the Greek word *aristokratia*, 'rule by the best'. It does not necessarily mean a hereditary nobility (there are, for example, military aristocracies, such as Sparta in the fifth century BCE), although when 'the best' are selected according to expertise or educational attainment, this nowadays tends to be known as 'meritocracy'. For **Aristotle**, aristocracy is rule by the best in the common interest, as distinct from 'oligarchy', which is rule by the wealthy few in their own interest. **Plato** and Aristotle are both aware of how easily the former can turn into the latter.

capitalism Capitalism is that system of economic organisation or 'mode of production' within which (1) the means of production and distribution are wholly or mainly privately owned, and (2) goods and services are exchanged at prices determined with a view to the profit of private owners. **Marx** believed that capitalism is inherently unjust, partly because it requires those whom it employs to sell their labour at less than its market value, the difference being the profit of the employer. It has in practice proved possible for elements of social ownership to exist within the capitalist mode of production without destroying or seriously disrupting it. Liberals tend to see capitalism as an important (for neo-liberals, the all-important) guarantee of human liberty.

civil rights Originally 'civil' rights were those rights deemed to belong to individuals simply as members of civil society. Especially in the 1960s, the phrase came to mean specifically the rights of ethnic (and especially black) minorities in the United States. It is in this sense that the phrase 'civil rights movement' is used. As part of this usage, 'civil rights' now often, or usually, refers to group rights as much as to individual ones.

civil society The term 'civil society' has been used in a number of ways by writers since the eighteenth century. It is now usually used in (more or less) the sense intended by **Hegel** to mean that sphere of society in which individuals associate freely in relationships and organisations – firms, voluntary associations and other corporate bodies – intermediate between the state and the family. It is, in other words, the field of all the public and social relationships in which the state does not ordinarily intervene. The general tendency of government in the twentieth century was to reduce the size of that field and hence to erode, however slowly, 'civil' rights. However, New Right government of the 1970s and 1980s sought to reverse this trend.

communism According to Marxist theory, communism is the final and highest stage of human development. It will come about following the communist revolution, although not immediately. The revolution will overthrow capitalism and bring the workers to power in a worldwide 'dictatorship of the proletariat', which has the task of creating the classless, stateless, equal society that is communism. However, after the first communist revolution in Russia in 1917, the revolutionaries (or 'Bolsheviks') led by Lenin argued that because the workers' revolution had not spread around the world, as Marx had predicted, it had to be protected by all means possible until the rest of the world caught up. This justified a gigantic state apparatus that dominated every aspect of Russian life. Lenin's regime, and those modelled on it (like China), came to be called 'communist' even though none of them claimed to have achieved genuine communism. In this way the term came to be associated with a totalitarian system in which the state owned and controlled everything: that is, the very opposite of what Marx understood by the term.

conservatism Conservatism, particularly in its traditional British form, is a set of beliefs, or an 'ideology', emphasising the preservation of traditional ways, mistrusting rapid or discontinuous change, and to that extent favouring only slow and piecemeal alterations to the existing order. Always a force of some kind in politics, it came into its own in Europe especially after, and in reaction to, the French Revolution of 1789. Forms of conservatism in Europe up to World War II tended to be more reactionary and nationalistic. In England and America during the 1970s and 1980s, conservative politics tended to identify itself with neo-classical or New Right liberal views on such subjects as economics and state intervention.

critical theory The term 'critical theory' was coined by the German social philosopher Max Horkheimer (1895–1973) and is associated with the Frankfurt School, of which he was a leading figure (along with Theodor Adorno and Herbert **Marcuse**). The School was inspired by Marx's early writings and its members were critical of his later works, which Marx regarded as more 'scientific'. 'Critical' theory is contrasted with 'traditional' theory, as exemplified in the natural sciences. Whereas the task of traditional theory is to investigate a stable and unchanging reality, that of critical theory is to identify the conditions necessary to a rational form of social existence: in other words, to work towards a state of affairs not yet realised. Traditional theory is an impartial and scholarly pursuit, while critical theory is committed to human emancipation and the achievement of radical social change. Jürgen **Habermas** is the thinker most associated with the later development of the Frankfurt School.

Enlightenment 'The Enlightenment', like 'Romanticism', is a term of notoriously elastic meaning. Roughly, it may be taken to denote the cultural and intellectual history of the eighteenth century in so far as that history is characterised by love of rational order, liberal politics, belief in progress, and faith in scientific reason as the engine of progress. It is customary, though not wholly satisfactory, to think in terms of a French, an American and a Scottish Enlightenment. The great philosophers of the seventeenth century – **Hobbes**, Descartes, **Locke**, Newton – are usually regarded as the fathers of Enlightenment thought. **Montesquieu** is the political thinker most associated with the French Enlightenment.

epistemology The term 'epistemology' means 'theory of knowledge'. It is the branch of philosophy concerned with origin, structure, methods and validity of knowledge: that is, with investigating what can be known and how. The philosophy of **Plato** is perhaps the best example of how epistemology may be adapted to the service of politics.

hedonism 'Ethical' hedonism identifies pleasure as the highest good; 'psychological' hedonism holds that the attainment of pleasure and the avoidance of pain are the chief or only explanations of human motivation. The one does not necessarily imply the other, but most ethical hedonists (see THOMAS HOBBES; JEREMY BENTHAM; JOHN STUART MILL) are also psychological hedonists, if only implicitly.

idealism See MATERIALISM.

ideology An ideology, broadly speaking, is a collection of ideas purporting to describe the world in which its exponents live and to prescribe for them the kind of political actions necessary to maintain that world or change it for the better. Coined by the eighteenth-century French philosopher Antoine Destutt de Tracy, the word has been used in a number of different, and not always compatible, ways. The degree of integration that ideologies exhibit is very variable. Thus, fascism and Marxism (see BENITO MUSSOLINI AND FASCISM; KARL MARX) are closely defined ideologies, with clear doctrines and a scriptural canon against which orthodoxy can be checked. Liberalism, by contrast, is a very loose and adaptable ideology. Conservatism is so lacking in 'doctrine' as to be hardly an ideology at all.

intellectualism The term 'intellectualism' has a number of applications. In medieval legal theory (see ST THOMAS AQUINAS), it is the doctrine that the essence of law is its conformity to reason (ultimately, to the Divine reason) and therefore that the validity of law depends upon its embodying rationally apprehensible moral standards: a bad or immoral law is not really a law at all. By contrast, 'voluntarism' (see MARSILIUS OF PADUA) holds that law derives its binding force from the will of a legislator, reinforced by coercion or the threat of coercion, and that moral content is not part of the definition of law. 'Voluntarism' in this sense is synonymous with 'legal positivism'.

Keynesianism 'Keynesianism' is a shorthand term for the economic and social doctrines associated with the British economist John Maynard Keynes (1883–1946), especially as set forth in his

General Theory of Employment, Interest and Money (1936). As generally understood, Keynesianism advocates government intervention in the economy to manipulate demand, in the interests of maintaining continuous steady growth and full employment. Keynes himself believed that these things could be accomplished without any serious disruption of the existing order. In the United Kingdom, very high levels of inflation and unemployment during the 1970s led to a general abandonment of Keynesian economics in favour of 'supply-side economics', which concentrates on controlling inflation and other obstacles to the optimum working of the free market.

laissez-faire *Laissez-faire* is the doctrine that economies work according to a 'natural law' that fixes prices according to the relation between supply and demand, and therefore should be 'left' to 'function' according to that law. The doctrine is associated particularly with exponents of classical and neo-classical liberalism (also called 'neo-liberalism'). It favours the idea of a minimal or non-interventionist state, which leaves individuals alone to pursue their interests in free markets. When economies are regulated by states or such business associations as cartels or 'trusts', this is, in effect, an interference with a natural process and can only lead to baneful consequences, such as inflation.

legal positivism See INTELLECTUALISM.

liberalism Liberalism is usually said to have originated in seventeenth-century England, as the ideology of the emergent middle class or 'gentry' whose members wished to assert their own political and economic status and oppose the 'divine right' absolutism of the Stuart kings (see JOHN LOCKE). It emphasises the rights and personal autonomy of the individual, private property, the rule of law, the importance of consent as creating political obligation, the need for a minimal or non-interventionist state, and *laissez-faire* economics. Towards the end of the nineteenth century, 'classical' liberalism gave place to a version of liberalism that accorded more emphasis to the idea of community and was more tolerant of provision of welfare by the state. This new 'social' or 'welfare' liberalism is particularly associated with the ideas of T.H. **Green** and L.T. Hobhouse. The revival of interest in individualism and *laissez-faire* economics that characterised politics in Britain and the United States during the 1970s and 1980s is often called 'New Right' or 'neo-classical' liberalism or 'neo-liberalism'.

materialism In politics and sociology, materialism is the view that the character of political and social experience – including how we think or feel about such experience – is wholly or mainly determined by the material conditions under which it occurs. The best-known exponent of materialism in this sense is Karl **Marx**. The opposite view, 'idealism', is that 'mind', 'consciousness', 'ideas', and so on, determine the nature of social being and shape its material conditions. **Kant** and **Hegel** are both 'idealists' in this sense. In philosophy, materialism is the doctrine that only matter exists; idealism is the opposite view, that only minds and mental representations exist or have true reality.

metaphysics Metaphysics, or 'what lies behind nature', is that branch of philosophy purporting to deal with the ultimate reality underlying the realm of sensory experience. It therefore has to do with such things as existence, substance, causality, and so on. The Ancient Greeks were the first philosophers to pursue it seriously. Much of what used to belong to metaphysics has either been abandoned altogether or 'hived-off' into other disciplines such as psychology, and the predominantly analytical character of philosophy in the twentieth century tended to have a discrediting effect on metaphysics. Largely thanks to Professor A.J. Ayer and like-minded positivists, there was a time during the second half of the twentieth century when 'metaphysics' was used more or less as a synonym for 'nonsense'.

minimal state See STATE.

mode of production In Marxist theory (see KARL MARX), a mode of production is the form taken by the organisation of economic or productive relations prevailing at any given period of history and therefore determining the social, political and other human institutions characteristic of that period.

monetarism Monetarism is the name given to the economic doctrine asserting (1) that changes in the money supply in an economy cause changes in the general level of prices; (2) that increases in the money supply are inflationary in tendency; and (3) that inflation can be controlled successfully only through restrictions in the growth of the money supply. In its modern form, the doctrine is especially associated with the Chicago School of economists, to which belong Milton Friedman and F.A. von **Hayek**. Monetarism especially commended itself during the 1980s to successive British governments, to whom the control of inflation sometimes seemed to be the sole aim of economic policy. Monetarism is the most extreme form of 'supply-side economics', which has dominated Western economic thinking since the late 1970s.

moral relativism Moral relativism is the doctrine that there are no absolutely, objectively discoverable moral standards, and that ideas of 'right' and 'wrong' are simply relative to the moral community whose ideas they are. On this view, universal moral prescription is impossible, and attempts to engage in it are probably no more than instances of cultural imperialism. Moral relativists characteristically ground their opinion on two things: (1) moral diversity (that is, the actual perceived differences of moral conviction as between one community and another); and (2) the apparent absence of any rational apparatus whereby moral disagreements may be resolved.

neo-classical liberalism/neo-liberalism See LIBERALISM.

Neoplatonism Neoplatonism is the name given to the revival and development, in the third century CE and after, of the philosophy of **Plato**. The tendency of Neoplatonism is to bring out the mysticism implicit in much of Plato's thought. Neoplatonism postulates an ultimate reality called the One, from which Mind, Soul and Matter – and therefore all sensible particulars – emanate as 'hypostases'. The chief exponents of Neoplatonism were Plotinus (205–70 CE), Iamblichus (*c.*245–326 CE) and Proclus (412–85 CE). The markedly Neoplatonist character of Christian philosophy down to the thirteenth century is due largely to the influence of Neoplatonism on the thought of St **Augustine**.

New Right liberalism See LIBERALISM.

nominalism Nominalism is (to put it crudely) a philosophical doctrine invented in the eleventh century to solve the problem of how 'universals' – that is, concepts that can be predicated of more than one subject – can be said to exist. Nominalists hold that abstract ideas have no independent existence or reality, and therefore that words expressing such ideas ('purple', 'two', 'good') have meaning only in so far as they are the 'names' of individual instances of them. Thus, **Hobbes**, **Bentham** and **Mill** all believe that 'good' and 'evil' are only 'names' that we give to the things which we find pleasurable and painful respectively.

normative political theory Political theory is 'normative' in so far as it is concerned with what *ought* to be: with what values we should live by, such as freedom and justice, and how they can be put into practice. It therefore deals with questions about how we should live, what kind of society we should strive to create and what laws we should have.

oligarchy Oligarchy refers to rule by the few, usually a wealthy minority. For **Aristotle**, oligarchy is the 'perverted' form of aristocracy: it is government by the wealthy few in their own interests. The word is not intrinsically evaluative, but nowadays it has almost always an unfavourable sense. Political theorists such as Robert Michels and Joseph Schumpeter have emphasised the oligarchical or elitist tendencies latent in all organisations.

patriarchy 'Patriarchy' is a word with several distinct meanings. In modern political writing, and especially in feminist writing, it refers to the alleged dominance, in most known human communities, by males of social, political and private life. Such writing typically takes it for granted that the normal relation of the sexes is exploitative, with women as the victims. It is suggested that the law – especially family law – and other mechanisms of social control and value-transmission systematically institutionalise and defend male values, or values that serve the purposes of male hegemony.

prerogative powers Prerogative powers are extra-legal powers that may be used at the discretion of a sovereign. The intention is that they will be deployed in an emergency or in circumstances not covered by the normal provisions and processes of the law, where a final arbiter is required. The idea of prerogative powers was first formulated – though not, of course, invented – by John **Locke**.

radicalism Radicalism, as the term is used in this book, is the political stance of those eighteenth- and nineteenth-century figures who directed their efforts towards such things as extension of the franchise, popular participation in politics, civil liberties, greater social welfare and religious toleration. It is associated also with non-conformism or scepticism in religion. The term is also used more generally, as in the expression 'radical right', to refer to any sustained attempt to challenge the existing order or widen the terms of political debate.

raisons d'état A term, originating in the seventeenth century, designating political matters, especially in the field of international relations, deemed to be of so urgent or important a character that they override all other considerations, including the 'normal' requirements of morality.

Renaissance humanism Renaissance humanism was an intellectual movement among scholars and teachers that developed in Italy in the Renaissance period and spread to the rest of Europe. It was a reaction against the scholasticism that dominated the universities of the time. Whereas scholastics emphasised the study of logic, metaphysics and Aristotelian science, the humanists regarded such studies as arid and of little use to the conduct of life. They instead advocated the study of history, literature, moral philosophy and, above all, languages. They were responsible for the revival of Ancient Greek and of a purer and more authentic Latin, and for making these the basis of European education until the twentieth century. More broadly, they promoted the view that Ancient Greece and Rome were the pinnacles of human civilisation, whose achievements should be emulated – though in a Christian context.

revolution Revolution is, literally, the 'turning around' of political power, usually (though not always) by sudden and violent means. Revolution is not, however, a mere *coup d'état*: not, that is, the mere replacement of one ruler by another. It involves the thorough and fundamental transformation of the social and political order affected by it. Thus, Marxists expect communism to be effected by a revolution of the proletariat; monarchy in France was abolished by the Revolution of 1789. The term is used in an extended sense also, to refer to such large-scale episodes of change as the Industrial 'Revolution'.

Romanticism The Romantic Movement began in the late eighteenth century as a reaction against the fashionable ideas of the Enlightenment, and indeed it is sometimes known as the 'Counter-Enlightenment'. Whereas the Enlightenment stressed reason and science and universality in understanding human affairs, Romantic thinkers insisted that these were at best limited. They stressed the particularity and uniqueness of every individual, society and culture, and they believed that it was history, literature and the arts in general that gave us greatest insight into the human condition. Romanticism expressed itself in a multitude of different and sometimes contradictory ways. In politics there were influences across the spectrum. The conservatism of **Burke** has a distinctly Romantic dimension, with its stress on unique history and traditions, while the liberalism of Wilhelm von Humboldt stressed the need for freedom so that each person could fully develop their unique individuality – he influenced John Stuart **Mill** and social liberalism. However, the greatest influence of Romanticism was probably on nationalism and the view that each people has its own special heritage and destiny.

scholasticism Scholasticism is an imprecise term for philosophy as practised in the medieval Christian universities: the 'schools'. Broadly speaking, it has the following features: (1) love of minute analysis; (2) respect for the intellectual authorities of the past, especially (from the mid-twelfth century) the authority of **Aristotle**; (3) preoccupation with the reconciliation of faith and reason; (4) logical precision, sometimes – especially in later scholasticism – carried to the point of mere hair-splitting; and (5) verbal disputation as a method of instruction and clarification. The beginning and end of scholasticism are hard to identify (university curricula were still largely 'scholastic' in the seventeenth century), but the thirteenth century is usually supposed to have been its heyday and St Thomas **Aquinas** its most distinguished exponent.

socialism Socialism represents a long tradition of political thought that stresses the values of social equality and social solidarity. Its modern form began in the early nineteenth century as a response to industrialisation and unrestricted capitalism. Many early forms of modern socialism were based on small self-governing communities (for example, Robert Owen and William Morris), but the twentieth century has seen a stress on state ownership and planning. Marxism is a revolutionary form of socialism with a history of its own (see KARL MARX), but most socialists have sought change by peaceful democratic means. In the late twentieth century, the experience of communist regimes led many socialists to give up the prospect of abolishing capitalism and instead see the ideal society in terms of state-managed capitalism and extensive welfare. This 'social democracy' has become the dominant form of socialism in the Western world.

sovereignty Sovereignty is the right to exercise, within given territorial borders or over a particular area of the world, a power than which there is none higher. Thus, in the United Kingdom, the authority of Parliament is 'sovereign' in the sense that everyone is bound by, and no agency may disregard or overturn, the laws that it makes and causes to be enforced. Again, Great Britain and Argentina have for many years been in dispute over the 'sovereignty' of the Falkland Islands: that is, over who has the right to own and control them.

state The word 'state' occurs in several different senses in the history of political thought; it is a mistake to suppose that the city-state of classical Athens, Machiavelli's *lo stato* and the modern nation-state are the 'same thing' in any but the most tenuous sense. 'The state' need mean no more than 'the governed community'. In most modern occurrences, it denotes all those agencies and institutions within given territorial boundaries that (1) are authorised to make and enforce law; (2) are responsible for protection and defence; and (3) possess a monopoly of legitimate coercive force. The phrase 'minimal state' expresses the conviction of classical and neo-classical liberals that liberty depends upon restricting or reducing the power of the state over the lives of individuals.

totalitarian An adjective used to describe regimes that seek to include every aspect of life within the sphere of governmental control, and thus hold sway over the 'totality' of human existence in the name of some doctrine. Because such regimes are characterised by extensive bureaucratic control, insistence upon ideological conformity, high levels of intervention and surveillance, and drastic legal and penal systems, the term is almost always used in a pejorative sense.

utopia 'Utopia' is a pseudo-Greek neologism meaning either 'no place' or 'good place'. The word originates with Sir Thomas **More**'s little book of which it is the title and theme. 'Utopian' has by extension come to denote a literary form depicting an imaginary ideal society. Such a society is typically one from which present evils have been eradicated and in which perfect peace, harmony and justice prevail. Anachronistically enough, the earliest 'utopia' is probably the 'Kallipolis' of **Plato**'s *Republic.* In relatively recent times, the word 'dystopia' has been coined as the name of a literary sub-form depicting imaginary societies in which present evils have become worse. Aldous Huxley's *Brave New World* is an example of 'dystopian' literature.

INDEX

Adorno, Theodor 211, 213, 214, 230, 231, 243
alienation 120, 123
anarchism 90–1, 92, 104, 150, 151–5, 228, 238, 241; anarcho-syndicalism 154, 156–8, 185
Aquinas, St Thomas 28–34, 35–6, 49, 75, 244, 250
Arendt, Hannah 188–190
aristocracy 8–9, 18, 75, 90, 91, 97
Aristotle 10, 11–19, 21, 28–31, 34, 35–6, 58, 75, 76, 77, 106, 143, 241, 248, 250
Augustine of Hippo, St 19–25, 28, 29–31, 247
authority, forms of 172–4
Averroes 29

Bacon, Sir Francis 50, 52
Bakunin, Michael 152, 153
Baudrillard, Jean 240
Beauvoir, Simone de 206–10
Bentham, Jeremy 73, 112–17, 134, 135, 136, 144, 218, 244, 247
Berlin, Sir Isaiah 144, 190–3, 204
Bernstein, Eduard 156, 159–164
black emancipation 175–81 *see also* racism
Bolshevik Party 165–6, 242
Bookchin, Murray 111
Bosanquet, Bernard 145, 192
Bradley, F.H. 135, 203
bureaucracy 90, 17, 171, 173, 174, 175, 188, 213, 231
Burke, Edmund 71, 73, 93, 95–9, 99, 101,194, 202, 205, 250

capitalism 118, 123, 125, 127–8,129, 153, 154, 157, 159, 160–2, 165, 166, 170, 171, 174, 184, 212–3, 231, 241–2, 250
Christianity 148–9, 170, 171, 250
Cicero 19, 22
citizenship 36, 37, 59–60, 80, 82–4, 143, 176, 179, 195, 223, 235
city state *see* polis
civil disobedience 197–8
civil rights 175–6, 178, 180, 181, 199, 242 *see also* natural rights
civil society 108–11, 143, 242
communism 103, 120, 121, 123, 124, 128, 129, 153, 167, 168, 188, 242, 249
communitarian movement 111
constitutions 17–18, 59–61, 68, 76, 82, 118, 195; American constitution 68, 77, 176, 176; English constitution 76–7, 96
conservatism 73, 96, 97, 98, 205, 238, 242, 244
critical theory 212, 231, 234, 243

Darwin, Charles 140, 141
democracy 8–9, 30, 75, 80–2, 84, 125, 131–3, 162, 163, 184, 186, 219; direct democracy 80, 83; representative democracy 80, 94, 115, 137–8, 174

Derrida, Jacques 236, 238, 240
despotism 75–6, 131, 132, 138, 186–7
dictatorship of the proletariat 128–9, 156, 167, 242
divine right of kings 30, 62, 65,68 (*see also* monarchy)

ecologism 224–7, 239, 120, 154
Engels, Frederik 120, 121–2, 123, 128, 159, 160, 161, 167
egalitarianism 48, 90, 131, 184 *see also* equality
Enlightenment, the 77–9, 87–8, 89, 90, 93, 102, 173, 191, 213, 214, 230, 231, 235, 237, 238, 240, 243,249
environmentalism *see* ecologism
equality 63, 79, 81, 90, 94, 115, 125, 132, 148, 150, 162, 222 *see also* egalitarianism
evolution 140–1, 143, 153, 154, 186
existentialism 188–9, 206–7, 212

Fabians, the 159
Farrakhan, Louis 181
fascism 111, 146, 150, 182–88, 155, 158, 213, 244 *see also* national socialism
feminism 82, 87, 94, 99–101, 118, 137, 150, 181, 206–10, 233, 239, 248
Filmer, Sir Robert 62
Foucault, Michel 216–20, 238, 240
Fourier, Charles 117–120
Franklin, Benjamin 92
Frankfurt School 111, 175, 211–16, 230, 231, 232, 233, 235, 243
freedom *see* liberty
Freudian psychology 118, 201, 208, 213–14, 215, 236, 237
Fromm, Eric 213

Gandhi, Mohandas 196–9, 225
Garvey, Marcus 175–81
Gentile, Giovanni 184
general will 81–4, 107, 109–10
Godwin, William 99, 101–4, 152
Green, T.H. 111, 135, 141, 142–6, 192, 204, 245
green ideas *see* ecologism

Habermas, Jürgen 215, 219, 230–236, 243
Harrington, James 57–61, 77, 190
Hayek, Friedrich von 98, 175, 193–6, 205, 246
hedonism 73, 113, 114, 135, 244
Hegel, G.F.W. 88, 91, 104–112, 121, 122, 142, 143, 156, 161, 184, 202, 203, 207, 212, 242, 246
Heidegger, Martin 188, 211
Herder, Johann Gottfried 88–92, 191
Herzen, Alexander 191
historicism 194, 201–2
Hitler, Adolf 146, 175, 180, 182, 183, 184, 185, 186, 187
Hobbes, Thomas 50–7, 58, 61, 63, 64, 68, 75, 113, 135, 243, 244, 247
Hobhouse, L.T. 145, 245
Hobson, J.A. 145
Horkheimer, Max 211, 212, 213, 214, 230, 231, 243
Hume, David 66, 68–73, 85, 95, 142, 200

ideology 124–5, 128, 129, 148, 172, 184, 188, 192, 205, 231, 232, 233, 237, 238, 239, 241, 243, 244
individualism 108, 120, 125, 132, 136, 147, 174, 184, 213, 235

John of Salisbury 25–8, 35
justice 5–7, 70, 220–4, 229

Kant, Immanuel 85–8, 107, 108, 109, 110, 142, 174, 200, 246
Kautsky, Karl 159, 160
Keynes, Maynard 194, 196, 244–5
King, Martin Luther 181, 199
Kropotkin, Prince Peter 151–5

labour theory of value 127, 161
Lenin, Vladimir Ilich 164–8, 242
liberalism 60, 68, 87, 88, 111, 118, 143, 145, 148, 150, 160, 163, 173, 182,202, 223, 241, 245; classical (*laissez fair*) liberalism 125, 141, 145,145, 195, 227, 229, 242, 244, 245, 246, 251 *see also* new right ;

new liberalism 141
liberty 63, 66, 76, 80, 87, 125, 131, 132, 136–7, 138, 140–1, 143, 144, 150, 174, 195, 207, 221, 229; positive and negative freedom 144, 192–3
Locke, John 61–8, 69, 71, 77, 94, 108, 109, 228, 243, 245, 248
Luxemburg, Rosa 159
Lyotard, Jean-François 235, 236–40

Machiavelli, Nicolo 38–46, 58, 190, 191, 251
Marcuse, Herbert 111, 175, 211–16, 230, 231, 243
Marsilius of Padua 35–8, 244
Marx, Karl 120, 121–30, 142, 156, 157, 159, 160, 161, 163, 164, 166, 168, 169, 182, 202, 211, 212, 214, 216, 231, 232, 233, 241, 242, 243, 244, 246, 250
Marxism 121–30, 157, 159, 161, 163, 164, 165, 166, 167, 168, 169, 171, 182, 208, 211, 212, 213, 215, 236 244, 246, 249; Marxism-Leninism 165–7, 211, 242
Mazzini, Joseph 157
Mill, James 115,134, 135
Mill, John Stuart 67, 131, 133, 134–9, 202, 244, 247, 250
modernity 169, 170, 171, 175, 183, 213, 230, 234, 235, 238, 239, 240
monarchy 30–1, 40, 55–6, 71, 75–6, 82, 90, 93, 95, 97, 100, 110, 111, 249
see also divine right of kings
Montesquieu, Baron de 73–7, 243
More, Sir Thomas 47–50, 251
Morris, William 120, 250
Mussolini, Benito 180, 182–88, 244
myth 157, 207, 209

Naess, Arne 224–7
national socialism 146, 174, 182, 183, 188, 213 *see also* fascism
nationalism 90, 91, 111, 128, 146, 157, 173, 176, 180, 181, 182–3, 185, 196, 250
natural law 31–3, 63–4, 66, 70, 72–3, 74, 245
natural rights 53, 63–4, 66, 73, 96, 98, 115, 123, 143, 180, 228 *see also* civil rights
nazism *see* national socialism
new left 154, 211, 214
new right 142, 175, 196, 227, 235, 242, 243, 246 *see also* liberalism (*laissez faire)*
Nietzsche, Friedrich 146–51, 156, 173, 183, 216, 218, 173, 174
Nicholas of Cusa 38
nominalism 52, 135, 247
Nozick, Robert 68, 139, 142, 227–30

Oakshott, Michael 96, 98, 175, 191, 203–6
oligarchy 3–4, 17–18, 30, 156, 248
Owen, Robert 119, 120, 250

Paine, Tom 92–5, 98, 102
Plato 3–11, 19, 21, 29, 49, 58, 77, 82, 108, 133, 134, 147, 188, 202, 241, 244, 247, 251; *see also* Socrates
Plotinus 19, 247
polis (city state) 15–17, 19, 21, 35–6, 80,82, 102, 108, 110, 150, 189
political sociology 75, 169, 172
Popper, Karl 98, 111, 191, 193,194, 199–203, 205, 235
positivism 212, 213, 231
postmodernism 147, 150, 154, 235, 236–7, 238, 239, 240
post-structuralism 147, 150, 216, 236, 240 *see also* structuralism
Priestley, Joseph 99, 102
property 63–4, 66–8, 79, 81, 94, 119, 123, 125, 126, 129, 152, 153, 157, 161, 198, 229
Protagoras 7
Proudhon, Pierre-Joseph 111, 152, 153

racism 91, 146, 175–6, 179, 181–2, 187
Rawls, John 116, 138, 220–4, 228, 229
republicanism 36–7, 44–5, 59, 71, 75–6, 86, 87, 156, 189
revisionism 156, 160
revolution 66, 68, 84, 90–1, 93, 95–8,

101, 103, 107, 115, 117–119, 121, 123, 125–6, 128, 130, 131, 152–33, 155, 156, 157, 158, 159, 160, 163, 165, 166, 190, 213, 242, 243, 249
rights-of-man *see* natural rights
romanticism 78, 89, 91, 106, 191, 249–50
Rousseau 69, 75, 78–85, 86, 107–8, 109, 110, 114, 118

Saint-Simon, Henri de 119, 120
Sartre, Jean-Paul 206, 207
Schopenhauer 147, 148
Smith, Adam 108,
social contract 64–5, 70, 71–2, 80, 90, 94, 96, 221–2, 228
social Darwinism *see* evolution
socialism 94, 117, 120, 148, 150, 154, 158, 159, 161, 162, 163, 167, 184, 194, 196, 250 *see also* new left, utopian socialism
Socrates 3–11, 108, 135, 147, 148 *see also* Plato
Sophists 4, 7, 8
Sorel, Georges 154, 155–8, 183
sovereignty of the people 82, 84, 91, 94
Spencer, Herbert 139–42, 143, 153
Spengler, Oswald 156
state of nature 53–4, 63–6, 79–80, 83, 221, 228
state, the 90–1, 109, 172, 184–5, 197–8, 228, 232, 251
structuralism 216- 17 *see also* post-structuralism

Tocqueville, Alexis de 130–3
totalitarianism 82, 84, 11, 167, 184, 188–9, 195, 211, 212, 213, 214, 238, 239, 251
trade unionism 154, 156–7, 160, 165, 195
Trotsky, Leon 166, 236

utilitarianism 73, 102, 112–16, 134-138, 140, 143–144, 202, 221, 228
utopias 47–9, 129, 157, 172, 195, 214, 251
utopian socialism 117–20, 161

Vico, Giambattista 191

Washington, Booker T. 176
Weber, Max 156, 169–75, 213, 230, 231, 234
welfare state 94, 115, 162, 194, 222, 228
Wittgenstein, Ludwig 149, 236, 239
Wollstonecraft, Mary 98, 99–101, 102